On Book Design

On Book Design

Richard Hendel

YALE UNIVERSITY PRESS · New Haven & London

Designed by Richard Hendel.
Set in Monotype Garamond and Meta type
by Julie Allred, B. Williams & Associates.
Printed in the United States of America
by Thomson-Shore.

Library of Congress
Cataloging-in-Publication Data
Hendel, Richard.
On book design / Richard Hendel.
    p. cm.
Includes bibliographical references and index.
ISBN 978-0-300-07570-0 (alk.paper)
1. Book design—United States. I. Title.
Z116.A3H46   1998
686—dc21   98-17186
            CIP

A catalogue record for this book is available from
the British Library.

The paper in this book meets the guidelines for
permanence and durability of the Committee on
Production Guidelines for Book Longevity of the
Council on Library Resources.
10 9 8 7 6 5 4

For Vicky

Just because something is legible doesn't mean it communicates; it could be communicating completely the wrong thing. Some traditional book titles, encyclopedias, or many books that young people wouldn't want to pick up, could be made more appealing. It is mostly a problem of publications sending the wrong message or not a strong enough message. You may be legible, but what is the emotion contained in the message?

— David Carson

Those predicting the end of print (i.e., its demise) will, without doubt, find little of interest in *this* book unless, of course, they are interested in the end of print (i.e., its purpose). Even so, their concept of purpose is likely to be something quite different from the ideas in this book. To them, this book will be too conventional, too boring, and naive in the belief that the primary role of the book designer is to make text as legible as possible.

Contents

Read Me

It would have been much easier to write this book years ago. I was certain then about how typography worked and how books should be designed. Now, after three decades of experience, I am more uncertain than ever about how to design books. I have no design philosophy; I subscribe to no theories of typography; I am willing to try anything (and often do, to my peril); I no longer know what the rules are supposed to be.

The last thing one discovers in writing a book is what to put first.
—Pascal

A while back, when a colleague, Iris Hill, suggested that I write a book about book design, I was less interested in the idea of setting forth my own views than I was in having an excuse to see how other designers worked. Book design is not an easy thing to learn because there is almost no place to find out about it. Even book designers who have been working professionally for a long time have only a glimmer of how their colleagues do it.

This book is neither a history of book design nor a guide to typography. It is a book about how books are designed. It is not a book on how to design books. This is not a tautology. My intention is not to write an instruction manual. Instruction manuals tell you how to do something, as if there were some formula or recipe. Book design is complicated, especially because there isn't a single way to proceed.

There is nothing wrong with instruction manuals. I would never have gotten a foot in the door without one. I knew almost nothing about book design when I conned my way into my first publishing job by reading Marshall Lee's *Bookmaking* the weekend before I started work. In addition to that inestimable volume, there are a handful of other books that explain in great detail methods for designing books. The reason this book isn't one of them is that I don't have a universal philosophy of design. I don't know how to design books—books in the abstract. I only know how to design the book I am working on at the moment. Each book, like all books, is unique.

The epigraphs that appear as sidebars throughout this book are sometimes meant to confirm or to contradict what I write. Although I believe what I think when I am thinking it, I can easily be persuaded that there are other, often better ways of designing. The particular problems of whichever book I am working on determine how much I follow the rules.

I am not implying that every violation of the rules is acceptable. Certainly, however, there are more ways of thinking about book design and typography than I once believed.

The designers who contributed chapters to this book often work in ways very different from the way I do and from the way the others do. The neophyte designer may find it confusing to be confronted with so many dissimilar models. Each has a commonality, however, and that is the real substance of this book: to show why designers make the decisions they do.

In my brief bibliography I have listed the most useful books on general typographic principles, along with other books on book design. In my chapters I have tried to use as little jargon as possible. Designers, production staff, and printers do not always agree on the meaning of technical terms, in any case. My definitions, given in the Glossary, are based on those in *Glossary of Typesetting Terms* (University of Chicago Press, 1994), which three of the contributors to this book also helped write: Richard Eckersley, Anita Walker Scott, and myself.

ACKNOWLEDGMENTS AND THANKS

Let me first thank the contributors, who have been patient during the many years since I first talked with them about working on this project: David Bullen, Ron Costley, Richard Eckersley, Sandy Hudson, Mary Mendell, Anita Walker Scott, Humphrey Stone, and Virginia Tan. They are as skilled in their work as they are articulate in discussing it. I am honored by their enthusiastic willingness to contribute essays.

In the many hours I spent talking with Alan Bartram, Gerald Cinamon, George Mackie, and John Ryder I learned much. Robert Bringhurst, in his books, essays, and letters to me, has said everything about typography I wish I had and better than I ever could. I am also grateful for the many helpful and instructive conversations that I have had with other designers and production managers: David Bann, Harry Ford, April Leidig-Higgins, Nancy Ovedovitz, Mary Ellen Podgorski, Cameron Poulter, Molly Renda, Steve Renick, Hans Schmoller, Christine Taylor, Kim Wiar, and Barbara Williams. They provided the best ideas in this book. Richard Angstadt, Eric Brooks, and Charles Ellertson have taught me how type should look by the example of their excellent typesetting. Paul Stiff did his best to try to make this a better book—that it isn't is not his fault but my own. Robert Cantwell, Deborah Greger, Sean Magee, and J. D. McClatchy gave me invaluable insights on the relationship between author and designer. Alexander Nesbitt not only introduced me to typography and book design but arranged for me to meet the formidable Beatrice Warde. I would not have been a book designer were it not for Alex. Leone Stein, director of the then fledgling University of Massachusetts Press, gave me the chance to learn book design on the job. Judy Metro's misguided notion that publishing a book on book design is not a futile exercise has encouraged me in this dubious venture. Mary Pasti's valiant editorial efforts made my prose less soporific than it might have been. Ron Maner's always wise advice got me through difficult problems. Designers are fortunate there are such sympathetic editors as Mary and Ron. Heidi Perov kept the Mac miraculously running through three operating systems. I thank my muse, Sam, for his constant companionship. Finally, I offer my reluctant gratitude to my wife, Vicky, who made me do it.

On Book Design

Introduction

If printing is the black art, book design may be the invisible one. Henry Petroski in his book *The Pencil* wrote: "This ubiquitous and deceptively simple object . . . is so familiar as to be a virtually invisible part of our general culture and experience." The same holds for book design. You don't have to understand how books are designed to read one with pleasure. If you accept the idea that the important thing about a book is the meaning of the words and not how they look, the very invisibility of the design is to its credit. I have always been surprised that, as omnipresent as books are, hardly anyone thinks about how they are designed or even comprehends that they are. The more mundane the object (a pencil, a book), the less we think about its design. The more efficiently it works and the more often we use it, the less we think about how it came to be. But the simplest object often has very complicated specifications for making it.

Book design is, indeed, an arcane subject. We need a context to understand it. Knowing a technical vocabulary does not provide that context; rather, we need to be aware of the specific problems that book designers must consider as they work.

Being musically illiterate, I know that when I listen to a piece of music, I am missing a lot. I remember hearing a lecture by Leonard Bernstein on Saint-Saëns's *Carnival of the Animals*—a piece that he found extremely funny. Bernstein recognized Saint-Saëns's clever allusions to other composers, while I just thought I was listening to a collection of pleasant tunes. Similarly, book designers may use old tunes and traditional material in their work. Someone who perceived this might appreciate the designer's cleverness, but, after all, just as in Saint-Saëns's composition, the design has to make sense whether or not its allusions are obvious.

Book design is a craft with its own traditions and a relatively small body of accepted rules. Whether the design of a book draws attention to itself or not depends as much on the reader's awareness of design in general as it does on the design of a particular book.

In spite of the ubiquity of books, it is not so easy to discover how they have come to look the way they do. The writers of books are much more fortunate than their designers. Writers yearning to know how other writers write have a plethora of sources. Hardly an author is unasked about how he or she creates.

Many book designers work in isolation, so they do not have the chance to see how their cohorts work. When designers meet, even if they do talk shop, they rarely discuss the process of how they design. The idea for this

If a little knowledge is dangerous, where is the man who has so much as to be out of danger?
—T. H. Huxley

book came from my own curiosity about how designers conceptualize what a book should look like as well as how they actually *do* their work.

I consulted British and American designers whose work I admire and asked if they would contribute design samples and describe their working methods. There are dozens of other designers whose work is as good as that of the designers included in this book, but my intention was to include a variety of designs done for a variety of publishers. I wanted both designers who were trained in design schools and those who learned on the job. I asked them to analyze their working styles and talk about the way they made their decisions. From each, I wanted a case history of a project and an explanation of how a design evolved: how much they knew about a manuscript before they designed it, how they visualized the book, how they chose the typefaces and made the necessary decisions.

Designers often work intuitively and in spite of problems presented by their clients. One told me that he did what he did

> 'cos I like it that way. Or, the publisher/author/artist/artist's widow/ artist's daughter told me to do it that way. That's all there is to book design really. It's a very lonely occupation, like a carpenter's but with less skill required.
>
> Even working for fairly enlightened publishers I am always constrained by what I know they will and won't accept. Many authors have strong views on what they want. Artists often have extremely decided views about things (and they are unfortunately not always very visually literate), and bereaved relations feel they are responsible for the artist's posthumous reputation. Long dead artists are best.
>
> I find the main problem is not the design, but getting the text out of editors and/or authors. The trick is to find a way of designing a book when you only have part of the text, or none.*

This isn't idle grumbling. Authors often do have right of approval over the design. Publishers do not always show the entire manuscript to the designer. Too often, editors make last-minute changes without knowing the havoc they have wreaked. Designers are not always responsible for the corruption of what might have begun as a carefully conceived piece of typography. In this regard, there are many book designers who, in addition to espousing "invisible" design, desire *themselves* to be invisible—or at least prefer to remain nameless. Seeing a finished book that only vaguely follows their original specifications, they know the value of design anonymity.

Some publishing houses have no acquaintance with book design at all. They care only about getting as much type on the page as possible. Their books have such a lack of style or elegance that I can only assume that no designer has ever come within breathing distance of the manuscripts they publish.

Some publishers ignore details that they consider insignificant. They in-

*Alan Bartram,
letter to author,
8 September 1993.

sist, for example, that complicated material, such as the copyright page, must blindly follow a house style. At least one university press insists that the Library of Congress cataloging data be set exactly as it comes from the library, even though there is no more reason to preserve the style of that computer printout than there is to typeset the entire book using the same line endings that the author used in the manuscript. The cataloging information isn't a poem but a piece of prose.

```
            Library of Congress Cataloging-in-Publication Data


  Hendel, Richard.
       On book design / Richard Hendel.
            p.    cm.
       Includes bibliographical references and index.
       ISBN 0-300-07570-7 (alk. paper)
       1. Book design--United States.    I. Title.
     Z116.A3H46   1998
     686--dc21                                              98-17186
                                                               CIP
```

The design of books is different from all other kinds of graphic design. The real work of a book designer isn't making things look nice, different, or pretty. It is finding out how to put one letter next to another so that an author's words seem to lift off the page. Book design doesn't delight in its own cleverness; it is done in the service of words. Good book design can be done only by people who read—by those who take the time to see what happens when words are set into type.

Few schools teach book design. The best way to learn it is to look at what experienced designers do—to try to figure out how they make their decisions. To reveal the virtues in their typography, I asked my colleagues to talk about their solutions, to make clear why their typography succeeds. Several of the designers helpfully selected a specific project and talked through the process of designing it, showing initial ideas and rejected layouts. Seeing why something doesn't work is often more revealing than seeing why it does. A proper design seems self-evident. "But of course," we say.

This book might well be of interest not just to other book designers but also to writers who wonder how their books end up looking the way they do, to readers who have never realized that books are designed at all, to others in publishing who assume that designers do what they do purely on whim or purely by formula, and to graphic designers who do not design books (in the hope of explaining why book design is different from other kinds of design).

Graphic design is an applied art (art for something other than itself). When I was a student, it was called "commercial art"—art for commerce. Graphic design is used to communicate some specific message in a visual way, and it is valued for the cleverness of how the design tells something. The message is as much in the telling, the way the words look, as in the words themselves. Sometimes, in fact, there aren't any words. The graphic designer supplies an attitude to the words to influence the way the reader sees and responds to them. The graphic designer is a propagandist.

If book design is not graphic design, it is not fine art, either. The graphic designer's work is to tell the viewer something, and if the message

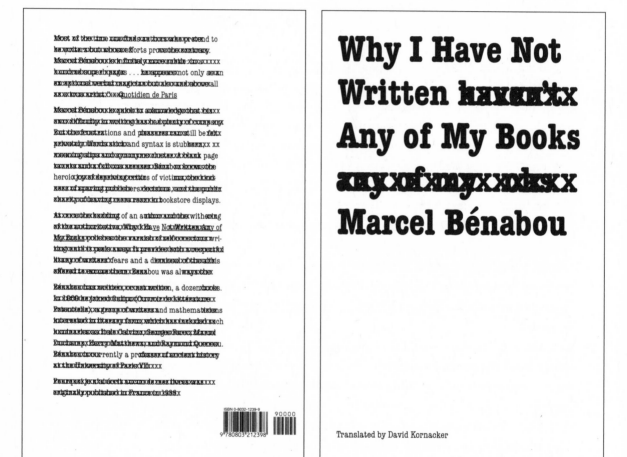

Jacket design for the University of Nebraska Press by Richard Eckersley

is not understood, the designer has failed. Fine artists tell their own story. A viewer's failure to understand isn't always important to them. Artists are often engaging in personal, private exploration.

There are many kinds of books and book design. One more thing this book is not is a book about fine printing. Fine-printed books are often made for collectors, and I agree with the designer Robert Josephy, who wrote that "fine printing" is synonymous with books "not printed to be read."* Those who do fine printing are commonly—but certainly not always—less interested in what the words say and more interested in how the type looks. They make books to be looked at. One designer I knew called such books "instant antiques."

I am using the term "book design" to mean what goes on *inside* the book, not on the book jacket. Although many people assume that a book designer does just the jacket, the opposite is generally the case. Book designers often do not design the jackets to their books. Book jacket design is so different a problem from interior design that it needs a book of its own.

This is an interesting time to be a book designer. By the mid-1990s many designers—even those who swore they would never use a computer—succumbed willingly. Never in the history of the printed book have most designers had a tool for working so easily with type. In the first century of the printed book, the designer not only set the type but also may have designed the typeface and done the printing. In time, the separation between typesetter and designer became a chasm. Whether through a failure of training in the printing trades or a general corruption of typographic standards, by 1947, when Jan Tschichold arrived in England to improve design at Penguin Books, designers had to provide the most exact instructions for the typesetter. George Mackie called this kind of typesetting "industrial typography," insisting that the only way to avoid expensive revisions was to provide the typesetter with unambiguous technical specifications. Hans Schmoller, who followed Tschichold at Penguin, wrote that specifications "should leave nothing for the printer to decide . . . one typographical point [that is, 1/72 inch] must be as important as one inch." Sometimes it was necessary to write such exact specifications for setting the type that printers resented what Beatrice Warde called the "thoroughly bad manners" of the designers.

Computers may increase this separation between typesetter and designer. Many designers, knowing exactly how they want something to look, and not knowing how or wanting to bother to specify it, set their own type for some or all of a book. If nothing else, computers have radically changed how designers work. What once took hours and days can now be done in minutes. Nearly every classical book typeface and many new ones of dubious design are available. Computers and computer fonts could not have come any too soon for me. I used to spend hours, even days, drawing out a title page. I was consummately proud of my skill at rendering letters. Now the computer has made all of this unnecessary. No longer dependent on my ability to draw letters, I can see precisely what the letters look like and can control every detail of their final placement.

The work of a book designer differs essentially from that of a graphic artist. The latter is constantly searching for new means of expression, driven at the very least by his desire for a "personal style." A book designer has to be the loyal and tactful servant of the printed word. . . . The aim of the graphic artist is self-expression, while the responsible book designer, conscious of his obligation, divests himself of this ambition. . . . Those who think in purely visual terms are useless as book designers.
—Jan Tschichold

The artist is the only man in modern society who is paid to do what he likes. . . . What he likes is to disturb us, pleasantly or not, by a visual message; and we like that quality in his paintings. So of course he is the last man to enjoy that disciplined exercise in the code-transmission of words—that is, typography—with all its conventional signalling of purpose and kind by format, by style and by orthography.
—Beatrice Warde

*"Trade Bookmaking," in Books and Printing, ed. Paul A. Bennett (Cleveland: World Publishing Company, 1951), p. 169.

Although computers have made preparing layouts infinitely easier, all too often the quest for design "perfection" has more than consumed the time saved. It is now possible for designers to try out every minuscule alteration in type size and letterfit where once they would have been more or less content to accept the way the type looked as it arrived from the typesetter.

Assuming that the designer prefers not to set all the type in a book, it is important to find a sympathetic typesetter. The problem is not new, but it seems more obvious than ever before. Because the design and fit of letters can now be altered so easily, knowing who will typeset a book is as critical as planning the design itself. The same specifications followed by different typesetters often result in typography that is considerably dissimilar. Skilled and sensitive typesetters will always modify the faces they set—refining the letterfit, kerning awkward letter combinations, and even extensively redrawing the typeface itself.

Books on design written just a few years ago could not have taken into account the enormous changes that the Macintosh computer and Post-Script fonts would bring. Even so, book design is inextricably tied to the dual tradition of how we read and what we think books should look like. The problems to be solved are the same ones we've always had. What is important is not the mechanics of making the layouts but finding exactly the right design and typeface for the author's words.

1. Looking Like Books

Book design is no field for those
who desire to "mint the style of
today" or to create something
"new." In the strict meaning of the
word there cannot be anything
"new" in the typography of books.
Though largely forgotten today,
methods and rules upon which it
is impossible to improve have
been developed over centuries. To
produce perfect books these rules
have to be brought back to life and
applied.

—Jan Tschichold

The design of everyday things is often invisible. Until the look of something becomes radically different from what we expect, we rarely think about its appearance. We assume that books are supposed to look like "books": upright rectangles with serifed type. Any deviation (no matter how subtle) suggests that something quite different is going on. The peculiarity may be ineffable, but it is genuine.

The typography of books is steeped (some might say mired) in tradition and convention. Designers must understand the history and conventions of book typography because there are good reasons for their existence. More than half a century ago, Stanley Morison and Oliver Simon reiterated what we have come to consider the principles of good typography. These presumed rules of good book design are not absolute, but they provide useful points of departure—what Robert Bringhurst calls "typographic etiquette."

Bringhurst suggests that the traditional rules of typography are indeed like rules of etiquette, which, if observed in moments of doubt, will prevent visual faux pas. Design novices would do well to know these conventions, but for more experienced designers to slavishly follow them will result in visual platitudes. The territory between tritely applying "the rules" and overdoing the design is quite narrow. Book design is not one of those crafts that allow for infinite and unfettered creativity.

The real reason for the number of deficiencies in books and other printed matter is the lack of—or the deliberate dispensation with—tradition, and the arrogant disdain for all convention. If we can comfortably read anything at all, it is exactly because we respect the usual, the commonplace. To be able to read implies conventions, knowledge of them, and regard for them.
—Jan Tschichold

Typography thrives as shared concern—and there are no paths at all where there are no shared desires and directions. A typographer determined to forge new routes must move, like other solitary travellers, through uninhabited country.
—Robert Bringhurst

I, like an usurp'd town, to another due,
Labour to admit You, but Oh, to no end!
Reason, Your viceroy in me, me should defend,
But is captiv'd, and proves weak or untrue...

The poet, of course, is John Donne, and both passages come from the *Holy Sonnets*. Coincidence? Possibly: but at least they show a persisting habit of mind, and a similar tendency to reach for a particular kind of simile in moments of intense introspection. Both Donne and Ausias March, one might say, are poets who submit their undisciplined lives to the discipline of verse, and in doing so create memorable poems. And one phrase of Ausias March stays in the mind as a superb expression of the state from which so much of his poetry derives: 'en tot lleig fet hagué lo cor salvatge' (LXVIII) [in every base action, his was a savage heart], an appropriate note on which to leave a poet whose sheer intelligence and energy enabled him to use the existing tradition to produce great poetry.

THE TEXT. The spelling of the Catalan text has been modernized, except where this would involve a change of pronunciation. This seems legitimate, and even essential, in an anthology that is intended for non-specialists, and those who require a more scholarly text may refer to the edition by Pere Bohigas listed in the Bibliography. It should also be noted that many editions follow the manuscript tradition of indicating the caesura after the fourth syllable—a constant feature of the decasyllabic line as used by Ausias March and earlier poets— by means of a space. Thus, in Bohigas's edition, the first stanza of I appears as follows:

Axí com cell   qui.n lo somni .s delita
e son delit   de foll pensament ve,
ne pren a mi,   que.l temps passat me té
l'imaginar,   qu. altre bé no.y habita,
sentint estar   en aguayt ma dolor,
sabent de cert   qu.en ses mans he de jaure.
Temps de .venir   en negun bé .m pot caure;
aquell passat   en mi és lo millor.

VERSIFICATION. As the orthography of the Bohigas text emphasizes, the correct scansion of such verse depends on a number of contracted forms (qui.n = qui + en, que.l = que + el, qu.altre = que + altre, etc.) which in modern

Text page by
George Mackie,
from Ausias March,
Selected Poems,
University of
Edinburgh Press

Books for Now

What the author writes in a book is not all that tells what a book is about. The physical shape of the book, as well as its typography, also defines it. Every choice made by a designer has some effect on the reader. The effect may be radical or subtle, but it is usually outside a reader's ability to describe.

A tall, thin novel or a small, square one makes a statement that the book is not what you would expect. George Mackie's small-format monographs (4 5/8 × 8 inches) for Edinburgh University Press in the 1970s certainly seemed more approachable than the bloated, oversized scholarly monograph of that time.

Some kinds of design—industrial design, for example—encourage variation and change. Automobile designers are expected to alter their designs significantly every few years. But when a change is too radical, as the design for the Edsel was thought to be, the object no longer corresponds to the image people have of it. A package of oatmeal all in black with typography redolent of a nineteenth-century circus poster might be a splendid piece of graphic design but would most likely confuse someone just looking for breakfast.

I once employed a young student who was eager to learn about book design. His first assignment was a book on seventeenth-century British military history. After a few weeks he returned with a design done in 8-point sans serif type, ragged right, set asymmetrically on the page. The design was handsome and exciting, but it didn't seem the right one for that book, whose readers might have found the typography difficult to read and the *look* of the book equally perplexing. To my comments the student replied that making readers see the words in an unexpected context might force them to think about what the author was saying. At that time I was sure the designer was completely wrong, but I now think that his attitude might be the right one in some circumstances.

Designers can travel two different paths. There are those who feel that book design should reflect no particular time or place, and there are those who feel it should reflect current taste. Each attitude has its virtues and its problems.

A production of *Richard II* set in Fascist times establishes a contemporary relevance that enhances the play while still being faithful to Shakespeare's text. So there is no reason why an edition of Shakespeare's plays could not be set in Bauhaus-style typography. Designers need to realize, however, that by using unexpected typography, they might make the reader more aware of how the words look than of what they say.

Novelty is not necessarily a virtue. If a design is to vary from what is expected, it should add some level of meaning to the text; otherwise, it is simply a flimsy excuse for the eccentric.

Books last. We keep them in libraries so that we can read them for years after they are printed. Those designers who attempt to make neutral, time-less books feel that overtly fashionable design comes between the author and the reader. But is it possible to design a book that doesn't in some way reflect the time in which it is made? Timelessness may be unattainable. It is easy to look at many books and know immediately when and where they were designed.

Among the many ways a book can be designed there are three main approaches:

1. typography that is as neutral as possible, suggesting no time or place
2. allusive typography, which purposely gives the flavor of an earlier time
3. new typography, which presents a text in a unique way

Making a flawless traditional design is as difficult as achieving a novel one. Classical typography, done correctly, is no easier to design than some-thing more in vogue; the traditionalist is not necessarily avoiding hard work. Traditional typography may even be more difficult to do because this kind of design rarely uses ornament and decoration; it is pure in the sense that the type style, size, and arrangement are in accordance with accepted rules of "good typography."

Allusive typography may be both easier and more dangerous than tradi-tional design. Embellishments, like printers' flowers (typographic orna-ments), or type styles that evoke other times provide ready-made handles. Their use may offer facile solutions instead of genuine problem solving— that is, finding how to relate the typography to the specific text. Or the allu-sions may prove confusing. The allusive designer assumes the reader will make the same visual connection he or she did. Too often, however, *allusive* becomes *elusive*. Occasionally there will be dissonance—as when the de-signer assumes that the design means one thing and the reader another.

I once used a turn-of-the-century sans serif type for the headings in a book about nineteenth-century Native Americans; the typeface suggested (to me) the Old West. Seeing it with different assumptions, the author could not understand why I would want to use a typeface that was so obviously out of keeping with the time and place of his book.

When I asked Robert Bringhurst about allusive typography, he acknowl-edged how tricky it could be.

When I read a manuscript I start immediately to look in the back of my mind for typographic allusions or relations. I ask myself automatically, What are the types that might do justice to this book? Is there a type that comes from the same time (seventeenth-century type for a seventeenth-century book, etc.), or a type from the same place (French type for a French book, etc.), or one that embodies a similar intellectual attitude (neoclassical type for a book about neoclassicism; avant-garde type for a book about the avant-garde or one *by* an avant-garde artist, etc.).

But things are not very often that easy.

There is no Native American type, no Afro-American type, no type from ancient Greece or ancient China or Papua New Guinea. So what do I do if I am designing a book of Native American literature in translation, or an anthology of African American writing, or a new translation of Plato or the *I Ching* . . . ?

Sometimes I find a cultural parallel within the tradition of European/American typography, and thus perform a kind of double-allusion. If I do so, I may feel very pleased with myself, though I will have to accept that very few readers, even if they are typographically well informed, are likely to understand the hypermetaphor. Often, in such cases, typographic neutrality is the best I can hope for.

Neutrality is necessary in other circumstances too. The most obvious example is when designing a series, such as the Library of America or Gallimard's excellent Editions de Pléiade. In some cases—the Penguin Classics, for example—a certain amount of typographic allusion or tailoring is possible. One can choose a different typeface for each book in the Penguin series but the page size and page shape and margins must ordinarily stay the same. That enforces a great overriding neutrality upon all subsequent typographic decisions.

Most typographic allusions are, of course, all but invisible to the average reader. But I choose to believe that people are sensitive even to perceptions and sensations of which they aren't aware. So I choose to believe that these allusions matter, even to readers who don't see them. But I like most typographic allusions to be subtle, so that even readers of great typographic acuity will not find them blatant or trite or overwhelming.

I could live, like Nicolas Jenson or Thomas Cobden-Sanderson, with one type for everything. And if I did live that way, I would have to make my typographic allusions very subtle indeed—or make them entirely outside the text, in the ornamentation and the mise-en-page. But such allusions are often heavy-handed. Allusions made from within the text, through the choice of type and handling of typographic details (the handling of block quotations, versals, etc.), are often much more subtle, and are, for me, therefore more satisfying.

The history of type is a subject I find very compelling, but it is a history that is pretty much confined to Europe and America and to the period 1460 to the present. This is a small part of human time and geography. The geometry of the written page is also a subject I find fascinating—and it has a much broader reach—to wherever and whenever manuscript books have been made. Allusions to these histories are among the pleasures of real literacy. But a lot of my work is with texts that lie entirely outside that historical fabric, and I would not give it up for any of the pleasures of allusion.*

On the other hand, even designers who reject any notion of allusion may not be able to avoid making some statement. Today, for example, the neutral typography of the sixties now seems typical of the time. Michael Rock has said, "Fonts are rich with the gesture and spirit of their own era—even Helvetica and Univers can seem downright evocative."**

Novelty makes its own rules. New design, like new music, can easily hide its flaws. Is that dissonance intended, or is it ineptitude?

Innovative typography is a kind of allusive typography. It proclaims its newness the way allusive typography intimates connections, but it, too, may be confusing to the reader and completely wrong for the text. One has to be careful to avoid excess, not to sacrifice the text to fashionable design or put the book into a ghetto of ephemeral typography. But that doesn't necessarily make traditional design the best solution.

The designer Merle Armitage once complained that book design had too much reverence for the past. Noting that the English printing historian Stanley Morison had advocated an obedience to convention, Armitage asked, "Where has holding fast to tradition placed the British Empire today?" He wanted design that looked ahead and was aggressively contemporary. "Looking backward forsakes . . . the opportunity to make new and significant statements allied to our particular times." He concluded *Rendezvous with the Book* with a call for present-mindedness: "Our responsibility therefore is to reflect our place, our time and our attitude . . . and although we are in a period of transition [1949], there never was just such a time, place, and attitude as ours."***

What would Armitage make of the typography of our time? David Byrne, in the foreword to David Carson's *The End of Print,* says that "every society gets the visual environment it deserves." But who is to decide what a society deserves? How aggressive should designers be in breaking tradition? Designers like Carson, who seem no longer interested in merely delivering the author's message, want to be equal partners with the author. They reject the idea that books should provide common experiences to multiple readers, wanting instead to substitute layers of ambiguity and multiple meaning, even to the point of arranging the text so arbitrarily that it is not always clear which words follow which. They want to use their own

*Letter to author, 23 November 1995.

**"Typefaces Are Rich with the Gesture and Spirit of Their Own Era," in* Looking Closer: Critical Writings on Graphic Design, *ed. Michael Bierut, William Drenttel, Steven Heller, and D. K. Holland (New York: Allworth Press, 1994), p. 123.

***"The New Forms—and Books," in* Graphic Forms: The Arts as Related to the Book *(Cambridge: Harvard University Press, 1949), p. 110;* A Rendezvous with the Book *(Brooklyn: George McKibbin & Son, 1949), pp. 21, 27–28.*

****EDITED AND
****DESIGNED BY
MERLE ARMITAGE
WITH ARTICLES BY

1938

GEORGE
GERSHWIN

PAUL WHITEMAN ★ OLIN DOWNES ★ WALTER DAMROSCH
GEORGE GERSHWIN ★ MERLE ARMITAGE ★ OTTO H. KAHN
ARNOLD SCHOENBERG ★ WILLIAM DALY ★ HAROLD ARLEN
OSCAR HAMMERSTEIN II ★ ISAMU NOGUCHI ★ DAVID EWEN
NANETTE KUTNER ★ LESTER DONAHUE ★ ISAAC GOLDBERG
ERMA TAYLOR ★ GILBERT SELDES ★ J. ROSAMOND JOHNSON
RUDY VALLEE ★ LEONARD LIEBLING ★ ALEXANDER STEINERT
ALBERT HEINK SENDREY ★ JEROME KERN ★ DuBOSE HEYWARD
HENRY A. BOTKIN ★ SAM H. HARRIS ★ ROUBEN MAMOULIAN
EVA GAUTHIER ★ FERDE GROFÉ ★ LOUIS DANZ ★ TODD DUNCAN
BEVERLEY NICHOLS ★ IRVING BERLIN ★ S. N. BEHRMAN
GEORGE ANTHEIL ★ IRA GERSHWIN ★ SERGE KOUSSEVITZKY

LONGMANS, GREEN & CO · LONDON · NEW YORK · TORONTO

A
MERLE ARMITAGE

BOOK

Igor
Strav insky

WORKS OF ART BY:

Pablo Picasso ● Russell Cowles
Edward John Stevens Jr. ● Paul Klee
Cady Wells ● Marc Chagall
Carlus Dyer ● Antonio Frasconi
P. G. Napolitano ● J. E. Blanche
Arnold Newman ● Fred Plaut
Edward Weston ● John Vachon

EDITED BY EDWIN CORLE

Two title-page spreads by Merle Armitage in 1938 (top) and 1949 (bottom) typefaces because, to them, the old faces are exhausted of meaning, seen too much. To them, legibility is anathema; it is passive, static.

Being hopelessly traditional, I don't want to be a coauthor, but no designer can completely avoid influencing how the text is read. My intention, at least, is to get out of the way of the text. Even the smallest detail gone wrong—an ornament in a running head that is just a bit too large—can be as irritating as nails scraping a chalkboard. I often listen to recorded books and know that how a reader reads out loud is very much like how a designer designs. In listening, I pay too much attention to the reader who reads too quickly or too slowly, or who has a slightly odd accent or an unpleasant voice, or who emphasizes the wrong syllables. "Speakos," the aural equivalent of typos, are insufferable.

Assuming that the designer manages to do no harm, to be invisible in that sense, design cannot help but color the text. In 1968, Hammermill Paper Company published *The Trial of Six Designers*. Six book designers were invited to design Franz Kafka's *The Trial*. This approach was especially useful, for readers rarely see the same book typeset in six different designs. Even readers who have never thought about book design or who are unable to distinguish one typeface from another can see how different the same words look when set in another way. Using the same book size, no two designers chose the same typeface or the same arrangement.

Because George Salter's design was the one I was already familiar with, it seemed correct to me. First impressions are powerful things. The first time something grasps our imagination, that version of it becomes the benchmark; we have nothing to judge it against. Only after seeing a variety of solutions can we make an informed judgment.

Title-page designs from *The Trial of Six Designers:* George Salter (top), Merle Armitage (bottom)

All illustrations from *The Trial of Six Designers* are courtesy of Hammermill Paper Company.

CHAPTER ONE

*The Arrest / Conversation with Frau Grubach
Then Fräulein Bürstner*

SOMEONE must have traduced Joseph K., for without
having done anything wrong he was arrested one fine
morning. His landlady's cook, who always brought him
his breakfast at eight o'clock, failed to appear on this
occasion. That had never happened before. K. waited for
a little while longer, watching from his pillow the old

3

GEORGE SALTER

11.5/14 Linotype Scotch. Initial words in 12-point Scotch caps. Chapter-title calligraphy by the designer.

ONE *The Arrest*

Conversation with Frau Grubach

Then Fräulein Bürstner

Someone must have traduced Joseph K., for without
having done anything wrong he was arrested one fine
morning. His landlady's cook, who always brought him
his breakfast at eight o'clock, failed to appear on this
occasion. That had never happened before. K. waited for
a little while longer, watching from his pillow the old
lady opposite, who seemed to be peering at him with a
curiosity unusual even for her, but then, feeling both put
out and hungry, he rang the bell. At once there was a
knock at the door and a man entered whom he had never
seen before in the house. He was slim and yet well knit,

3

P. J. CONKWRIGHT

10/13 Linotype Palatino. Chapter title in Amsterdam Mistral.

Chapter One

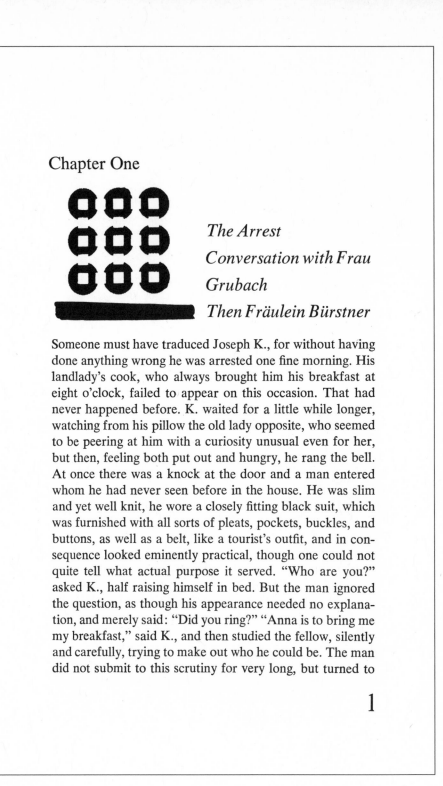

The Arrest

Conversation with Frau Grubach

Then Fräulein Bürstner

Someone must have traduced Joseph K., for without having done anything wrong he was arrested one fine morning. His landlady's cook, who always brought him his breakfast at eight o'clock, failed to appear on this occasion. That had never happened before. K. waited for a little while longer, watching from his pillow the old lady opposite, who seemed to be peering at him with a curiosity unusual even for her, but then, feeling both put out and hungry, he rang the bell. At once there was a knock at the door and a man entered whom he had never seen before in the house. He was slim and yet well knit, he wore a closely fitting black suit, which was furnished with all sorts of pleats, pockets, buckles, and buttons, as well as a belt, like a tourist's outfit, and in consequence looked eminently practical, though one could not quite tell what actual purpose it served. "Who are you?" asked K., half raising himself in bed. But the man ignored the question, as though his appearance needed no explanation, and merely said: "Did you ring?" "Anna is to bring me my breakfast," said K., and then studied the fellow, silently and carefully, trying to make out who he could be. The man did not submit to this scrutiny for very long, but turned to

1

MERLE ARMITAGE

10/14 Linotype Times Roman. Chapter-opening drawing by the designer.

THE ARREST

Someone must have traduced Joseph K., for without having done anything wrong he was arrested one fine morning. His landlady's cook,
who always brought him his breakfast at eight o'clock, failed to appear
on this occasion. That had never happened before. K. waited for a little
while longer, watching from his pillow the old lady opposite, who
seemed to be peering at him with a curiosity unusual even for her, but
then, feeling both put out and hungry, he rang the bell. At once there
was a knock at the door and a man entered whom he had never seen
before in the house. He was slim and yet well knit, he wore a closely
fitting black suit, which was furnished with all sorts of pleats, pockets,
buckles, and buttons, as well as a belt, like a tourist's outfit, and in consequence looked eminently practical, though one could not quite tell
what actual purpose it served. "Who are you?" asked K., half raising
himself in bed. But the man ignored the question, as though his appearance needed no explanation, and merely said: "Did you ring?"
"Anna is to bring me my breakfast," said K., and then studied the fellow, silently and carefully, trying to make out who he could be. The
man did not submit to this scrutiny for very long, but turned to the door
and opened it slightly so as to report to someone who was evidently
standing just behind it: "He says Anna is to bring him his breakfast."
A short guffaw from the next room came in answer; and it rather
sounded as if several people had joined in. Although the strange man
could not have learned anything from it that he did not know already,
he now said to K., as if passing on a statement: "It can't be done."
"This is news indeed," cried K., springing out of bed and quickly pulling on his trousers. "I must see what people these are next door, and
how Frau Grubach can account to me for such behavior." Yet it occurred to him at once that he should not have said this aloud and that
by doing so he had in a way admitted the stranger's right to superin-
tend his actions; still, that did not seem important to him at the moment. The stranger, however, took his words in some such sense, for
he asked: "Hadn't you better stay here?" "I shall neither stay here
nor let you address me until you have introduced yourself." "I meant

8

CARL ZAHN

8/12 Helvetica. Chapter title on a separate page.

The Arrest

Conversation with Frau Grubach

Then with Fräulein Bürstner

Sᴏᴍᴇᴏɴᴇ must have traduced Joseph K., for without having done anything wrong he was arrested one fine morning. His landlady's cook, who always brought him his breakfast at eight o'clock, failed to appear on this occasion. That had never happened before. K. waited for a little while longer, watching from his pillow the old lady opposite, who seemed to be peering at him with a curiosity unusual even for her, but then, feeling both put out and hungry, he rang the bell. At once there was a knock at the door and a man entered whom he had never seen before in the house. He was slim and yet well knit, he wore a closely fitting black suit, which was furnished with all sorts of pleats, pockets, buckles, and buttons, as well as a belt, like a tourist's outfit, and in consequence looked eminently practical, though one could not quite tell what actual purpose it served. "Who are you?" asked

9

JOSEPH BLUMENTHAL

12/16 Monotype Emerson. Woodcut by Fritz Kredel.

THE TRIAL

The arrest : Conversation with
Frau Grubach, then Fräulein Bürstner

13   Someone must have traduced Joseph K., for without
having done anything wrong he was arrested one fine
morning. His landlady's cook, who always brought him
his breakfast at eight o'clock, failed to appear on this
occasion. That had never happened before. K. waited for
a little while longer, watching from his pillow the old
lady opposite, who seemed to be peering at him with a
curiosity unusual even for her, but then, feeling both put
out and hungry, he rang the bell. At once there was a
knock at the door and a man entered whom he had never
seen before in the house. He was slim and yet well knit,
he wore a closely fitting black suit, which was furnished
with all sorts of pleats, pockets, buckles, and buttons, as
well as a belt, like a tourist's outfit, and in consequence

MARSHALL LEE

10/13 Linotype Devinne. Title in Berthold Standard Medium.

The Ephemeral Verities

I once believed that there were certain absolute truths about book design and typography. To violate them was not just unsound; it was heresy. I had total faith in what I thought were the eternal typographic verities. Stanley Morison's *First Principles of Typography,* Oliver Simon's *Introduction to Typography,* and Marshall Lee's *Bookmaking* were my articles of faith.

I came across the term "ephemeral verities" in an essay by Joseph Epstein. He was using it in an ironic sense, although it could honestly apply to the rules of book design. In a rampantly revisionist intellectual world constantly constructing and deconstructing itself, who is to say that one must always follow the rules? What rules?

Clichés and conventional wisdom about design blind us to what the oft-repeated words originally meant. We no longer even question if the truths still hold. All rules and conventions have something of the cliché about them. They become so entrenched that we don't bother to reevaluate them. There must be, or must once have been, enough validity to make them useful.

But fashions and tastes change. The traditional rules of typography need to be examined again. They aren't obsolete, but neither are they absolute. Writers today write differently from the way writers wrote in the seventeenth century. These days we constantly see type used innovatively. How would Bruce Rogers—an American typographer who worked in the first part of the twentieth century—design Jacques Derrida or John Cage?

Just as there are no guidelines for designing the nontraditional writings of our day, there is no single complete set of typographic rules that applies to designing more coventional manuscripts. There may be assumptions about how a conventional book should look, but book design needs to grow out of the author's words, not from abstract theory. No two books can be designed exactly the same way, any more than two books can be written using the same words. And, although a design can serve as a model for a series of books, parts of some books based on that format will be flawed.

The design for every book is a series of compromises. Only if every page of every text and every chapter title used the same words would book design be perfectly solvable. The design for a book has to account for the worst extremes of the text—the chapter title of two words and the one of seventeen, the unbroken text page and the one with numerous extracts and subheads.

So What?

Often when I find myself struggling to come up with the right design for a particular project, cranking out one hopelessly common and uninspired title-page idea after another, I wonder what difference it makes. Do readers ever look at title pages? Do they look at copyright pages, half titles, epigraphs, dedications—at any of those pesky details that make up the preliminary pages of a book? I myself, picking up the latest Elmore Leonard novel, go straight to page 1 and begin to read. Who, other than the author, the author's mother or spouse, and a librarian or two, cares what the title page looks like?

The time spent designing pages that are rarely or never looked at is hugely out of proportion to the time spent designing an ordinary text page. Should designers stop wasting publishers' time and money on the self-indulgence of designing copyright pages? How can we ever know what impact design has in publishing? Take the list of best-sellers to the book-store and look at their designs. It is dishearteningly rare to find a good one. The books that sell the best are too often those with marginless pages filled with repulsive typesetting.

Next, look at the books in the book-show design catalogs. You'll rarely see those books in a bookstore. There isn't any correlation between what books look like and how they sell. Design seems to make no difference. No matter how brilliantly they are done, books from small publishers or some university presses sell only a few thousand or a few hundred copies.

It may be true that more people have bought a book because it was well designed than have not bought a book because it wasn't. But designers may be the only ones who have refused to buy a book because it was ugly. Design bothers most people only when it is so execrable that the text is difficult to read.

According to conventional wisdom, it doesn't cost any more to make a book look good than it does to make it ugly. But good design and good printing do have a price. The smaller the publisher or the fewer the copies printed, the greater the impact of the cost of good design. A publisher who issues a small number of new titles or who prints only a few copies of each accounts for the cost of design by spreading the amount across those few projects. The design expense per book can be very high.

Many publishers, being aware of this, try to do without unique specifications for each new project. Instead, they use the designs for earlier books as models and hope that all the pieces fit, or else they attempt to establish a house design style.

A large part of the western world manages well enough without design. Go into a shopping centre in any town, and look at the signs announcing "sale": they will be off-the-peg notices, used by jewellers as well as clothes shops. . . . Any Japanese tourist walking by knows at once what is going on here. No "design" can ever beat this. . . .

We designers are working more for ourselves—typography for typographers—than we like to admit, or, even less, to contemplate. There is a world going on outside where we are not wanted, and where we couldn't help anyway.
—Fred Smeijers

Jan Tschichold was hired by Allen Lane to improve and standardize the design for Penguin Books in 1947. He established a now famous and still useful set of rules for compositors on the use of space and letterfit. But these were guidelines, not inflexible instructions.

Jeremy Aynsley, in his history of Penguin Books, commented, "Within these ground-rules each book was designed separately, its typeface, tone of page and finer detail such as headings, borders and chapter openings varying according to subject. Such a blend became an essential ingredient of Penguin typography, recognized by the awards given by the National Book League. However, it was a costly exercise, which could be justified in 1949 only by print runs of 20,000 or over." Aynsley repeated a comment by Hans Schmoller, who succeeded Tschichold: "A printer's bill of £160 for corrections, partly of a typographic nature (fine adjustments in leading, spacing, and many revisions before arriving at the final form of title and preliminary pages), would spell the economic ruin of a book with an edition of say 3,000 copies. But in an edition of 50,000 or 100,000 the total cost of production is such that £160 will not seriously prejudice the profit and loss account."*

The success of the house style for Penguin Books under Tschichold and later Schmoller was not due to its innovative design but to the quality and care in the details of the typesetting. Good design is just as much the careful arrangement of the most ordinary typefaces in the most conventional formats as it is the use of unusual typefaces in brilliant juxtapositions.

There are a few commercial houses whose names can be used in the same sentence with the words "good design." Among those, Faber & Faber, for example, uses for many of its titles a standard and controlled design style, one developed by Gerald Cinamon. Not only are the trim sizes of the books specified, but the typefaces and their sizes are as well. There is an overall design intelligence, which, as in books from Knopf, assures a consistent and high level of excellence.

Smaller, less commercially successful publishers appreciate the cachet of making consistently attractive books and, in fact, have built their reputation partly on the quality of their production. Design can be a useful asset in acquiring good manuscripts. Some authors are sufficiently attracted by the prospect of having a beautifully made book to choose to publish with a small house with a name for good design. These publishers have a style—a consistent attitude about design—but not a rigid format for all books. MIT Press under the design direction of Muriel Cooper in the 1970s did not use the same typefaces or formats for all its books, but the books were often instantly recognizable as coming from MIT.

When the University of Nebraska Press began to publish Derrida, Avital Ronell, and contemporary European literature in translation, it was fortunate that Richard Eckersley was in Lincoln. This was the perfect coincidence of designer and text. Eckersley's designs helped the press attract a completely different kind of author than before.

*Fifty Penguin Years
(Harmondsworth,
England: Penguin Books,
1985), p. 116.

Is the Crystal Goblet Broken?

In a legendary essay, "The Crystal Goblet," Beatrice Warde wrote that book typography should be as plain as a crystal goblet. She assumed that anyone drinking from an excessively designed jeweled cup would pay more attention to the cup itself than to the wine therein. Extending the idea, she claimed that excessive design would be just as distracting in a book. Extravagant typography would intrude between the author and the reader.

Book designers who prefer doing timeless crystal-goblet typography know precisely what Beatrice Warde meant. They are on typographic good behavior and would prefer never to violate Morison's "first principles of typography." They would agree with the type designer Fred Goudy, who (it is alleged) said that anyone who would letterspace lowercase letters would steal sheep. These folks know the rules.

Then there are the designers who flounder about, attempting to do something different. For years I did what I hoped were crystal goblets. I had carefully studied all the principles of good typography, which, if followed, were certain to lead to design paradise. Although the concepts themselves were sound, my application was so rigid that every book looked nearly the same. After a while I began to think that I should do something more unusual. Lurking in the back of my mind was a comment made about one of my books by a book show juror: "Nothing new here."

Having discovered Jan Tschichold's *Asymmetric Typography,* I memorized it all. There I was, working in the wilderness of western Massachusetts trying to make little Swiss books. The result was the typographic equivalent of ersatz Alpine lodges. Later I discovered that Tschichold had changed his mind.

Failing at asymmetry, I next read Geoffrey Dowding's *Finer Points in the Spacing & Arrangement of Type* and the typographic manuals of Oliver Simon, Stanley Morison, and Hugh Williamson, which led me to half-baked pastiches of British book design.

Frustrated as ever, I acquired what the British designer Ron Costley calls "the American designer's restless urge to find a new place for the folio." This was the dawn of the Herb Lubalin jam-all-the-type-together school of typesetting. Letters were bashed into each other, half of them looking as if they were mating. I was grafting misunderstood New York advertising typography onto books with titles like *German Peasants and Conservative Agrarian Politics, 1914–1924: A Study of Rhineland and Westphalia.* The books looked more like Kmart than Knopf.

I had long conversations with P. J. Conkwright, the legendary designer at Princeton University Press, and I looked at everything that I could find of

Typography may be defined as the art of rightly disposing printed materials in accordance with specific purpose: of so arranging the letters, distributing the space, and controlling the type as to aid to the maximum the reader's comprehension of the text. Typography is the efficient means to an essentially utilitarian and only accidentally aesthetic end, for enjoyment of patterns is rarely the reader's chief aim. Therefore, any disposition of printing material which, whatever the intention, has the effect of coming between the author and reader is wrong. It follows that in the printing of books meant to be read there is little room for "bright" typography. Even dullness and monotony in the typesetting are far less vicious to a reader than typographic eccentricity or pleasantry. Cunning of this sort is desirable, even essential in the typography of propaganda, whether for commerce, politics, or religion, because in such printing only the freshest survives inattention. But the typography of books, apart from the category of narrowly limited editions, requires an obedience to convention which is almost absolute—and with reason.
—Stanley Morison, *First Principles of Typography*

Hermann Zapf's. I set all my books in Palatino—everything from West-phalian peasants to Shakespeare.

The design rot really set in when I designed an entire book in Gill Sans Light. Thinking myself clever for such audacity, I was unprepared for pub-lic chastisement when John Updike reviewed the book in the *New Yorker,* complaining that the typeface was unreadable. It was.

I set another book in Helvetica with tight word spacing. It was so tight that the book seemed to be a single word, 160 pages long.

Nothing worked. If I tried to do what Beatrice Warde wanted, the books looked ordinary. If I tried to follow fashion, the books looked like tarts. And all of this because some book show judge had hinted that I hadn't done anything new.

I went back to the first books that I had designed to see if I could under-stand why they seemed so much better than my more recent work and began to understand that the more straightforwardly I worked, the better the books were.

I still worry that the publishers I design for might be disappointed to pay good money for something that looks like nothing new. Lurking in the back of my mind is the thought that I should make my books look different, new, revolutionary—designed!

Because there are no absolutes in design, book shows have come to be the point of reference for designers; for us, design shows are our only mea-sure of success. But shows, which are meant to foster good design, often encourage the worst. Their theme music should be Cole Porter's "Anything Goes" or "Let's Misbehave." I look at the book show catalogs every year and wonder why some miserable-looking books are chosen. What could have appealed to the judges? Even so, what the judges select this year sets our direction for next year. No matter how independent we might think we are or how certain of our designs, what the judges say does make a difference.

The pressure for designing books for book shows—designing for other designers—can be a corrupting influence. Design shows may have been es-tablished to foster better design, but they have often done just the opposite. Book shows encourage us all to try to be cleverer than our colleagues and much too clever for our authors.

In the face of all of these influences I find it impossible to make rules for myself. The longer I work as a designer, the less sure I am about my theories of design, for I know that I will have revised my theories by the time I have the next job to do. I'm not sure that I even have such a thing as a theory of design. I question what I once thought was good or corrupt and find myself doing things with type that I would have thought inexcusable a year ago. Times change more rapidly than ever. Perhaps book designers need to take a vow of design celibacy: avoid the temptations of typographic trendiness, work with one typeface, and be pure. But to hold rigidly to rules and theo-ries blinds a designer to more creative and appropriate possibilities.

The best title for this book might have been *It Depends*. Understanding the traditions of good book typography is the basis of book design. How those traditions should be observed, or even *if* they should be observed, depends on the book being designed. I wish I could write this book without using the word "should," because one of the very few things the designer *should* do is to know the text. On that depends everything else.

Designers just need to think less about designing books and more about designing for reading.
—Paul Stiff

2. The Design Begins Here

The text may be set up in dozens of
different types but only when the spacing
of all elements and margins correlate and
the size of the letters chosen fit precisely
the measure of the text-line, will the eye
of the reader work without strain. Space
on the page reveals the message as space
in the city reveals architectural details.

—John Ryder

In my Introduction I say that this book is not about how to design books but about how books are designed. Still, those who aren't familiar with book design need some context to understand what designers do. For those who already know what designers do, this section will contain nothing new. For those who do not, here are at least some of the problems designers deal with when they work.

Give full typographical attention *especially* to incidental details.
—Robert Bringhurst

Designers are to books what architects are to buildings. Designers write specifications for making books just as architects write them for constructing buildings. Even the most seemingly mundane detail needs to be decided, and it is just these tiny particulars that make a design successful. The parts of the book that are most ignored by readers are the ones that often need the most attention from the designer. You may not be able to tell a book by its cover, but you can tell a book design by its copyright page.

The author's words are the heart of book design. To solve the design problem for a book, a designer needs to know both *what* an author is saying (what a book is about) and *how* it is being said (the actual words being used). This doesn't mean that the designer always understands some (let alone all) of what an author is writing about, as I quickly learned on the first book I was hired to design—a specialized study of the American philosopher Charles Sanders Peirce. Most designers tell me they rarely read much of the books they design, not only because there isn't the time to do it but also because they all too often have no interest in the content. But they do have to know generally what the book is about and who the book is for. Conventions of design make one kind of typography seem normal to one group of readers but eccentric to another. Books meant for architects often look different from books for scholars of seventeenth-century European history.

Assuming I can understand the subject of the book, I usually read the introduction or first chapter, and I read some of every few pages to get a sense of the author's style. It is important for me to see the words the author uses. The author's vocabulary often dictates the typeface I use.

Book designers serve two clients: the author and the reader. For me, the goal is to make the communication between them as clear as possible. A third client is the publisher. Design decisions have to be made in relation to how publishing costs fit within a manufacturing budget, which is usually determined long before designing starts.

A publisher first determines how much text the author has written. The quantity of text can be as important in its way as the quality of the writing. All decisions about legibility and aesthetics have to be made in terms of the amount of text and the practical, financial considerations of printing and selling that text. Estimating length is a mechanical and simple business, but a miscalculation can make for major problems after the fact; it is just another of those seemingly unimportant details in book designing that needs to be right.

Authors and publishers use a word count, but to a typographer, the word count is too imprecise a measure. How many words fit on a page depends on how long the words are, so a typographer prefers to count characters— that is, every keystroke (letters, punctuation, spaces). This exercise is not quite as onerous as it sounds. Unless a manuscript is typed in many different kinds of formats, it is relatively easy to count an average number of characters per line from a representative sample of text, multiply that by the number of lines of text on a typical manuscript page, and multiply that by the total number of manuscript pages. Counting is even easier on manuscripts prepared on a computer because most word-processing software will calculate the characters. At the same time, it is important to keep track of text that will be designed differently from other kinds of text, for example, notes, bibliographies, appendixes. Only after quantity and kinds of text are observed can the design begin.

TRIM SIZE

The design starts with a book's physical shape—its "trim size." Books can be any format, but the upright rectangle that we think of as normal became the standard through both custom and practicality.

Since Gutenberg's time, books have been most often printed as upright rectangles that conform loosely, if not precisely, to the Golden Section (1:1.618), a Renaissance concept of the ideal proportion. The typographer-designer Jan Tschichold claimed that "many books produced between 1550 and 1770 show these proportions exactly, to within half a millimeter."*

Tschichold, Jost Hochuli, Robert Bringhurst, and others show numerous diagrams of book formats based on ideal page proportions, but designers do not commonly have complete freedom to specify nonstandard formats. More often than not, the format is decided long before the designer begins work.

Papermakers and printers have standardized certain book sizes, making customized formats impractical and expensive. The more closely paper and press size match each other, the more efficient and less expensive it is to manufacture a book. Books are printed on large sheets of paper that are folded to make signatures of (generally) thirty-two pages. That is, sixteen pages are printed on one side of the sheet and sixteen on the other. Press sizes and paper sizes evolved to produce efficiently only a certain number of formats. And no matter what other noble attributes a publisher may ascribe to books, they are commodities and need to be sold for a profit if publishers are going to survive. Books must be manufactured with as little waste as possible to allow a publisher to sell them for a reasonable price, and that

*The Form of the Book, trans. Hajo Hadeler (Port Roberts, Wash.: Hartley & Marks, 1991), p. 28.

requires the standardization of book sizes and materials. Any element that varies even moderately from the standard will increase costs.

In the United States, paper and books are measured in inches; much of the rest of the world uses metric units. For a conventional book of prose sizes range between approximately 5 × 8 inches and 6 1/8 × 9 1/4 inches; the first number is the width, the second the height. The difference of 1/8 inch can add greatly to the cost. To change the shape of a book—making it wider than it is tall—also risks situations that will add both extra expense and manufacturing problems. One reason that it is not so simple to change the size of a book from 6 × 9 to 9 × 6 is because the wider format requires folding the paper against the grain. The fibers that make up a sheet of paper align themselves in a certain direction when paper is being made. This is the grain, and paper folds best in the direction of the grain. Book papers are made on the assumption that the trim size will be an upright rectangle. To avoid problems in the bindery, wide formats require specially ordered paper with grain in the other direction.

MARGINS

Conventional wisdom says that in books of text meant for continuous reading, facing pages should be positioned in relation to each other such that the reader thinks of them as a single unit. In a traditional design, the gutter margin—the margin by the spine—is therefore smaller than the front margin, the margin opposite the gutter, so that the two facing blocks of text are close together and the space to the outside of them is greater. The top margin is smaller than the bottom margin, which is the largest of all. Some writers suggest that the bottom margin should be large enough for the reader's thumbs to hold the book, but what if the reader prefers to hold the book on the side of the page instead of the bottom? The large bottom margin is another of those conventions of ideal Renaissance proportion that we now think of as rules. These proportions have become so accepted that a radically different layout is a sign that the text is somehow unconventional. Or the design is simply ugly. The text block that sits square in the center of the page can look arbitrarily placed. Books with large top margins and small bottom margins sometimes feel as though they met some mishap in the bindery. Explanations of why these margins have become standardized may only be rationalizations for what we have become used to seeing, but that doesn't mean they can be ignored.

Perhaps fifty percent of the character and integrity of the printed page lies in its letter forms. Much of the other fifty percent resides in its margins.
—Robert Bringhurst

When opened, a book shows mirror symmetry. Its axis is the spine, around which the pages are turned. Thus any typographic approach, including an asymmetric one, has always to take account of the symmetry that is inherent in the physical object of the book.
—Jost Hochuli

TEXT TYPEFACE

Although some designers claim to be able to design a book in all its essentials before choosing a typeface, I cannot. The typeface I use influences so many other parts of the page that until I can settle on which to use, I am unable to carry on. It is the basis for everything else. Choosing a typeface can be the most vexing, infuriating, time-consuming, and pleasurable part of designing a book. Unlimited choice is a false blessing. There are so many typefaces and so many ways to use them that freedom itself becomes a problem. In the days when books were set in metal type, designers had a relatively limited selection of faces suitable for text. Typesetters who specialized in book setting might stock only a few dozen faces—and then in only a limited number of sizes, because just a few sizes of one typeface could cost thousands of dollars. Making separate molds (from which each letter was cast) was an expensive and labor-intensive business. As film setting replaced metal, and digitized type replaced film, typefaces became much cheaper to produce.

So-called desktop publishing changed that. The typefaces available for the personal computer are inexpensive to acquire. They are so cheap that they are often given away by the dozens, and because they are readily reproduced from their digitized formulas, they can easily be redesigned, altered, stretched, compressed, and otherwise abused—or improved. Designers and typesetters who once had only a few choices can now own entire libraries of faces—thousands of fonts that can be set in every size—for less than the cost of a single font of one metal face. What this means is that it is possible to choose virtually any typeface to use in a book. There are hundreds to choose from, almost too many. At one time, most book designers could identify any text face, but now that would be unlikely even for the keenest eye and the most capacious brain. Every month fistfuls of advertisements for new types arrive. I have always thought it was nonsense to categorize faces as masculine or feminine, but this may be the reason there are so many of them—they're breeding.

When typesetters offered only a limited selection of typefaces, designers generally had a good understanding of each face and its peculiarities. They used the same faces over and over and came to know them well—how they looked in various sizes and set to different measures with varying amounts of leading. Because there wasn't much choice, designers literally made the best of what they had.

Personal feelings about a face narrowed the choices further. The printer D. B. Updike found charm in the ungainliness of Caslon and thought that ungainliness made the face more readable. Other designers, not so forgiving, reject Caslon for the very reasons that it appealed to Updike. One virtue of ugliness is that it immediately eliminates some typefaces from consideration. Beyond the perceived beauty of a face, the way the letters are drawn or the way they are set might create special problems that are revealed only when the designer uses some of the author's actual words. The front of the Monotype Garamond "f" is so wide that it appears to crash into any ascender that follows it. So a book about Kafka might be better set in a typeface like Times Roman, whose "f" is narrower and will not continually seem to touch the "k" following. But it is not just obviously awkward combinations such as "fk" and "gy" that expose design flaws, as is evident when one looks at the letterfit of the rest of the word.

Kafka Kafka Kafka

Foggy Foggy Foggy Monotype Garamond, Times Roman, Galliard

PostScript was revolutionary. When film setting and digitized typesetting drove metal to its death, the type foundries, in their rush to reissue their libraries of faces for computerized setting, did not always take the trouble to translate their old designs with care. Often the letterfit was atrocious, and letter combinations that looked good enough in metal weren't adjusted with the skill that they had been before. Nor was there much consideration given to the weight of the stroke, so that the letters often looked too thin. The original designs had been made assuming that the weight of the letters would thicken from the impression of ink onto paper.

But the old faults and the new ones in digitized type could be corrected, and fonts could be completely customized. Once it was possible to change the letterfit, everyone wanted to. Adjusting the spacing of a typeface takes time, and there isn't enough time to fix every typeface. Using a familiar typeface is a matter of knowing not just how it looks but how it sets. The designer should want to know if the typesetter has adjusted the face to the designer's taste.

The official foggy morning
The official foggy morning letterfit adjusted and special ligatures ("ffi" and "ggy")

Complicating choice is the flood of new typefaces. Being able to digitize type deindustrialized it. Where it once took years to design a new face, cut punches, prepare molds, cast letters, and try the new type design, it is now possible for designers to create completely new faces quickly and have more or less complete control over their appearance. Even with the most expertly designed faces, however, the book designer who wants to use one faces hazards. The first use of any new face, especially when there are few examples done by others to study, is like going on a first date. You think you like the face, and you want to take it out to see how you get along with each other, but you're not quite sure how you'll relate to it. My own experience is that I need more than a few attempts with any new typeface before I feel I have any sense of how to use it.

The designer looks for special problems. Does the author use a lot of words needing italic or small caps? Are there many numbers? Will various levels of subheadings require a face with good boldface? Designers should have some acquaintance with typographic history—knowing who designed a typeface or when and where a typeface was designed—especially when designing books dealing with former times. Confronted with every possi-

A true advantage of present-day conditions is that production of typefaces can be implemented quicker than ever before and under your total control. What you make today is tested tomorrow, in any size you want.
—Fred Smeijers

bility, a designer might want to narrow the field by first limiting the choice to faces that have historical connections to the time period or subject matter of the text (for example, using an eighteenth-century English typeface such as Baskerville or Caslon in a book on colonial America).

Design allusiveness, carried too far, is a problem, however. Allusiveness can be a trap. Sometimes the design requires using a typeface that is more suitable to the requirements of the text than to the subject matter of the book.

A designer can find inspiration outside history. The name of the typeface might suggest its use. A colleague of mine used Eagle for the display type in a book by an author with the same name. But as Bringhurst says, the "typographic page so well designed that it attains a life of its own must be based on more than an inside joke."*

Most beginning designers want to try out a different typeface for every new project. Experienced designers find themselves working with a handful of faces, often using the same one for many books in a row. Suddenly, the only typeface that feels right for everything is Galliard, or Garamond, or Baskerville. Picasso had his Blue period and his Rose period. Book designers have their Palatino period. Inevitably, a typeface is used so much that it becomes stale for the designer exactly at the time a project comes along that it is just the right one for. And the designer, unfortunately, uses something else out of boredom.

Some studies show that serif type is easier to read than sans serif type, and others prove the opposite. As Marshall Lee suggests, people are probably not born with a preference for one kind of type design over another. The old story is that we read most easily any letterforms that we are most used to seeing. If sans serif is not a style of type commonly used in books, then, the argument goes, it probably isn't a typeface that *should* be used in books. But sans serif letters are not inherently illegible; they are used (often badly) for highway signs and in other places where information must be read quickly. Even comic strips use sans serif letters; the letter style is common enough to be used for the most casual readers.

How a typeface is used, not the typeface itself, defines how readable it is. Book designers may think that sans serif type is unsuitable for books because they have little experience using it for extended text. Certainly, the best-designed serif typeface can be rendered unreadable without much effort.

I once believed that there were no bad typefaces, just misunderstood ones. I am no longer so sure when I see faces from designers like Zuzana Licko. Her typefaces for *Emigre* have sometimes pushed design to the edge. Yet within the context of a publication like *Emigre* even these eccentric designs look right.

Until I could set type samples so easily on my Macintosh, I would not have suspected that the differences between faces could be so great. In pre-

If a text calls for Renaissance type it calls for Renaissance typography as well. This usually means Renaissance page proportions and margins, and the absence of bold-face.
—Robert Bringhurst

A child born today is no more accustomed to the Roman type forms than was a child of the Paleolithic era. A new form would not be strange to people growing up with it. For adults, a change would be a temporary inconvenience.
—Marshall Lee

If people read "ugly" against-the-rules typography every day they will eventually get used to it and be able to read it without any problems. It's just a matter of giving it to them again and again and again.
—Rudy VanderLans

*The Elements of Typographic Style, 2d ed. (Port Roberts, Wash.: Hartley and Marks, 1996), p. 99.

suburban

abcdefghijk
lmnopqrstuvwx
yzABCDEFGHI
JKLMNOPQRSTU
VWXYZ1234567
890 " ! ? * @ ↕ ↕

**abcdefghijk
lmnopqrstuvwx
yzABCDEFGHI
JKLMNOPQRSTU
VWXYZ1234567
890 " ! ? * @ ↕ ↕**

Typefaces are not intrinsically legible;
rather, it is the reader's familiarity with
**Typefaces are not intrinsically legible;
rather, it is the reader's familiarity with
faces that accounts for their legibility.**

DEMO
craTica

abcdefghijkl
mnopqrstuvwxyz
ABCDEFGHIJKLM
NOPQRSTUVWXYZ
1234567890
1234567890&?#!

abcdefghijkl
mnopqrstuvwxyz
ABCDEFGHIJKLM
NOPQRSTUVWXYZ
1234567890
1234567890&?!

Typefaces are not intrinsically legible; rather, it is the reader's
familiarity with faces that accounts for their legibility. studies have
shown that readers read best what they read most. legibility is also a
dynamic process, as readers' habits are ever changing. it seems curious
Typefaces are not intrinsically legible; rather, it is the reader's
familiarity with faces that accounts for their legibility. studies have
shown that readers read best what they read most. legibility is also a
dynamic process, as readers' habits are ever changing. it seems

Emigre fonts

computer days, to see how a typeface might look for a particular text, I had to trace or draw out type, get sample settings from typesetters, or simply guess. Like many other designers, I usually worked with a small group of faces over and over because I knew how they would perform. I never truly knew what would happen in a new job because different authors rarely write in the same way. Even using the same typographic specifications, one book might look very different from another simply because of the peculiarities of the writing—the words used in the titles, the structure of the text, even the author's vocabulary. This is why books that are forced into typographic formats often have design bumps and why the design for many journals is so bland.

Being able to set a large sample of actual text on the computer makes it possible to see what happens with different sizes and styles of type as I try to find which one suits the author's words best. In sorting through the possibilities, I am seeking the right combination of type style and size to fit the words: to make sure the spaces will be reasonably uniform and the frequency of hyphenated words at the ends of lines will be minimized.

So much about book design is not obvious, and even the smallest changes are significant. Most people cannot distinguish between one simi-

Good typographers can make good use of almost anything. The typeface is a point of departure, not a destination. In using new typefaces the essential ingredient is imagination, because unlike with old typefaces, the possibilities have not been exhausted. . . . It is always possible to do *good* typography with old typefaces. But why are so many typographers insistent on trying to do the impossible—*new* typography with old faces?
—Jeffery Keedy

lar typeface and another, but there are large differences between the way two seemingly similar versions of, say, Garamond may set. A type size change of half a point (1/150 inch) can have an important effect on the readability of the type.

The size of the typeface and how it is set are of the same importance as the choice of the face itself. No matter how well designed a face, it has to be large enough to be readable, yet not so large as to look too big for the page. The conventional ideal measure is something close to 65 characters per line,

Being able to set a large sample of actual text on the computer makes it possible to see what happens with different sizes and styles of type as I try to find which one suits the author's words best. In sorting through the possibilities, I am seeking the right combination of type style and size to fit the words: to make sure the spaces will be reasonably uniform and the fre-

Adobe Garamond 11.2/15

Being able to set a large sample of actual text on the computer makes it possible to see what happens with different sizes and styles of type as I try to find which one suits the author's words best. In sorting through the possibilities, I am seeking the right combination of type style and size to fit the words: to make sure the spaces will be reasonably uniform

Simoncini Garamond 11.2/15

Being able to set a large sample of actual text on the computer makes it possible to see what happens with different sizes and styles of type as I try to find which one suits the author's words best. In sorting through the possibilities, I am seeking the right combination of type style and size to fit the

Monotype Garamond 11.2/15

Being able to set a large sample of actual text on the computer makes it possible to see what happens with different sizes and styles of type as I try to find which one suits the author's words best. In sorting through the possibilities, I am seeking the right combination of type style and size to fit the words: to make sure the spaces will be reasonably uniform

Monotype Garamond 11.8/15

Being able to set a large sample of actual text on the computer makes it possible to see what happens with different sizes and styles of type as I try to find which one suits the author's words best. In sorting through the possibilities, I am seeking the right combination of type style and size to fit the words:

Monotype Garamond 10.8/15

but, as with everything else in book design, it depends. It depends on how the type is designed and on the author's vocabulary. In some instances, it might be possible to set a handsome line of type fewer than 50 characters long or more than 70. And a satisfactory choice of typeface depends on the leading—the amount of space between one line of type and the next. The accepted idea is that long lines of type are somewhat balanced by adding extra space between them, so that a reader's eyes go readily to the beginning of the next line.

Being able to set a large sample of actual text on the computer makes it possible to see what happens with different sizes and styles of type as I try to find which one suits the author's words best. In sorting through the possibilities, I am seeking the right combination of type style and size to fit the words: to make sure the spaces will be reasonably uniform and the frequency of

Monotype Garamond 11.2/13

Being able to set a large sample of actual text on the computer makes it possible to see what

happens with different sizes and styles of type as I try to find which one suits the author's words

best. In sorting through the possibilities, I am seeking the right combination of type style and

size to fit the words: to make sure the spaces will be reasonably uniform and the frequency of

Monotype Garamond 11.2/18

There is no sure formula for how to do this. A change in one part of the type page means rethinking another. Widely leaded lines of type often need to have generous margins to make the type block look as if it fits on the page.

The line measure—the length of the line of type—also depends on whether the type is set justified (evened up on both sides) or ragged (with an uneven margin, generally on the right side). Customarily, type set in a narrow measure is set with ragged right, and the spaces between words are uniform. When type is set in a narrow measure and justified (as in a newspaper column), the word spacing varies so much that sometimes the word spaces may be greater than some of the words.

The line measure—the length of the line of type— also depends on whether the type is set justified (evened up on both sides) or ragged (with an uneven margin, generally

Ragged right to a narrow measure

The line measure—the length of the line of type—also depends on whether the type is set justified (evened up on both sides) or ragged (with an uneven margin, generally on the right

Justified to a narrow measure

Type specification is generally expressed in the form
    10/12 Garamond × 26 picas
which stands for
    the size of the typeface (10 point)
    the leading (the space measured from the base of one line of type to
        the base of the next, here 12 points, giving a 2-point space
        between lines)
    the name of the typeface (Garamond)
    the width to which the type is set (26 picas, where a pica is 12 points,
        or about 1/6 inch)

The expression would be read "ten on twelve Garamond by twenty-six picas."

DETAILS

Paragraphs

What happens between paragraphs? Many designers use an em space to begin a new paragraph. Other designers feel that a space the width of a letter "M" is not enough, and others would use less space, not more. One of the first books I designed was with the artist Leonard Baskin, who insisted on half an em space. A journal editor with whom I worked was uncomfortable with 1 em and wanted 3 ems. We compromised on 2. In *Questioning Edmond Jabès,* the designer, Richard Eckersley, used what he called "outdents"—hanging indents with the first line of each paragraph flush left and the rest of paragraph indented. Eric Gill's *Essay on Typography* has no paragraph indents but instead uses the symbol ¶ (known as a pilcrow). Other designers use no indentations but prefer space between paragraphs.

---

he elaborates his dictionary of obsessional words, he implies that in one
    of its aspects at least, the Book will be precisely that: a dictionary.
Other words might well be added: *dwelling, desert, sand, void, margin,*
    scream. Still others, even more frequent and connotatively charged,
    Jabès uses, exploiting the poetic potential of tautology, to denote

Paragraph style by Richard Eckersley in *Questioning Edmond Jabès*

**would be no one to build the Forth Bridge but plenty
to build houses; and the printing of books would be
done slowly & painfully by hand. ¶ All these things
are said in amity & not in bitterness. An industrial-
ism which really completes itself will have many
admirable and noble features. The architecture of**

Paragraph style by Eric Gill in *Essay on Typography*

Jan Tschichold wrote an entire essay on why paragraphs must be in-dented: because indention guarantees that no reader will miss the begin-ning of a paragraph and because it does not compromise the design. Spaces between paragraphs are "flagrant interruptions and at times leave the reader in doubt whenever a new page indeed begins with a new paragraph." Tschichold also felt that a lack of indention compromised the text. Flush-left paragraph beginnings give the reader

> the impression that everything on the page is connected . . . that he is reading a single paragraph. Yet a good writer chooses his paragraph breaks with great forethought and wants them to be recognized as such. . . . While blunt beginnings seem to create a uniform and consistent impression when compared with normal typesetting, this impression is paid for with serious loss of comprehension.*

But what about the first paragraph of a chapter or section? Should it be flush left or indented? Even with so explicit a philosophy, Tschichold him-self allowed that sometimes paragraphs *could* begin without indention—after centered headings, for example.

Numbers

Some numbers align at the same height, and others (called old-style figures) have a range of heights. Those that align, called "lining figures," can be of two kinds: the figures can be approximately the same height as capital letters, or the figures can be the same height as the lowercase letters (Bell) or a middle height (Melior).

lining 0 1 2 3 4 5 6 7 8 9   Bell 0 1 2 3 4 5 6 7 8 9
old-style 0 1 2 3 4 5 6 7 8 9   Melior 0 1 2 3 4 5 6 7 8 9

In texts with many numbers, old-style figures will be less obtrusive. But using old-style figures in a line of full caps can be awkward. Using small caps with old-style figures is often preferable.

YALE UNIVERSITY PRESS 1998 caps and lining figures
YALE UNIVERSITY PRESS 1998 caps and old-style figures
YALE UNIVERSITY PRESS 1998 small caps and old-style figures

The seemingly benign choice of figure style can open up a range of prob-lems that designers need to be aware of, especially when situations arise in text, such as B-52 when B-52 (using a small cap for the "B") might be visually preferable.

Caps Versus Small Caps

Just as old-style figures in text may look better than lining figures, small caps are a particularly useful alternative when a text has many acronyms. Small caps are not just smaller sizes of a full cap; they are specially designed

*The Form of the Book, *p. 108*.

letters, their weight matching that of the rest of the font. Reducing the size of capital letters to simulate small caps simply will not do.

NATO genuine small caps   NATO imitation small caps

Although using small caps for A.M. and P.M. may pose little danger, using them for acronyms is not always a decision that editors are willing to give up to a designer. When a designer chooses to use small caps for acronyms, where does it end? Should "U.S." be small caps? Or if a sentence begins with an acronym ("NATO war planes . . .") should the acronym be caps and small caps, all small caps, all caps?

Dashes

The design of the em dash dictated its questionable use. When it was first used in machine-set type, the dash was made to fill the width of the piece of metal, with no space left and right, so that when a 2- or 3-em dash was required, the dashes would connect into a single line. This worked well for multiple dashes, but when the em dash was used in text—like this—it naturally became common American usage to set it up close to the neighboring letters. The arbiter of American editorial correctness, *The Chicago Manual of Style,* shows the em dash with no space around it. But British style uses an en dash with space around it. Hans Schmoller, who was production director at Penguin, disapproved of the American style, pointing out that the closed-up dash *connects* two phrases when its intent should be to *separate* them.

In some fonts the em dash is narrower than the ordinary em dash, with space already designed around it. It is also possible for the designer or typesetter to create a 3/4-em dash with a small amount of space on either side—as has been done for this book.

On pages 45–47 Richard Eckersley shows how much better a text page can look when the conventional rules of typography are ignored.

Extracts

Extracted material—long passages of text quoted from another author—is meant to be read as part of the main text but is usually set off from it in some way. Some designers prefer to set prose extracts in a smaller size, whereas others prefer to set them the same size as the text and indent the extract or set it ragged right to distinguish it from justified text; still others use italic type. It is easy to overdo the distinction between main text and extract.

The length of the extracted material and the frequency with which extracts occur should be considered in how quoted text is styled. Long extracts that carry over from one page to another easily lose their special identity, so that simply indenting the extract is not necessarily a useful answer.

Setting the extract smaller (generally by one point size) is common, but

em dash—unspaced
em dash — with space
en dash–unspaced
en dash – with space

The unspaced em dash is not only ugly, it also lacks logic, for it is meant to separate, not to connect.
—Hans Schmoller

Use an en dash (not a hyphen) with word space either side.
—James Sutton
  and Alan Bartram

Dashes should be separated from the word or words they relate to by a hair space only.
—Geoffrey Dowding

"Mr. Cassadessius" was actually a parody of his own elapsed father. Pinecoffin elaborates this thesis ad nauseam (P.P.B.A., pp. 109–573) and with frequent references to some "tête-à-tête" with Gottlieb in the tea rooms of the Printemps department store. "The anecdote of the Café Julienne," as it has subsequently become known—and with no discouragement from its perpetrator—compounded by gullible Gottlieb's oleaginous biographers and students, has been even further corrupted by the patently false accounts given in Gransky's "Homage au Maître de Seumart-des-Deux-Bains"—mercifully out of print.

My motive for scuttling this ghost ship is disinterested—but not "uninterested" or, I'll venture, "uninteresting," (certainly not to those scholars who, like myself, "deign to look askance at purpled doctors gowns and rather, chalked their sleeves on the cracked slates of slat- terns' 'ABCs.'" I believe myself to be uniquely qualified in this under- taking. "For what reason," do you ask? Simply this—I was there: indeed, I paid the waiter's bill, (much inflated by Gottlieb's excess).

Mr. Cassadessius sat between us. In the hatband of a thumbed and fingered trilby hat was the salmon-pink betting slip askew, with face turned from the world—and its back turned towards me; and, confidentially, it advised me of his programme "de ce soir," boldly blotted in biro by his addlepated masters. First "memo to driver no. 14, Martin Cole, Esq. [*sic*]? Then cryptically what I took for his agenda—"Dr. and Mrs. Martinson, and J. W. F. Cornwallis—total weight 4 cwts. 9 lbs. 2 ozs.—To be collected from no. 120, Doughty St., at 4 p.m.—Be furnished with plenty of John Jamieson and H2O if temperature at time of departure falls below 52 F.—Cornwallis has 4to and Bacon 1st. folio—missing p. 1—with slipcase 9 x 7—to be deposited at Messrs. Lloyds for collection by the UNIVEX agent—then on to the "Rosy Turbot" for snacks, before returning to Eel Pie Island, S.E. 17, by the left fork of the V to "The Green Man," "The Pied Sheep," "The Suffolk Punch," and "The Prospect of Whitby"—"on no account leave the Alsatian alone in the back—sit tight—'Drive safely'—Gutteridge." And so the agenda concluded. I noted by the ormolu hunter before me that the hour was nearer to 4 than 5p.m., without surprise—Cassadessius had been tardy ever, and particularly towards the "cocktail hour." Gottlieb, mean while, was emptying his pockets at the nagging insistence of some creditor. First she

The first example is something of a caricature of bad practice: wide paragraph indents, double word spaces between sentences, lack of ligatures, use of letterspacing to disguise loose lines. The text is set in 10/12.2 Galliard, but this typeface requires more generous leading, particularly when the text includes such a rash of capital letters, figures, and punctuation marks.

'Mr Cassadessius' was actually a parody of his own elapsed father. Pinecoffin elaborates this thesis ad nauseam (PPBA, pp.109–573) and with frequent references to some 'tête-à-tête' with Gottlieb in the tea rooms of the Printemps department store. 'The anecdote of the Café Julienne,' as it has subsequently become known—and with no discouragement from its perpetrator—compounded by gullible Gottlieb's oleaginous biographers and students, has been even further corrupted by the patently false accounts given in Gransky's 'Homage au Maître de Seumart-des-Deux-Bains'—mercifully out of print.

My motive for scuttling this ghost ship is disinterested—but not 'uninterested' or, I'll venture, 'uninteresting,' (certainly not to those scholars who, like myself, 'deign to look askance at purpled doctors gowns and rather, chalked their sleeves on the cracked slates of slat- terns' ABCs.' I believe myself to be uniquely qualified in this under- taking. 'For what reason,' do you ask? Simply this—I was there: indeed, I paid the waiter's bill, (much inflated by Gottlieb's excess).

Mr Cassadessius sat between us. In the hatband of a thumbed and fingered trilby hat was the salmon-pink betting slip askew, with face turned from the world—and its back turned towards me; and, confidentially, it advised me of his programme 'de ce soir,' boldly blotted in biro by his addlepated masters. First 'memo to driver no.14, Mar- tin Cole, Esq [sic].' Then cryptically what I took for his agenda—'Dr and Mrs Martinson, and J W F Cornwallis—total weight 4cwts 9lbs 2ozs—To be collected from no.120, Doughty St, at 4pm—Be furnished with plenty of John Jamieson and H^{2}O if temperature at time of departure falls below 52f—Cornwallis has 4to and Bacon 1st folio—missing p.1—with slipcase 9 x 7—to be deposited at Messrs Lloyds for collection by the UNIVEX agent—then on to the 'Rosy Turbot' for snacks, before returning to Eel Pie Island, SE17, by the left fork of the V to 'The Green Man,' 'The Pied Sheep,' 'The Suffolk Punch,' and 'The Prospect of Whitby'—'on no account leave the Alsatian alone in the back—sit tight—"Drive safely"— Gutteridge.' And so the agenda concluded. I noted by the ormolu hunter before me that the hour was nearer to 4 than 5pm, without surprise—Cassadessius had been tardy ever, and particularly towards the 'cocktail hour.' Gottlieb, mean while, was emptying his

The type size is 9.8/12.8. Other changes: letterspacing and double word spaces between sentences have been banished, "fi" and "fl" ligatures have been used, acronyms have been set in small caps, old-style figures have replaced lining figures, single quotation marks have become the primary order, periods have been deleted with acronyms and contractions, word spaces have been removed between abbreviations and their related numbers, and the gothic "V" has been reset in the text font. Despite all this, the paragraph breaks are uglier than ever.

'Mr Cassadessius' was actually a parody of his own elapsed father. Pinecoffin elaborates this thesis ad nauseam (PPBA, pp.109–573) and with frequent references to some 'tête-à-tête' with Gottlieb in the tea rooms of the Printemps department store. 'The anecdote of the Café Julienne,' as it has subsequently become known – & with no discouragement from its perpetrator – compounded by gullible Gottlieb's oleaginous biographers & students, has been even further corrupted by the patently false accounts given in Gransky's 'Homage au Maître de Seumart-des-Deux-Bains' – mercifully out of print.

My motive for scuttling this ghost ship is disinterested – but not 'uninterested' or, I'll venture, 'uninteresting,' (certainly not to those scholars who, like myself, 'deign to look askance at purpled doctors' gowns and rather, chalked their sleeves on the cracked slates of slatterns' ABCs.' I believe myself to be uniquely qualified in this undertaking. 'For what reason,' do you ask? Simply this – I was there: indeed, I paid the waiter's bill, (much inflated by Gottlieb's excess).

Mr Cassadessius sat between us. In the hatband of a thumbed and fingered trilby hat was the salmon-pink betting slip askew, with face turned from the world – and its back turned towards me; and, confidentially, it advised me of his programme 'de ce soir,' boldly blotted in biro by his addlepated masters. First 'memo to driver no.14, Martin Cole, Esq [sic].' Then cryptically what I took for his agenda –'Dr and Mrs Martinson, and JWF Cornwallis – total weight 4cwts 9lbs 2ozs –To be collected from no.120, Doughty St, at 4pm – Be furnished with plenty of John Jamieson and H^2O if temperature at time of departure falls below 52f – Cornwallis has 4to and Bacon 1st folio – missing p.1 – with slipcase 9 x 7 – to be deposited at Messrs Lloyds for collection by the UNIVEX agent – then on to the 'Rosy Turbot' for snacks, before returning to Eel Pie Island, SE17, by the left fork of the V to 'The Green Man,' 'The Pied Sheep,' 'The Suffolk Punch,' and 'The Prospect of Whitby' – 'on no account leave the Alsatian alone in the back – sit tight – "Drive safely"– Gutteridge.' And so the agenda concluded. I noted by the ormolu hunter before me that the hour was nearer to 4 than 5pm, without surprise – Cassadessius had been tardy ever, & particularly towards the 'cocktail hour.' Gottlieb, meanwhile, was emptying his pockets at the nagging insistence of some creditor. First she demanded 10,000 francs, then 7,500, & then 5,000. 500 was what she got, for that was all I could afford. But what was in

The type remains 9.8/12.8. Punctuation hangs in the margins, paragraph indents have been reduced to 1 em, and the small cap ampersand has been employed on an ad hoc basis to resolve remaining word space problems. Examples prepared by Richard Eckersley.

THE DESIGN BEGINS HERE   47

when there are many extracts within the text, the type page begins to take on a decidedly odd and unsettled look.

Poetry extracts are usually set in the same size type as prose extracts and line for line, with the end-of-line breaks specified in the manuscript. Whether they are indented and by how much depends on the nature of the poetry. The occasional verse extract is often centered on the longest line of the quoted poem—that is, the longest line is centered on the normal width of the surrounding text, and the remaining lines of poetry are aligned with it on the left. When there are numerous verse extracts, establishing a common indent is often a good idea, for it gives stability to the whole page, the text block.

---

by the wind), Dobyns moves past a "dog panting at the foot of the stairs" to a bedroom upstairs, where

> a man lies naked on white sheets smoking a cigarette. His wife, also naked,
> sleeps with her head on his chest. As he smokes, the man carelessly strokes
> her back and stares up at the lines and angles of the white ceiling until it
> seems he's looking down from some high place, a plane or hilltop.

It is here that Dobyns draws a parallel between the elevated perspective of his narrator and the consciousness of the man, who is alone among the characters in the poem in being able to see something beyond the confines of this property: "he can just see / the roofs of other houses and he imagines his neighbors / drowsing their way through the August afternoon." This is the only thought he has here in the first section of the poem. Next, he watches his cigarette smoke "turn blue / as it rises through bars of sunlight to the ceiling," and he hears

> the sound of people
> playing tennis—an occasional shout and the plonk
> of the ball against the webbing of the racket;
> from the porch, he hears the tinkling of wind chimes
> like a miniature orchestra forever warming up.

Thus ends the first section of this poem, with a glance back at one of its opening images, the image of the title. The man is in a state of languid alertness as he experiences a defining moment in his life, a moment of particular emotional and sensual poignancy.

Or so it will seem "Years later," in the second section of the poem, when "the same man is lying fully clothed / on his bed in a city hotel . . . / waiting for a friend / and soon they will go out to dinner." The only light is from the street and from "a blinking / red sign outside his window." He again stares at the ceiling, and either that action or "some combination of sounds from the street" reminds him of the wind chimes. Much has changed in the intervening years—

STEPHEN DOBYNS : 71

Two verse extracts with a common indent, from Peter Stitt, *Uncertainty & Plenitude*, University of Iowa Press

Books of Poetry

The choice of typeface and type size is nowhere quite so critical as in setting books of poetry.

My daughter's young friend once told me how clever she thought authors were because they could pick just the right words to make every line end at the same place. Although I wish that authors were all so visually sophisticated, many don't seem to think about design when they write. I have always wondered why poets don't seem to understand that books have a finite width, and write to make sure that lines do not have to be broken. When I raised this issue with the poet J. D. McClatchy, his response was that "poets write lines that must be broken because they are writing an ideal poem, not one that's cut to the size of someone else's bed. You speak as if you'd have every poet be a Dickinson, and none a Whitman! I hate broken lines myself, and would try to revise a poem to avoid them. Many others are less compromising."*

Even though books of verse are often much shorter than books of prose, they are considerably more work for the designer. Poems by the same author within the same book can have entirely different formats, frequently requiring slight adjustments because they do not have the same length, width, or complexity of structure. Making each one fit as well as possible within the design calls for very detailed specifications and often many separate layouts.

Display Type

The choice of a display face is no easier than the choice of a text face. Some designers prefer to begin the plan for the book with the display type because the design of the letters is more distinguishable than with a text face. The typeface for the chapter titles can more obviously establish the visual tone for the book, and in determining the size and placement of display type, there is more freedom of choice than there is in doing so for text type.

Often designers shuttle back and forth between the text and the display faces, adjusting one after deciding what works best for the other. The type for the chapter titles can be the same typeface as the text face — only larger. But it may also be a contrasting typeface. If a contrasting typeface is used for the chapter titles, should it be used for subheadings within the text? Or is it preferable to use some variation of the text face for the subheadings? The nature of the text — the physical words themselves — usually supplies the clue, which is why preconceived, standardized, or model designs for books often look so wrong.

How the display type is used is as critical as what it is. The frequency with which display type is used in the text and the actual words for the titles make the difference. When the author writes a two-word title for one chap-

Yes, there is a type that I especially like for poetry —Baskerville. I think that Baskerville monotype, 169 E, makes the best looking poetry pages I've seen printed. I particularly dislike those light type faces some publishers seem to think appropriate for poetry. It seems to me that the Baskerville monotype 169 E, eleven-point, would be perfect—but eleven-point might be too big—it might make too many run-over lines—maybe they could try and see. It would all depend on the size of the page.
—Elizabeth Bishop

*Letter to author,
28 February 1994.

ter and a fifteen-word title for another, the designer must figure out how to give them both the correct visual weight in relation to the rest of the text page.

Some designers begin with the most awkward chapter title, assuming that if it can be made to look good, the others will, too. That isn't always so. For example, in a book of ten chapters, with nine having one- or two-word titles and the tenth a much longer title, choosing a small type size for the majority of the titles to accommodate the longest one might be a mistake.

Designers often have an idealized text page in their heads, and they may be so confident about its satisfactoriness that they do not draw it or print it out. This is less likely the case for display type, because it is generally necessary to know *exactly* how long some titles are going to be and how the words might break when set in the chosen typeface and type size. Before the advent of the computer, designers either had to trace out each title or guess at how lines would break. Now it is easy for a designer to set every chapter opening, and many do this, making layout after layout.

Subheadings within the text can be even more problematic than chapter titles because there are a seemingly infinite number of problems attached to them. I always want to know how many levels of subhead there are, how frequently they occur, what the longest and shortest subheads within each level are, whether there are any words in full caps or italics, whether the subheads are stacked (that is, two or more levels of subhead appear one after the other without intervening text), and whether a subhead begins the chapter. Not only do subheads have to be designed so their hierarchy is evident; they must not be confused with running heads or other type elements on the page. Because authors rarely think in visual terms, they give little consideration to the problem subheads present to the designer who must reconcile extreme variations in length. Inevitably, the designer becomes a typographic Procrustes, figuring out the least awkward compromise to make them all fit—more or less.

If the designer has chosen to work with a single style of type throughout the book for display and text, the choice of what to do with the subheads is limited. In books with only one or two levels of subhead, this may be a minor problem. But if there are three or more levels of subhead, the designer needs to be especially judicious in determining the size and style of type (italics, full caps, small caps) and establishing the position of each level of subhead (centered, flush left or right, indented, hanging in the margin, etc.). Sometimes there is no recourse but to rethink the entire design using two styles of type (serif and sans serif) or to introduce boldface type.

When subheads occur frequently, the space used around them is especially critical. The space between the subhead and the following text must be small enough to make it clear that they belong together. Too much space destroys the unity of the text and creates recurring trouble when subheads fall near the bottom of the page. A factor in determining the space around subheads should be the leading of the main text. Using spacing around subheads that does not total whole lines of text means that facing pages will not be evenly aligned with each other when there is a subhead on one page but not on the other. By this I mean that if the text is 10/12 (10-point type leaded 2 points), the subhead and the space around it should add up to even units of 12. When a subhead occurs at the top of a page, using an uneven amount of space around it causes an additional problem. If the subhead is to begin on the first text line and there is an uneven amount of leading between it and the text that follows it, the bottom of that page will not be aligned with the bottom of the opposite page.

The design or position of the running head must be different enough from that of the subheads so that when a subhead begins a new page, the two elements neither look uncomfortable together nor can be mistaken for one another. One advantage of running feet is that they are never immediately adjacent to a subhead.

Running Heads and Folios

Running heads are a peculiar convention. They show up even in books for which they seem to serve no obvious purpose. In books of complex organization they do help the reader locate material quickly, but in works of fiction, nothing is gained by repeating either the author's name or the book title page after page. In a time of rampant photocopying, however, the running head at least provides a provenance to purloined pages.

Repeated page heads and folios (page numbers) have no stipulated placement. Their style and position on the page are related to the reason for having them. How prominent they need to be depends on the text. In books with few pages, running heads might be unnecessary altogether, and folios could be positioned in less obvious places—at the inside margin rather than the outside margin, for example. Some designers feel that the running heads should be part of the text and so have only the minimum amount of space between the running head and the text. Others feel that running heads should be clearly separate from the text. Some prefer running feet—at the bottom of the page—and others mix feet and heads or omit heads or folios on, say, left-hand pages.

Like all other matters of aesthetics, taste changes. Once it was popular to set running heads larger than the text face. Designers can evoke a certain typographic era by using these out-of-fashion styles, but should do so with some care.

The Half-Title and Title Pages

I often think that the amount of time spent on designing the half title (or what was once called the "bastard title") and title page of a book is in inverse ratio to the time a reader spends consulting them; the most time-consuming page designs are the least looked at. What reason is there now

Under this necessity to make the book novel and startling, so it will sell, you seize upon little elements like running heads and primp them up with neckties and ribbons and things running heads oughtn't to have (because that makes them conspicuous, and they oughtn't to be conspicuous because that takes your eye off the reading). Folios, too, are easy spots for the ornamentalist to seize upon. He puts brackets around them, and wings on the brackets, and curls on the ends of the wings.
—W. A. Dwiggins

for a half-title page? Once, when books were sold unbound, the half title kept the title page clean, but now it serves no real purpose. To add to its uselessness, many designers treat this page in the most thoughtless way. Because it is of so little real purpose, designers might be more creative with this page—setting up the design for the title page and the scene for the rest of the book.

If the half title isn't important, the title page surely is. It is the page of record. The design for the title page has to belong in some way to the design for other display type in the book, but often the words that appear on the title page are very different from the words used for all other headings. There is no other page in the book so dissimilar. Many times it isn't possible to use a larger size of the chapter title type, nor is it necessary to do so. The title page can relate to the rest of the design in understated and subtle ways, and the type need not be any larger than the type used for the chapter or part openings.

When books were set in metal type, very large sizes were rare. Typesetters kept only a limited range of display type because it was expensive to buy. And because metal type was cast in a limited range of sizes, the perfect size of large type for a given display was hard to find. Some designers sought to make a virtue of this by avoiding large type altogether.

In a long essay on title-page design Tschichold advised that "a proper title page has to be set from the same type family that has been used for the book." He also said that in only a few exceptional cases was it necessary to use more than three sizes of type in a book; he preferred two, used no boldface, and set titles in full caps that were letterspaced.

The words of the title page, their meaning, and their relative importance to each other are challenges to the designer's skill. Typographers like Richard Eckersley have shown how liberated the title page can be.

The Rest of the Front Matter

The copyright page, like the half title, is another of those pages that often escape the designer's attention. Copyright pages have become more complicated than ever with the addition of Library of Congress cataloging-in-publication (CIP) data, statements on the acidity of the paper, and portentous warnings meant to deter those attempting to violate the author's intellectual rights. Tschichold likened these particulars "to the endless list of credits before a film finally begins . . . they are as obtrusive as they are unwanted." He would have preferred them at the end of the book.

The copyright page needs to be handled as carefully as any other page in the book. It is the legal notice of who owns the contents, and it contains the cataloging information, which (one hopes) is of use to librarians. Relating these fragments by design to the rest of the book is not always a simple matter. The problem is deciding not just the type size, leading, line breaks, and space between elements but the position for the block of type contain-

LES VASES COMMUNICANTS

COMMUNICATING

VeSsels

ANDRÉ BRETON

Translated by Mary Ann Caws &
Geoffrey T. Harris, with notes &
introduction by Mary Ann Caws

University of Nebraska Press: Lincoln & London

Design by Richard Eckersley

THE CUBIST POETS

POETS

AN ANTHOLOGY

University of Nebraska Press: Lincoln and London

IN PARIS

EDITED BY L. C. BREUNIG

Design by Richard Eckersley

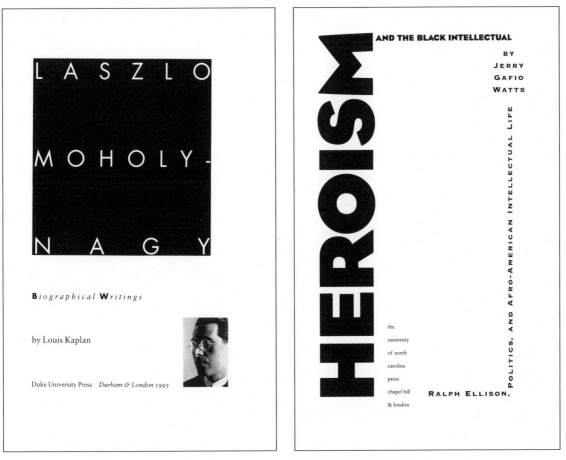

Design by Mary Mendell

Design by April Leidig-Higgins

Design by April Leidig-Higgins

ing all of them. Should it be indented? Should it align at the top of the page, align with the chapter-opening text, or have some place of its own? Too often designers don't see the complete copy for this page at the time that the design for the rest of the book is being planned. They may never see it at all. One publisher whom I knew seemed astounded that I would want to design the page, and another was bemused by my use of a two-column format.

The minimalism of the dedication page presents its own difficulties. What does a designer do with only two or three words? No other text page is so spare. Authors care about their dedicatees. More than once, I have had authors change the inscription while the book was in production, replacing the name of one pal with that of another, not realizing the design implications of adding a few more words or a different name. How the designer presents the dedication can make it either a line of mundane typography or a valentine. The conundrum is how to make the page important to both the dedicator and dedicatee and, at the same time, to ensure that it is modest and unassuming.

The design for the epigraph depends on its words. The design style for longer texts easily relates to that of the main text of the book, but shorter epigraphs can present the same kind of problems that the dedication does, especially when (as often happens) the source for the epigraph is more complicated than the epigraph itself.

Likewise, the design for the preface or acknowledgments depends on what is said and and at what length. Copy running a page or more might be set the same as the main text, but a paragraph or two could be set differently. Front and back matter text is often so different from the main text that its design may vary from that of the main text—especially in the style, size, and position of the headings.

The headings for the front matter pages need not always be an exact copy of the chapter titles, especially because the material that follows the front matter headings may be very different from the text that follows chapter titles. This is evident in the contents page, list of illustrations, and other lists appearing as part of the prelims. The design of these pages should be based on their text.

A few of the design problems for the contents page are

how to define the relative importance of the elements
how to relate visually the part titles, chapter numbers, chapter titles, chapter subtitles, and, in texts with muliple contributors, the authors' names
how to group various elements, such as sections within parts, and distinguish front and back matter titles from chapter titles
how to style the folios so that they are clearly not part of the titles, especially when the titles have many dates or other figures
how to break the lines of text so that the page has a visual unity—

INTRODUCTION

EGYPT

RACE

THE NEAR EAST

The quotation marks hang so that the chapter titles can align even when the chapter title is not a quotation. The folios are set in roman to distinguish them from the subtitles, which are set in italic.

avoiding both very long lines and very short ones while keeping the sense of what the words are saying

Occasionally chapter subtitles contain more critical information than the chapter titles do. In some books, the parts are the principal elements and the chapters are considerably subordinate to them. In some multiauthor books, the names of contributors are primary. The design should reflect this.

Common practice is to begin the contents on a recto (right-hand) page. If the contents list is especially long and complicated, I will begin the contents on the verso page so that a reader can see the entire information on a double-page spread.

The Back Matter and Everything Else

Back matter texts are as different in content from each other as they are from the rest of the book. Most nonfiction books have notes, bibliography, and index. Once upon a time, notes in serious nonfiction books would be on the same page as the reference in the text (footnotes). The expense and extra complications of making up pages with footnotes led publishers to put the notes at the end of the chapter or at the end of the book (endnotes). Although authors may be unhappy with this repositioning, designers are not. The typographic style of notes can be extremely finicky and difficult to make look inviting, especially when notes are set smaller than the rest of the text on the page. If the purpose of notes is to certify something the author has said, they might just as well appear some place other than on the page of reference. But if notes are meant to constitute a dialogue that the author is having with the main text or a further commentary on it, the editor might just as well incorporate that material directly into the text itself or treat it as an appendix.

Unquestionably, readers who like to check the author's references find it irritating to flip from the text to another page for the note. Publishers for whom I have worked have often excused the use of endnotes by saying that footnotes are off-putting to most readers. There is probably no hard evidence for this, just as there is little information about whether most readers interrupt their reading to check a reference, be it footnote or endnote.

Electronic page makeup has made the use of footnotes relatively easy. If there are footnotes, the usual style is to set them at least a size smaller than the text — and even smaller if extracts have been set down a size. Their reference to the text can be handled in any number of ways: numbered or lettered (with note numbers or letters set on line with the text or set as superscripts), with asterisks or daggers, by line reference, with the first line indented or flush left. The style for endnotes — either at the end of the chapter or the end of the book — depends on the notes themselves. Note numbers should

It is nice to think of trade publishers arguing against footnotes on grounds of usability ("they disrupt reading"). But "look and feel" is far more important. The message given to "non-academics" by footnotes is "Not for you." And, footnote readers are a tiny fraction of the book-reading population. So, the design decision was based on marketing priorities: Trade publishers think first of the choices people make before they are readers — that is, when they are potential buyers. Their rule is: At all costs avoid a look and feel that scares people off — so no footnotes. What people can't see won't hurt them.
—Paul Stiff

Footnotes, preferred to *end notes* . . . by reviewers and authors and probably by most readers, are often difficult to present really well.
—Hugh Williamson

be easy to find. Short notes might be set paragraph style (with the note number indented as in a paragraph), but when notes have paragraphs within them, hanging numbers are easier to locate.

Bibliographies can be set justified or ragged right. My own preference is to set bibliographies and indexes ragged right without hyphenation because the entries rarely take more than a line or two of type. Disallowing hyphenation in bibliographies assures that there will be no awkward breaks of, say, a publisher's name, but, as with everything else in book design, it depends. When there are many long German words, an unhyphenated bibliography can make for some very short lines.

Tables and lists are a problem unto themselves because their design depends so much on the information in them. No amount of good design can fix a badly prepared table. Not all tables in a book can be designed the same way unless each table contains the same kind of information. More often than not, each table needs its own design. I prefer to keep tables horizontal — running them across two pages when they won't fit on one — and to use as few rules (lines) and boxes as possible, but some tables insist on being turned sideways and need the visual assistance of rules.

Tables often require close communication among author, editor, designer, and typesetter. Authors and editors who fail to remember the size and finite limits of the text page make problems that are truly unsolvable. John Ryder calls this the absence of "visual editing."

When photographs are integrated with the text, captions have to be typographically distinct from the text and other headings. Captions may or may not be in the same typeface as other display type or the text. Whether captions align at one side of the illustration or the other, or whether they are ragged right, justified, or centered, depends as much on what information the captions contain as on what the design for the rest of the book is.

A designer who fails to examine every manuscript page does so at his or her peril. Book design is not exempt from chaos theory. Authors rarely understand that the singular use of a tiny subhead in the middle of a long manuscript can change an entire design. The visual significance of that one modest line of type ripples through the whole text.

SPECIFICATIONS

When the design is done, specifications must be prepared. What exists in the imagination of the designer must be recorded in some way so that those who carry out the work know how to do it. Until recently, the work of the designer was usually realized by others, and although, at this writing, so-called desktop publishing is widespread, many designers still must, or choose to, rely on others to set the type for their books.

How much or how little the designer says in the written instructions to the typesetter depends as much on the skills of the designer writing them as

1. This is an example of a note set in paragraph style.

2. Another note set in paragraph style.

1. This is an example of a note set in hang and indent style.

2. Another note set in hang and indent style.

on the craft and intelligence of the typesetter. Some designers only add confusion by writing specifications that disagree with the layout. The compositor is left with the choice of making the work look like the sample design or following a conflicting instruction. Other designers, having no confidence in the typesetter or not knowing who the typesetter might be, overspecify a job and may not realize that their request is perhaps no better than the typesetter's default or may not even be possible.

The relationship between designer and typesetter is more codependent now than it ever was, given that both have more control of the way type looks. What is said or unsaid in specifications is critical.

Writing specifications forces the designer to think about the rationality of the design, which is why specifications ought to be formally written even when the designer is also the typesetter.

The Design of *High Lonesome*

What follows is an example of how I designed a particular book, *High Lonesome,* an academic text about popular culture — specifically, the relation between the lyrics of country music and the rest of American literature and art. The design had to reflect its serious intent while not neglecting the rich visual aspects of the subject matter. The author had spent considerable effort and money collecting over a hundred illustrations of everything from record covers to paintings by Edward Hopper and Grant Wood, and she wanted them used prominently. But it was important not to make the book look like a picture book.

No publisher can guess exactly the number of copies of a book to print, but most have a good enough sense of the market to establish a quantity with some confidence. Because of the unusual subject of this book, the publisher was unsure whether it might be seen as too highbrow for country music fans and too lowbrow for academics. The publisher decided on a modest initial quantity of three thousand copies, which meant that the budget would be a major factor in how the book was produced.

The trim size was as much of an issue as the quantity. The publisher's usual format, 6 1/8 × 9 1/4 inches, was too small to display the illustrations, but a much larger format might have cost too much and could have upset the balance between text and illustrations. Many of the photographs were record album covers, which suggested a squarish book. Variations on 8 1/2 × 11 were tried, but that format was difficult. The text was lengthy, and I don't like reading a line longer than 75 characters. The large format meant that the text would have to be set either in a single wide column in a larger than normal type size or in two columns in 10- or 11-point type. The most practical solution seemed to be 7 × 10 inches, which allowed the text to be in a single column of standard-size type and a page to be large enough to give adequate space for the illustrations.

I always try to have some visual handle when I begin a design. If I don't have something specific in mind, I do at least try to decide on the look or feel I want the book to have. This can be as vague as wanting a serious, sober, understated semblance or as specific as an unapologetic typographic pastiche. It is not easy to design a book about which I have no feeling whatsoever.

I shamelessly admit I love clichés. It is foolish to reject something so visually useful. Still, I know that clichés can be nothing more than a facile and mindless way to communicate an idea. I wish that I always used them as cleverly as does Richard Eckersley, who has the knack of turning them on their heads.

I like allusiveness in design, and I am happiest when I have a book that allows for it. I had an idea of what *High Lonesome* should look like right from the start, but not until I actually began to read the text did I know what to do with it.

Unless I have a special interest in the subject of a book I am designing, I usually read only the preface or introduction. I always hope that I'll find a statement from the author, editor, or publisher giving me the book's raison d'être. I look at every page of the manuscript and flag everything that will need design attention. I check each chapter opening to see what the titles, subtitles, and epigraphs look like and whether there are those most awkward and detested of elements — subheadings on the chapter-opening page, right after the chapter title.

Knowing how the text begins in each chapter tells me if I can use a large or decorative opening initial letter (drop cap). I prefer not to when the text opens with a word in italic or a quotation, even though the *Chicago Manual* permits the removal of quotation marks when there is an initial. I myself find it confusing to read a sentence only to discover at its end that I have been reading a quotation.

I take note of each level of subheading, looking especially for the longest and shortest subheadings, stacked subheadings (one right under another, without intervening text), and the nature of the text after each of them — an extract, a list, whatever.

The text for *High Lonesome* was relatively uncomplicated: there were no subheadings, few extracts, no unusual tabular matter or lists, and only an interview to be styled differently from the rest. But the chapter titles varied considerably: chapter 1 was called "Pathos, Miseries, Happiness, Life Itself: An Introduction"; chapter 3, just "Road." Each chapter opened with epigraphs: chapter 9 had three short ones, and chapter 10 had a single extended statement.

The manuscript editor had skillfully reduced the running heads to no more than three words each. Many captions were short — fewer than twenty words — but sometimes one caption related to two or three illustrations. In addition to the usual front and back matter, there was a discography. It was enough like the bibliography for me to want to make the two elements typographically the same.

The plan was to make a book of 320 pages, so I knew how much type had to be on an average text page. When starting the design I sometimes import a sample of the author's electronic manuscript, if there is one, but I often prefer to keyboard two or three pages of actual text myself. Doing so is time consuming, especially with my dubious typing skills, but it seems no slower than the way I used to do it — drawing out pages of parallel rules to simulate the look of the type. When I am looking for a passage to typeset, I try to find a section of text in which the author talks about the purpose of the book, and in doing my own typing I acquire not only a sample of manuscript for the design but an inroad to the author's subject and approach.

For the typeface I first chose Bodoni Book. It is a face that I have used only rarely for book setting because I find it difficult to read, and it seldom typesets to suit the way I design. When I want a face that has some of the characteristics of Bodoni (contrast of light and dark strokes, an upright stress, a nineteenth-century feeling), I choose Century Expanded. It sets better and seems more readable. Because I use Bodoni so rarely, I think of it as an exotic face. For this book I thought that Bodoni might have the right weight and texture in 11- or 12-point type. The book was going to be *See page 64.* printed on uncoated paper, which would reduce some of the sparkle of Bodoni's contrasty design, and the larger-than-usual page size would show off a bit more of the type's design, too.

Before I had a computer on which I could set samples of the author's words, I could only guess at how they would look in one face or another. Now, because I keyboard samples of the text, I can see exactly how they react in the face and size that I propose using. In addition to seeing how readable the type is, I look to see how many awkward line endings there are and how the pages break. The text in my samples is hardly ever made up the way it will really appear in the book, but if the lines and pages don't break right in my layouts, they probably won't break right in the book either.

I began with a measure of 32 picas, which made for a fairly long line to read (86 characters), and the short running heads looked awkward no matter where I put them. Many books that I design need to have a lot of type on the page, and I have discovered that running feet often allow for an extra line of text. Apparently, the running foot, being less obtrusive than a full line of text, gives the appearance of leaving space at the bottom of the page, where I prefer a larger margin, and allows the first text line to set as close as half an inch from the top of the page. In this book, however, a short running foot under the wide text block made the page look unsteady, so I tried "running" sideheads. With the running heads moved to the side in a separate column I could reduce the width of the text block to make the line shorter and less difficult to read and could add a line of type to the page to compensate for the reduced measure. I was reasonably sure that the short sideheads would fit. The outside column for the sideheads could also be used for captions, and I could let the photos expand into that space. An additional consideration was to make sure that the design of the captions and running heads was different enough that they could not be confused with one another.

But I didn't like the way the Bodoni running sideheads looked. Roman or italic—it didn't seem to make any difference. They were either too large or too small, and I could not decide what to do with the folios. In lining figures the folios looked too important when they were set the same size as the sideheads, but they seemed to look too thin when I tried them in a smaller size. Making them boldface only got me back to where I started.

I set all the sideheads to see how they looked in different typefaces. The

Carl Belew the launch for his own song, "Lonely Street." This song, in turn,
comes our make-believe video screen from a 1959 Andy Williams hit (and a ▼ ▼ ▼ ▼ ▼ ▼
song Williams still sings in the 1990s). "Lonely Street" has been a country *High*
music perennial, recorded by Kitty Wells and then by Patsy Cline on the al- *Lonesome*
bum *Sentimentally Yours* (1962) and by Tammy Wynette (*Golden Memories*,
1972–81), finally by Emmylou Harris (*Bluebird*, 1988). There is no question
about the soundtrack here: we are listening to a country music classic-in-the-
making.

The story is of a search, even quest. Afflicted and burdened with a sorrowful story from the past, the singer seeks a place of emotional release to "weep"
and tell all. Patsy Cline's version (like Tammy Wynette's, suggests a progression toward a street that feels very real, an asphalt strip with curbs and gutters. There, on Lonely Street, this singer hopes to find a kindred soul who is
also keeping a death watch over dying love and shattered dreams—but who
would presumably also be a good listener.

This book does country—does it with a head-on recognition that *country*
is synonymous with *nation*. When TV and newspaper reporters speak or write
of "the country," they usually mean the United States of America. "Country"
is their shorthand term for both rural areas and for cities and suburbs too. We
understand and accept the all embracing reference immediately. Country
means nation—just as in this book, country music is emphatically national
music. Its belongs not solely to the locales. Carl Belew the launch for his own
song, "Lonely Street." This song, in turn, comes our make-believe video
screen from a 1959 Andy Williams hit (and a song Williams still sings in the
1990s). "Lonely Street" has been a country music perennial, recorded by
Kitty Wells and then by Patsy Cline on the album *Sentimentally Yours* (1962)
and by Tammy Wynette (*Golden Memories*, 1972–81), finally by Emmylou
Harris (*Bluebird*, 1988). There is no question about the soundtrack here: we
are listening to a country music classic-in-the-making. The story is of a
search, even quest.

Afflicted and burdened with a sorrowful story from the past, the singer
seeks a place of emotional release to "weep" and tell all. Patsy Cline's version
(like Tammy Wynette's, suggests a progression toward a street that feels very
real, an asphalt strip with curbs and gutters. There, on Lonely Street, this
singer hopes to find a kindred soul who is also keeping a death watch over
dying love and shattered dreams—but who would presumably also be a good
listener. This book does country—does it with a head-on recognition that
country is synonymous with *nation*. When TV and newspaper reporters speak
or write of "the country," they usually mean the United States of America.
"Country" is their shorthand term for both rural areas and for cities and suburbs too. We understand and accept the all embracing reference immediately.

12/15 Bodoni Book (reproduced at 82 percent)

The entryway features an oversize photo of Hank Williams at the mike in his Nudie-tailored western wear with his band, the Drifting Cowboys, and wall-mounted guitars are a major decorative motif (even a

10.5/15 Century Expanded

The entryway features an oversize photo of Hank Williams at the mike in his Nudie-tailored western wear with his band, the Drifting Cowboys, and wall-mounted guitars are a major decorative motif (even a

12/15 Bodoni Book

The entryway features an oversize photo of Hank Williams at the mike in his Nudie-tailored western wear with his band, the Drifting Cowboys, and wall-mounted guitars are a major decorative motif (even a

12/16 Monotype Garamond

best was Monotype Garamond, which had the advantage of setting tightly and had clear, nicely designed old-style figures. I also thought that Garamond looked good for the text, even though it was a much more neutral typeface than I had thought I wanted when I began the design. Equally important to me was who would set the book. Only two or three typesetters I worked with had adjusted the PostScript version of the face. Monotype had not taken much care when they made the face available for the computer, and I needed to be sure that the kerning pairs were adjusted and that the space around parentheses had been fixed. The space following words ending in "f" also seemed excessive.

I decided on 12/16 × 30 (12-point type with 4 points of leading set to a See page 66. width of 30 picas), which gave me the required amount of type on the page. The smallish x-height and the large ascenders of Garamond increased the look of the leading, which compensated for the long text line of about 75 characters. All of my typographic training, all of those design manuals, had warned me to avoid such an excessively long line of type. I never would have done such a thing in the first years that I was a book designer. But, as with all rules, there are ways to break them, and I have found that within reason a longer line can be set if there is enough space between the lines of type. I have also realized that as the space between lines increases, so does the space around the type, so the margins become more critical as the leading grows.

Even with the wider than normal measure, I kept the paragraph indent at 1 em. The 30-pica measure let the last lines of most paragraphs end far short of the right margin, and there seemed no reason to add more than a trinaire, Calvinist sister. He feels his orphanage most keenly in their respectable but alien household. Retreating to his room, he is not a moody preadolescent but a soul deeply alienated from his culture when he tells us, "I felt so lonesome I almost wished I was dead."

And soon he is, in a manner of speaking. Vowing to run away, Huck stages an elaborate hoax to lead townspeople (including his knife-wielding father) to believe he has met a violent end and washed away in that lonesome river. In effect, he stages his own death. Involving an ax and pig blood, his plan is so ingenious, and Huck's resourcefulness so fascinating, that neither he nor the reader thinks ahead to the moment when it's all over, when Huck is an escapee on the Mississippi. Inevitably, the let-down comes. Then, "by-and-by it got sort of lonesome," Huck says, faced with his own isolation, the absence of community and of his only friend, Tom Sawyer. Like an insomniac counting sheep, he counts stars, drifting logs, rafts. "There ain't no better way to put in time when you are lonesome; you can't stay so, you soon get over it."

But essentially, he never gets over it. Even weather triggers the feeling of desolation. Separated from the raft he shares with Jim, the runaway slave, Huck describes the whiteout of zero-visibility fog. "If you think it ain't dismal and lonesome out in a fog that way, by yourself, in the night, you try it once—you'll see." He is not talking about weather as such, but about his state of mind. This is the isolation of disorientation, when one has no access to the world beyond the self. And the "down-hearted" feeling overtakes Huck when he sees firsthand the violence and predation of "sivilized" life. Reentry into it at the close of the novel brings back that sense of desolation. Downriver, approaching the household of Tom Sawyer's aunt, Huck says it feels "Sunday-like," dead still, "so lonesome and like everybody's dead and gone; and if a breeze fans along and quivers the leaves, it makes you feel mournful, because you feel like it's spirits whispering—spirits that's been dead ever so many years. . . . As a general thing, it makes a body wish he was dead." Within minutes, Huck hears the hum and "wail" of a spinning wheel, the signature sound of a family and household of which he has never been a part. "And then I knowed for certain I wished I was dead—for that *is* the lonesomest sound in the whole world."

Are Mark Twain's readers' ears cocked for that lonesomest sound? Usually not. *The Adventures of Huckleberry Finn* is offered as a boys' adventure novel and a masterpiece of American fiction, to be enjoyed for its humor and admired for its important themes of individualism, racial consciousness-raising, zestful colloquial language, social satire. As for loneliness, it is a motif marked, at most, in passing.

Which brings us full circle from Huckleberry Finn right back to the world of the Little House on the Prairie. Twain's river, like Wilder's prairie, is pocked with

12/16 Monotype Garamond (reduced)

single-em indent, for there was already space enough at the end of the preceding paragraph to define the break.

My standard gutter margin is 3/4 inch (4.5 picas), which seems just right to make facing pages appear to belong together but not so small as to force the type into the gutter. Over the years I have moved the text higher and higher on the page. My visual default is now 1/2 inch, or 3 picas.

If *High Lonesome* had been a monograph, I might have been satisfied with the decisions made so far, but because the book was to be more "designed," I felt that the page needed a touch of something else. Unable to decide what to do, I put aside the text page and went ahead with the chapter openings, trusting that they might suggest a way to tart up the text page.

I was uncertain about what to use for the display type. Monotype Garamond was too polite for this book. I wanted something that would feel like the "West" or "country." The Garamond text was neutral enough to give me a lot of choice in the display face to use with it.

I started with the long chapter titles, those for the first and tenth chapters. Both had subtitles, so I felt the main titles should fit on one line to avoid a lot of clutter on the chapter openings. I wanted a typeface that would be in contrast to the Garamond but that would not overwhelm it, so I dug out Rob Roy Kelly's book on wood type for inspiration. When I had first seen Adobe's wood-type faces, I detested them and never thought I would find a use for them. They had been part of a package of free type that had come with some computer software, so I had them to try out. Willow, a tall, condensed type, had the right sort of design and weight, or color, and I liked the design of the figures. The long chapter titles could all fit on one line.

I first made the chapter number large and the title small, but the one-word titles looked insignificant. I kept increasing the size of the longest title until it filled the measure. I also threw in a few rules—my usual refuge—because the type didn't seem to have enough weight on its own. But the design now looked a lot like that for a book I had designed for another publisher a few years earlier. *See page 68.*

This being a book about the West, I thought maybe bullets would do, but I didn't like them. I once designed a book about Mary Austin using Zapf dingbat triangles as ornaments in the hope that they suggested Native American art. Ever since, I've thought of them as being as western. The rule made up of triangles seemed agreeable visually, but I couldn't decide how large the triangles should be, how many to use, or exactly where to put them. I shifted the rule around, first putting it close to the title and then close to the text. No matter where I put the rule, I could not find a place for the long epigraphs.

● ● ● ● ● ●

bullets

▼ ▼ ▼ ▼ ▼ ▼ ▼

dingbats

So the epigraphs were the problem. I decided to concentrate on them. I liked what they were saying and thought the author had chosen them well. With other books I haven't been shy about asking an editor to consider in-

5 Wild, Wild West

Walk west through urban canyons, west from the Avenue of the Americas and along Fifty-second Street between money mountains – Chase Manhattan, Paine Webber, Credit Lyonnais. Then cross Broadway into New York's theater district, where you stop at a building whose facade is a red-and-silver bus, like a Greyhound or Trailways. It is the Lone Star Café Roadhouse, "the official Texas embassy in New York City."

Red neon signs for Lone Star beer decorate the bar thought the distributror has stopped East Coast delivery, and Colorado-based Coors is the closest you can get in longnecks. Patrons come here for the western side of country-western music, and the Lone Star tries to oblige. The entryway features an oversize photo of Hank Williams at the mike in his Nudie-tailored western wear with his band, the Driftying Cowboys, And wall-mounted guitars are a major decorative motif (even a Chet Atkins-model Gibson). Texas license plates are nailed to a barroom-rafter. On a Sunday night in January, a patron with a New Jersey accent is overheard to say, "Thats why I wanted to go somewhere that's Texas-oriented."

By Texas, she means the West – not the New Yorker's sense of the "upper West Side," of course, but the mental map of the great American West. She means boots, hats, cowboys, and all that comes with them. On the job by day she might send data through a computer, telemarket, push retail merchandise over a counter. At night, however, in boots and jeans in the Lone Star, listening to country acts like Dan Seals, Delbert McClinton, or the Marshall Tucker Band, she is somewhere and somebody else. Walk west through urban canyons, west from the Avenue of the Americas and along Fifty-second Street between money mountains – Chase Manhattan, Paine Webber, Credit Lyonnais. Then cross Broadway into New York's theater district, where you stop at a building whose facade is a red-and-silver bus, like a Greyhound or Trailways. It is the Lone Star Café Road-house, "the official Texas embassy in New York City."

Red neon signs for Lone Star beer decorate the bar thought the distributor has stopped East Coast delivery, and Colorado-based Coors is the closest you can get in longnecks. Patrons come here for the western side of

The West of which I speak is but another name for the Wild.
—Henry David Thoreau, "Walking"

All in all, my years on the trail are the happiest I ever lived. . . . Most of the time we were solitary adventurers in a great land as fresh and new as a spring morning, and we were free and full of the zest of darers.
—Charlie Goodnight, cowboy (wall placard, Museum of Westward Expansion, St. Louis, Missouri)

A drunken cowboy got aboard a Santa Fe Train. "Where do you want to go?" asked the conductor. "To Hell," replied the cowboy. "Well, give me $2.50 and get off at Dodge,"
—Wall placard, Museum of Western Expansion, St. Louis. Missouri

You've got your hip country music, but out in the real world you have your cowboy stuff as well.
—John Jarvis, country music pianist/ keyboardist, magazine interview

First chapter-opening design, with rules and Willow display type tegrating long epigraphs into the text as extracts or editing them down. After all, epigraphs are meant to set the scene, not be the main show. Because the epigraphs in *High Lonesome* were so long, I abandoned the idea of putting them in the outside column. No matter how small I set them, they wouldn't fit. I set the text on the chapter-opening page wider, to fill the entire two columns—the text column and the narrower outside column—and moved the epigraphs to a four-column grid at the top of the page. I tried out every chapter opening to determine the length of each group of epigraphs and established a sinkage for the chapter title.

See page 70.

The epigraphs now seemed where they belonged, but I still had to decide what to do with the chapter number, chapter title, and subtitle. On the chapter openings with short titles and epigraphs the titles looked awkward. To give the display type more presence, I changed the chapter number from Willow to another Adobe wood-type face, Madrone, which was heavy and squat. Nineteenth-century typographers were skilled at mixing expanded and condensed faces—they made it look easy. But I've never found a way to make a creditable imitation. Dwiggins was right when he commented that we can't fully mimic the aesthetic of a different time and place because we aren't there and then, we are here and now.

See page 71.

I put back Bodoni as the text face but again rejected it and went back to Garamond. The text line on the chapter openings was just too long, so I decided to make the chapter-opening pages match the text width of the rest of the book. This meant adjusting the four-column grid I had established for the epigraphs and determining a new sinkage for the chapter titles.

I had been using the four-column grid established for the epigraphs to position the chapter number, title, ornament (the triangle rule), and text opening—aligning everything on the second column. The Madrone chapter numbers looked okay as long as they were used with titles of three or more words, but chapter 2 had a single word for its title. I moved the number flush left and moved the ornaments to the gutter, allowing them to extend to the right side of the third column of epigraphs. I retained the second-column indent for the title and first text line.

See page 72.

I varied this arrangement for the two long titles, allowing them to begin flush left. But with the long titles *and* the chapter numbers flush left, the opening seemed unbalanced. So for the two chapters where the titles began flush left I shifted the *number* to the second column, making these chapter openings different from the rest but continuing the idea of having the display type indent to the second column.

See page 72.

I had decided on the size of the chapter titles so that the longest would fit in a single line, but now I made two imperceptible changes: I increased slightly the size of the shorter chapter titles and let the quotation marks—single rather than double—on chapter 10 hang in the margin.

I then went back to the text page to try various sizes and arrangements of the triangles. I employed them as a decorative rule bleeding off the page

All in all, my years on the trail are the happiest I ever lived. . . . Most of the time we were solitary adventurers in a great land as fresh and new as a spring morning, and we were free and full of the zest of darers.
—Charlie Goodnight, cowboy (wall placard, Museum of Westward Expansion, St. Louis, Missouri)

The West of which I speak is but another name for the Wild.
—Henry David Thoreau, "Walking"

A drunken cowboy got aboard a Santa Fe Train.
"Where do you want to go?" asked the conductor.
"To Hell," replied the cowboy.
"Well, give me $2.50 and get off at Dodge,"
—Wall placard, Museum of Western Expansion, St. Louis. Missouri

You've got your hip country music, but out in the real world you have your cowboy stuff as well.
—John Jarvis, country music pianist/ keyboardist, magazine interview

5
Wild, Wild West

▼▼▼▼▼▼▼▼▼▼▼▼▼▼▼▼▼▼▼▼▼▼▼▼▼▼

Walk west through urban canyons, west from the Avenue of the Americas and along Fifty-second Street between money mountains – Chase Manhattan, Paine Webber, Credit Lyonnais. Then cross Broadway into New York's theater district, where you stop at a building whose facade is a red-and-silver bus, like a Greyhound or Trailways. It is the Lone Star Café Roadhouse, "the official Texas embassy in New York City."

Red neon signs for Lone Star beer decorate the bar thought the distributor has stopped East Coast delivery, and Colorado-based Coors is the closest you can get in longnecks. Patrons come here for the western side of country-western music, and the Lone Star tries to oblige. The entryway features an oversize photo of Hank Williams at the mike in his Nudie-

The epigraphs changed to a multicolumn format

5
Wild, Wild West

▼▼▼▼▼▼▼▼▼▼▼▼▼▼▼▼▼▼▼▼▼▼▼▼▼▼▼

Walk west through urban canyons, west from the Avenue of the Americas and along Fifty-second Street between money mountains – Chase Manhattan, Paine Webber, Credit Lyonnais. Then cross Broadway into New York's theater district, where you stop at a building whose facade is a red-and-silver bus, like a Greyhound or Trailways. It is the Lone Star Café Roadhouse, "the official Texas embassy in New York City."

Red neon signs for Lone Star beer decorate the bar thought the distributor has stopped East Coast delivery, and Colorado-based Coors is the closest you can get in longnecks. Patrons come here for the western side of country-western music, and the Lone Star tries to oblige. The entryway features an oversize photo of Hank Williams at

The chapter number changed to Madrone

This, indeed, was a home, —home. —Harriet Beecher Stowe, Uncle Tom's Cabin

Be it ever so humble, there's no place like home." —John Howard Payne, "Home, Sweet Home"

To the ramblers and the drifters, the seekers and the travelers and all the wanderers out there on the back roads and the highways... I hope that in some small way for even a minute or two I've been able to Sing You Back Home one more time... —Merle Haggard, Sing Me Back Home: My Story

Home still rocks my soul Steals my dreams each night —Holly Tashian, "Home"

Few have wealth, but all must have a home. —Ralph Waldo Emerson, "Domestic Life"

2
Home

Walk west through urban canyons, west from the Avenue of the Americas and along Fifty-second Street between money mountains. Then cross Broadway into New York's theater district, where you stop at a building whose facade is a red-and-silver bus, like a Greyhound or Trailways. It is the Lone Star Café Roadhouse, "the official Texas embassy in New York City."

Red neon signs for Lone Star beer decorate the bar thought the distributor has stopped East Coast delivery, and Colorado-based Coors is the closest you can get in longnecks. Patrons come here for the western side of country-western music, and the Lone Star tries to oblige. The entryway features an oversize photo of Hank Williams at the mike in his western wear with his band, the Drifting Cowboys,

Few have wealth, but all must have a home. —Ralph Waldo Emerson, "Domestic Life"

This, indeed, was a home, —home. —Harriet Beecher Stowe, Uncle Tom's Cabin

Be it ever so humble, there's no place like home. —John Howard Payne, "Home, Sweet Home"

To the ramblers and the drifters, the seekers and the travelers and all the wanderers out there on the back roads and the highways... I hope that in some small way for even a minute or two Sing You Back Home one more time... —Merle Haggard, Sing Me Back Home: My Story

Home still rocks my soul, Steals my dreams each night. —Holly Tashian, "Home"

2
Home

In July and August 1927, Ralph Peer, a New York–based producer for the Victor Talking Machine Company, drove to Bristol, Tennessee, the northeasternmost part of a state shaped like a parallelogram—or maybe a gunstock. In Bristol, Peer rented the third floor of a former furniture store, draped blankets over the walls, set up electrical recording equipment, and arguably launched contemporary country music by recording wax masters of commercially profitable ballads, spirituals, even comedy routines by figures like the Tennessee Mountaineers, Jimmie Rodgers, the Carter Family, and the Ernest Stoneman Family.

Chapter number and short title aligned with each other (left)

Chapter number moved flush left (right)

I'm really a country singer at heart.... I don't try to categorize my music, but it's always been the same—real honky soul.... It doesn't bother me to be labeled "country."... Elvis was a country singer, so were the Everly Brothers.... Those that think it's a problem are misinformed.

I feel an obligation to carry on the music of my dad's time, the music of Hank Williams and Jimmie Rodgers. Their talents and their symbolism forged the style, and we draw upon a kind of universal storehouse of country music knowledge.

Younger people really owe it to themselves to trace the roots of this stuff [country music] back to where it came from. And by the same token, the country fans... owe it to themselves not to have closed minds about such cool things as came out of England in the early sixties.

The real gratification comes from writing and singing the song. It's like painting a complete picture from start to finish.

Songwriting is my form of keeping a journal. —Rodney Crowell, newspaper and magazine interviews

10
'What Serious Songwriting Is All About'
An Interview with Rodney Crowell

"I stand by my words."

It is Rodney Crowell's parting line. Hair tousled, wearing sleek black running pants and an ivory sweatshirt, he is saying farewell, bound now for the lakeside trail he will walk after spending a spring Saturday morning recording a cassette full of words—words reflective, critical, analytical, even whimsical on the subject of country music songwriting.

The longest chapter title and the only subtitle

between folio and sideheads. At the time, the page seemed to need more ornamentation, but as with all my work, I now question whether I overdid it by adding this conceit.

I still had to consider what to do with the captions. Because I already had three different typefaces in the book, I was uneasy about adding yet another. I thought Garamond might work for the captions, but smaller versions of it in roman were too small for legibility, and italic in larger sizes only looked confusing with the sideheads. I finally settled on Gill Bold in 7.5-point type, which was readable and which allowed the captions to fit in the narrow outside column. I let the longer captions take whatever space they needed, placing them below their photos. I didn't establish a uniform measure for them and instead varied them according to the way the photos were sized.

See page 74.

For the front and back matter headings I used the same size of Willow I had used for the chapter subtitles. Instead of lining them up with the chapter titles, I put them at the top of the page and established the text sinkage based on the design for the contents page. The text that follows front and back matter headings is often very different from the text that follows chapter titles, so it has seemed better to me to establish a different design for them—but one that is clearly related in some way to the chapter titles. Because the text on the contents page is so problematic, I usually let the heading for that page determine what I do with the other front and back matter headings.

The diverse length of chapter titles continued to plague me on the contents page for *High Lonesome,* and I tried setting the list of titles in two columns to minimize the disparity among them. But with only seventeen lines of type each, the two short columns looked insignificant. I did not want to increase the type size, having tried that in other books with the uneasy result that the attempt just to fill up space was obvious. Instead, I set the titles line for line, except for the title of chapter 10, which had to break. In retrospect, I can see that I should have broken the long title for the first chapter as well, but it is too late to fix it now. Something diabolical in the realm of book design makes flaws evident only upon opening the printed book.

See page 75.

I used the sinkage for the contents to determine where to put the copyright information and the dedication. I like fancying up the dedication and am surprised when some authors think I have made too much of it. The dedication page is difficult because it is the only one with so little text-size type on it. It has to relate not only to the copyright page facing it but also to the text that follows. The type can't be so small that the words look like a speck on the page, nor can it be so much larger than the text that the dedication page looks like a part title. In this book, the dedication was set in widely letterspaced small caps, indented to align with the second epigraph column in the imaginary superimposed grid—which fortunately made the dedication seem centered on the page.

See page 77.

places, the phrase indicating access to power and influence, becomes Garth Brooks's pledge of allegiance to his "Friends in Low Places." The *real* people, country music says, are those who value honest labor, loyalty, independence, and fairness over and against the false values of the opportunists, social climbers, snobs, materialists, and the well-to-do whose lives are backed by undeserved wealth and white-collar crime.

Typically, then, country responds to class-based hauteur with a self-defensive and aggressive stance of pride and defiance, though sometimes the poignance of the have-not shows through. In "Amanda," a poor husband laments that his lovely wife was cheated of the chance to be a "gentleman's wife." He struggles in vain for worldly success, his wife's facial lines a calendar of his futile striving. "Take This Job and Shove It" expresses in its title the pain and anger of a worker trapped in a dead-end job. Such songs seem haunted by the economics-based conviction of a Harlan Howard song: "The rich is smart and the poor is a fool" ("Mississippi Delta Land").

Spoofing hillbillies: Henry Haynes and Kenneth Burns as "hick" comedians Homer and Jethro. By the 1950s, they preferred suits and sportswear to the hayseed image emphasized here. (Courtesy Country Music Foundation, Nashville)

Text page with photo and caption

Contents

▼▼▼▼▼▼▼▼▼▼▼▼▼▼▼▼▼▼▼▼▼▼▼

A section of color illustrations follows page 144.

Contents page

The American Culture of Country Music

High Lonesome

The University of North Carolina Press · *Chapel Hill & London*

CECELIA TICHI

Title page

I like designing the copyright page when I have the complete copy for it. This rarely happens, because publishers seldom have the CIP data at the time that I start the design. Some publishers never show me the copy for markup. Inevitably, no matter how carefully I specify what I want, it turns out wrong—especially with full caps used where I wanted small caps. In *High Lonesome* I had the complete copy and decided to let the copyright page follow the design for the contents. I negotiated with the editor to establish the order of material to appear on the copyright page.

I knew I had set myself up for problems with the title page. The very prominent chapter openings with the huge Madrone chapter numbers meant that the title page had to have some presence. I don't entirely disagree with Eric Gill about making title-page type no larger than the text type, but this didn't seem the place for understatement. The title page, for me, is a preview of the design of the rest of the book, so the natural place for me to start was with the 72-point Madrone used for the chapter numbers. But the title wouldn't fit. When I tried the Willow in the same size, it did. I still wanted to use Madrone on the title page; I felt that it needed to be introduced in the front matter because it was used so prominently throughout the book. A smaller size seemed right for the author's name. Illustrated title pages appeal to me. William Allard's photo of a lone cowboy riding across a deserted plain felt like the right metaphor for the book and the title.

FOR BILL, CLAIRE, JULIA

Sources

▼ ▼ ▼ ▼ ▼ ▼ ▼ ▼ ▼ ▼ ▼ ▼ ▼ ▼ ▼ ▼ ▼ ▼

The listings below give the sources that are quoted or used as references in the text, for the most part in the order in which they occur in each chapter. To avoid repetition of the same sources, page numbers relevant to an entire chapter are listed with the first citation of each source. Songs and albums mentioned or quoted in the text can be found in the discography preceding this section.

PREFACE

Williams, "Nashville Numbering System," 41, 43.

1. PATHOS, MISERIES, HAPPINESS, LIFE ITSELF

Malone, *Country Music U.S.A.*, 1; Lomax, "Bluegrass Background"; Kerouac, *On the Road*; Walt Whitman, "Song of Myself" and "Song of the Open Road," in *Leaves of Grass*, 65, 83, 149–59; Twain, *Huckleberry Finn*, 68, 94, 96, 171, 35–36, 8; Rodgers, *Country Music Message, Revisited*; Cantwell, *Bluegrass Breakdown*; Roger M. Williams, *Sing a Sad Song*; Nash, *Behind Closed Doors*, 38–39, 49, 65, 68, 100, 117, 119, 127, 163, 189, 191, 196, 383, 466, 384, 329, 351, 144, 466; Lee Smith, *Devil's Dream*; Carr et al., *Illustrated History of Country Music*, 272; Flippo, *Your Cheatin' Heart*, 235; Herbert,

"Laurie Lewis"; Nash, *Dolly*, 107, 131; "In the Hank Williams Tradition" (includes comments by Randy Travis and Emmylou Harris on Hank Williams's music as poetry; Travis on country music as stories; and Chet Atkins on Hank Williams's vocal registers and superb yodelling); Scoby, liner notes for *Delta Momma Blues*; Clark, Harris, and Cash, liner notes for *Diamonds and Dirt*; Holly Tashian interview; Painton, "Country Rocks the Boomers"; Ferris, *Blues from the Delta* and discussion with author, April–May 1993; Richard Bennett interview; Sandmel, liner notes for *After Awhile*; Farlekas, "Harris Returns to Mid-Hudson"; Ardoin, *Callas Legacy*, 109, 110, 205; Robinson, *Opera and Ideas*, 48; Scott, *Great Caruso*, 59–60.

2. HOME

Wolfe, liner notes for *The Bristol Sessions*, vol. 2; Malone, *Country Music U.S.A.*, 64–65; Silber, *Songs of the Civil War*, 120–21, 145–44. Crèvecoeur, *Letters from an American Farmer*, 1–91; Ralph Waldo Emerson, "The American Scholar," in *Selections from Ralph Waldo Emerson*, 63–80; Emerson, "Considerations by the Way," in *Conduct of Life*, 274; Emerson, "Domestic Life," "Farming," and "Notes," in *Society and Solitude*, 105–33, 135–54, 380; Emerson, "Self-Reliance," in *Selections from Ralph*

Dedication (left)   Sources (right)

Index

▼ ▼

Index

I generally set only the index in two columns, but in *High Lonesome* I set all of the back matter that way. The wider text measure allowed me to set the bibliography, discography, and notes in two columns without too many short lines. I prefer not to hyphenate bibliographies when they are set ragged right because many of the word breaks are inevitably awkward. With the short measure here, I did allow hyphenation, although the index and discography (having shorter entries than the bibliography) were not hyphenated.

The Design of *On Book Design*

Being designer for myself as author, I could take liberties with the manuscript I would otherwise never have dared. This was useful, for not until I was into my final revision of the manuscript did I begin to think of what this book might look like. I was surprised to find that I was as guilty as most authors in my obliviousness to the design problems my own words would create.

Don't overdo it.
—Bert Brown

Authors had told me how differently they felt about what they had written when they saw their text set into type. I didn't understand this until I saw the typeset samples of my manuscript. It was nearly as disconcerting as first hearing my voice on a tape recorder: Did I truly sound like *that?*

I began with two givens. The first was that I wanted to be able to reproduce illustrated examples at full size, when practical, which meant a format larger than 6 × 9 inches. I dislike 8 1/2 × 11 because it seems to require either a single block of text too wide for comfortable reading or a multicolumn format. Neither option appealed to me. I had recently designed a book that was 7 1/4 × 11 and thought that the narrower size would be right for my book.

The second was my choice of typeface. Months ago I decided which one I wanted to use. Even though I had given no thought to the particulars of designing this book, I felt that Monotype Garamond would present few problems no matter what I did. It has always seemed one of the most versatile faces, and it would be my desert island choice. Some of my British colleagues who worked with the original metal version of Garamond consider the digitized version much too light. It doesn't feel so to me. A typographer friend fine-tuned the face for me.

As a neophyte designer, I began every job with the ideal of a 65-character text line. Nowadays, I don't mind a slightly wider line of type as long as I have room to lead generously. Because I often design very long manuscripts and need to fit a lot of type on the page, a line of 70–75 characters now seems acceptable to me. Monotype Garamond has a fairly small x-height, which means that it appears smaller than other typefaces, and it needs less leading because the visual space around the ascenders and descenders adds to the openness between lines of type.

All too often, especially when I am hired as a freelancer, I feel that I'm expected to make the design obvious—to slightly overdo things so customers can see what their money has bought. But this time (assuming my publisher's indulgence) I was my own client. Still, this *was* a book about book *design*. Even after more than three decades of designing books, I am continually surprised at how ephemeral my sense of "good" design is. What seemed like a lovely piece of work at the end of the day, looks stale and ugly the next morning. The permanence of books just makes it worse; the ineptitude lives forever.

These days I am trying to take my own advice. I aim for typographic celibacy—no fooling around. There is a fine line between dull and just right. Others, like Jan Tschichold, P. J. Conkwright, and George Mackie, knew how to exercise restraint, but I have to struggle to stop myself from adding one too many ornamental rules or letting my type sizes balloon and multiply. What I learned from Richard Eckersley (though, alas, have not always applied as well as he can) was that it is better to begin smaller and only go larger when absolutely necessary.

For some years I have kept a notebook about what other designers have written on book design. I consult these notes from time to time, especially when I am trying to think of a better way to solve some knotty problem. At first I incorporated selected comments directly into the text of *On Book Design* as extracts, but they were so numerous that it was difficult to follow my own line of thought. The idea of positioning them adjacent to relevant portions of the text appealed to me because I could then easily include comments that disagreed with my own. The thesis for this book being that there is no single way to design books, these notes both support and/or contradict my own ideas.

I wanted a contrasting face for the sidebars—one that would be different enough from the Garamond in design but not in color. The sidebars had to be in a smaller face because they were longer and more numerous than I was aware of when I was putting the manuscript together. I chose the typeface Meta because, even in small sizes, it was legible, and I liked the idea that it had old-style figures and small caps. Not so long ago no sans serif type had either. Because the sidebars would be in a narrow column, ragged right was the only solution.

Normally, the margins of my text page are 3 picas at the top and 4 1/2 picas at the gutter. Garamond at 11.5 point seemed about the right size and, when set to 27 picas, gave me a line of approximately 70 characters. This left a generous enough space at the front (opposite the gutter) for the sidebars. I thought the front margin should be no smaller than the gutter margin. The ragged right setting meant that sidebars on recto pages could be closer to the front margin than 4.5 picas (because *visually* the margin of the ragged edge is not the length of the longest line), but this would be a problem when lengthy sidebars fell on verso pages (because the left margin presents a solid edge). Accordingly, I decided that 4.5 picas would do for both the gutter and the front margins.

One pica between the text and the sidebars seemed a sufficient amount of space to keep the two elements visually attached to each other. This left 6.5 picas for the sidebars. As I was going to do the typesetting myself, I could control the line breaks. I like to keep a fairly tight ragged edge but dislike hyphenating words in small blocks of unjustified type. The Yale Uni-

Being designer for myself as author, I could take liberties with the manuscript I would otherwise never have dared. This was useful, for not until I was into my final revision of the manuscript did I begin to think of what this book might look like. I was surprised to find that I was as guilty as most authors in my obliviousness to the design problems my own words would create.

11.5/14 Garamond

Being designer for myself as author, I could take liberties with the manuscript I would otherwise never have dared. This was useful, for not until I was into my final revision of the manuscript did I begin to think of what this book might look like. I was surprised to find that I was as guilty as most authors in my obliviousness to the design problems my own words would create.

11/14 Garamond

Typography may be defined as the art of rightly disposing printed materials in accordance with specific purpose: of so arranging the letters, distributing the space, and controlling the type

7.5/11 Meta

Typography may be defined as the art of rightly disposing printed materials in accordance with specific purpose: of so arranging the letters, distributing the space, and controlling the type as to aid to the maximum the

7/10 Meta

versity Press editorial staff were unhappy about my desire to identify the source of these marginal comments in such a minimal way (using only the name of the person being quoted and not the location from which the quotation was taken), but any longer source would have made the sidebars unwieldy.

In the first layout the text was 11.5/14 Garamond, the sidebars 7.5/11 Meta. When I ran out a couple of pages on the Macintosh, my words looked acceptable enough; there were neither an excessive number of line breaks nor awkward spaces between words, but I was unhappy about how stolid the page seemed. I dropped the text to 11/14, which felt just too small. I eventually settled on 11.2/15 Garamond and reduced the sidebar to 7/10 Meta, which made for better line breaks and lessened the necessity for hyphenated words.

The interview with Ron Costley needed special styling. (Unlike the other contributors, he submitted to an interview rather than submit an essay.) My first inclination in designing interviews is to set questions in italic and answers in roman. Here, though, I felt that this material was not so much an interview as a dialogue between the two of us. That suggested keeping both question and answer in the same style. Having designed many books of plays, my preferred style—especially when the speakers' names are more or less uniform in length—is to set the names in small caps followed by a colon and a word space. The text is run in, and the turnover lines indent, both of which help differentiate the break between one speaker and the next without having to add space between each exchange.

Each statement was only a few lines long. The differences in word spacing from one line to another in justified type is more obvious in such cases. To solve that problem, I specified ragged right, which also allowed me to avoid awkward last lines in each entry by letting me break the text as it *looked* best.

I prefer running feet to running heads. They present fewer problems, being less likely to be mistaken for subheads, among other things. At first I thought I might use the Meta for the running feet and/or the folio, but I decided to use the sans serif for comments by other designers, captions, and headnotes. In general, I try to keep the style of the running head or running foot different from that of subheads, but because I had few subheads in this book, whichever style of Garamond I chose for the running foot would not be a problem. The entries for the running feet were short but, I felt, important. Contrary to Yale's house style, I wanted them to appear on every text page, even ones where there were only illustrations and no text. I made them small caps and letterspaced them. I usually make running feet a point size smaller than the text, but 10-point letterspaced small caps felt too large, so I dropped the size to 9.5 point.

In recent years I have moved the running head or foot ever closer to the text, believing that having these elements as close as possible creates a more unified page. Here, however, I wanted to be able to run the illustrations as large as possible, so I moved the running foot lower on the page and positioned the folios flush outside the text. I did not letterspace the folios, a practice I've accepted because the typesetters I normally use once found it difficult to set letterspaced folios (their programs did not allow folios to be set automatically with the extra space).

I made one further adjustment by adding 6 points to the top margin. Text set with generous leading seems to require generous margins to hold the text block in place. It may have been the larger than usual trim size or the larger than usual front margin (even with the sidebar filling up the outside column), but the top margin seemed just a bit too small at only 3 picas.

The chapter titles were more or less uniform in length. As some chapters were only a few pages long, it was especially important to keep the design of the opening page of each modest. I began with 16-point Garamond for the titles but dropped it to 15 point when I reduced the text size from 11.5 to 11.2.

The front matter turned out to be more problematic than usual because of the oversized format. The shortness of the chapter titles, which had been welcome elsewhere, made the contents page feel empty. Against my self-inflicted "rule" that the type size for the contents page should not be any larger than that for the text, I have lately felt that there is no reason not to use a size that is moderately, if not obviously, larger. I decided that the heading for the contents page could not exceed 15 point (the size of type in the chapter titles), and I wanted the heading to be visibly larger than the text of the contents. I used 15-point type for the heading and 13/22 for the text and indented the contents list so that the longest title was flush right with the text page, letting the folios hang in the front margin. Since there were no numbers in the chapter titles (which meant that I did not have to worry about confusing a page number with a number in a title), I was more or less free to treat the folios as I chose. Having decided to hang the part numbers as roman old-style figures, I set the folios as italic old-style figures.

The book epigraph was very important to me, although I was sure few readers would pay the slightest attention to it. The problem was how to make it clear that the second paragraph was my response to the David Carson quote. My editor had found the manuscript unclear. I hoped that Meta for Carson and Garamond for me would clarify matters. I decided that my comment would be in 13/22 Garamond, the same size as the list on the contents page, but the Meta's larger x-height and uniform weight of line required it to be reduced to 11/22 to have the same weight as the Garamond. I decided to indent the page 15 picas to parallel that same indent on the contents page.

One of my teachers had said that a skilled designer ought to be able to avoid hyphenating words in small blocks of display text. Although this is sometimes unavoidable, it is an ideal I still attempt to achieve. No matter how I arranged the text of these two paragraphs, I ended up with either hyphenated lines or an awkward shape, especially where the first paragraph ended and the second paragraph began. So I tried moving the Carson paragraph to the left margin while leaving my comment indented — an allusion to the two-column format of the rest of the book. This also avoided the visual problem of the juxtaposition of the two paragraphs and reinforced the differences between Carson's words and my response.

Now that I had established another point of reference — the 15-pica indent — the title page was easier to design. Having too few words to design can be as baleful a curse as having too many. I decided that the title should be in one column and the author in the other and that I needed to use Meta somehow to prepare for its use inside the book. I am also fond of the Yale logo and wanted to include it.

Just to see how the arrangement looked, I set the book title to fill the first column and the author to fill the second. By sheer luck, the design worked on the first try. I left things just as they were, with the title at the top of the page (as with the other titles) and the author on the fifth text line (the same sinkage as for the chapter openings).

To finish, I used Meta small caps for the publisher's name and letter-spaced them to suggest the letterspacing of the small cap running feet. I set "New Haven & London" in Garamond italic as much to establish a contrast as to indulge my passion for the Garamond italic ampersand. The place names are indented 15 picas (to align with the author), and the logo is centered between publisher and place.

The final pieces of the preliminary design were the half title and the part titles. I positioned the part title and part-title epigraphs on the 15-pica indent in order to integrate the indent employed in the front matter into the rest of the book. I wanted the part titles to be slightly larger than the chapter titles, and I also wanted to keep the part epigraphs in the same style as the book's epigraph (11/22 Meta). I set the half title in the same 19-point Garamond indented 15 picas at the top but wished it didn't look quite so lonely.

ON BOOK DESIGN *Typesetting specifications*
Book trim size: 7.25 x 11
Margins: 3.5 picas top, 4.5 picas gutter
Typefaces: Monotype Garamond, Meta Book
Figures: old-style
Main text: 11.2/15 Garamond x 27, 44 text lines
    Paragraph indent: 1 pica
    OK 1 line short facing pages
    3/4-em dashes, thin-spaced left and right
    Fractions set as on-line fractions (1/2)
Interview style: 11.2/15 Garamond
    Speaker's name in even small caps letterspaced as on layout
            Flush left, followed by colon
    Dialogue ragged right, 27 picas maximum
            No hyphenation unless a line runs shorter than 24 picas
            Turnovers in text indent 1 pica
    No extra space between entries
Extract: 11.2/15 Garamond, ragged right, 27 picas maximum
    Indent 1 pica from left. No hyphenation unless marked
    22.5 points base to base above and below
Numbered lists: 11.2/15 Garamond, ragged right, no hyphenation
    Hang and indent style. Numbers indent 1 pica
    Align text
    22.5 points base to base above and below
Sidebars: 7/10 Meta, ragged right, 6 picas + 7 points maximum
    Minimal hyphenation
    Paragraph indent: 6 points
    Sidebars are in an outside column, 1 pica ditch between text
            and sidebar

Captions: 7/10 Meta, ragged right

Running feet and folios: Folios flush outside with outside column

    5 picas + 2 points from base of running foot to bottom trim

    Running foot: 9.5 Garamond, even small caps, letterspaced

        as on layout

    Em space between running foot and folio

    Folio: 9.5 Garamond old-style figures, no letterspace

A-heads: 12 Garamond, even small caps, letterspaced as on layout

    Indent 1 pica. 30 points base to base above, no extra space below

    Begin text indented 1 pica

B-heads: 12 Garamond italic, caps & lowercase

    Indent 1 pica. 30 points base to base above, no extra space below

    Begin text indented 1 pica

    When A & B are stacked: no extra space between

Space break: 30 points base to base.

    Begin text flush left, caps & lowercase

Footnotes: 9/12 Garamond italic, ragged right, 6 picas + 7 points

    maximum, no hyphenation. Position in the outside column

    at bottom of the page

Chapter openings: recto or verso

    15 Garamond, caps & lowercase, flush left at top

    Begin text on 5th line (or as marked), caps & lowercase, flush left

    Folio will show on the opening page

    Headnotes: 9/15 Meta x 27

        30 points base to base of text, which begins caps & lowercase,

        flush left

Part openings: recto

    Part title: 19 Garamond, caps & lowercase, indent 15 picas at top

    Epigraphs: 11/22 Meta, ragged right as broken

        Begin on 5th line, indent 15 picas

Half title: 19 Garamond, caps & lowercase, indent 15 picas at top

Title page:

    Title: 27 Garamond, caps & lowercase, flush left at top

    Author: 24 Garamond, caps & lowercase, indent 15 picas on 5th line

    Publisher: 11 Meta, even small caps, letterspaced as on layout

        Flush left on 9th line

    Address: 14 Garamond italic, caps & lowercase, indent 15 picas

        on 9th line

    Yale logo between publisher and address

Copyright: 9/15 Garamond, ragged right, 15 picas maximum

    No hyphenation

    Begin flush left on 5th line

Dedication: 16 Garamond italic, caps & lowercase, indent 15 picas

    on 5th line

Epigraph: 11/22 Meta as broken, begin on 5th line

 13/22 Garamond, ragged right as broken, indented

Contents: Indent all 15 picas

 Heading: 15 Garamond, caps & lowercase at top

 First entry begins on 5th line

 13/22 Garamond line for line

 Part numbers and titles:

  Part numbers: 13 old-style figures and even small caps
   letterspaced

   Hang 1 en to the left

  Part titles: 13 even small caps letterspaced

Glossary: [new recto]

 Heading: 15 Garamond, caps & lowercase at top

 Begin text on 5th line

 11.2/15, ragged right, no hyphenation

  Turnovers indent 1 pica

Bibliography: [new recto]

 Heading: 15 Garamond, caps & lowercase at top

 Begin text on 5th line

 11.2/15, ragged right, no hyphenation

  Turnovers indent 1 pica

Index: [new recto]

 Heading: 15 Garamond, caps & lowercase at top

 Begin text on 5th line

 10/14, ragged right, 13 picas maximum, no hyphenation

  Turnovers indent 1 pica

 Two columns, 1 pica ditch

 28 points base to base between alphabetic sections

3. How Designers Work

NO RULES!

—Cameron Poulter

Here a group of designers talk about how they work—or, more precisely, how they have worked. The process of designing books alters with time and technology. Designers continually change the way they think about solving problems, and they learn new things from each job. They are always experimenting, testing the typographic conventions. Surprisingly, the most valuable insights come from the most minor revisions to one's usual way of working.

Mary Mendell calls the design in her head that she starts with her "default"—like the settings in her computer. It is merely a jumping-off point—the preferences that automatically come to mind when beginning on a new assignment. Intuition, experience, practical problems in the text, and influences from other designers all affect the design.

Sometimes when I'm particularly pleased with a new solution (usually a typographic trick that I fall in love with), I want to keep using it. What was so exactly right the first time, however, probably isn't the second time. Such subsidiary uses of the "great insight" are rarely the best answer, but acknowledging it—and moving on—can require a long struggle.

Why does Janson, for example, become the type du jour (or much longer) and then suddenly seem not to be right for anything? Design decisions cannot always be explained. Where you end up depends on where you started from—your experiences, failures, quirks, and preferences—so no two designers are likely to arrive at the same conclusion.

In spite of all the traditions of book design and the acknowledged rules of good typography, what any designer designs today is influenced by what happened yesterday. The designers in the following chapters would probably not design the book they talk about in the same way now as they did before.

I suppose I do have current favorite types (they may vary from month to month). But practical considerations may have to override preferences: for instance, do I need a particularly strong bold, or particularly good and neat figures such as Sabon non-lining. Also, now, if the typesetter holds mainly Monotype, I have to find one that hasn't been PostScripted out of sight (Monotype Garamond* . . . is now so light as to be unusable).
—Alan Bartram

*This book is set in Monotype Garamond.

David Bullen

David Bullen is a graduate of the English literature program at the University of California, Berkeley, where he was a recipient of the Eisner Award for poetry. He was a cofounder, publisher, and editor of Cloud Marauder Press. He then found employment in typesetting and print shops prior to becoming designer, art director, and production manager for North Point Press, where he spent eleven years. After North Point closed, he founded his own freelance design office in the San Francisco Bay area, where he designs a wide variety of books, mostly for trade publishers. He is the recipient of many design awards, including those presented by AIGA, Bookbuilders West, and the Chicago Book Clinic.

Like many graphic designers, I now find myself working entirely on the computer. This has both expansive and limiting effects. The ease and speed with which I can view different ideas or create variations on them has opened up new possibilities. Yet I find it a constant battle to keep the designs clean and direct. With so many possible alternatives a few keystrokes away the challenge of design is now as much in realizing when you have arrived at the solution as it is in getting there. I worry that the potential for manipulation of type and image that the computer provides, and the ease with which manipulation is accomplished, diminishes the value of contemplation, which is necessary to find the substance of the work. And because the time frame is now hours instead of days, I feel bound to use typefaces that I have or can easily and quickly obtain. Less often do I use type or images that I must order from outside sources, which creates a constant demand to upgrade my type library.

The design begins with a page turn through the entire manuscript. On a sheet of paper I make a list of all the elements and the pages on which they occur, noting the longest and shortest examples of each. I also make note of any copy that is out of the ordinary and that will require special attention. On the same sheet I list the front matter pagination and display pages. This process gives me a feel for the basic structure of the book, a kind of skeletal view. In addition, it provides a quick reference document for checking on the relations of the various elements while working on the layout.

In most cases, the publisher has already determined the final trim size based on budget and marketing concerns. I try to comply with the publisher's wishes, but if the material seems too crowded or the type must be small and tightly leaded to fit, I will suggest that either the trim size be adjusted or the page count lengthened. I prefer a line of approximately 70 characters, depending, of course, on typeface, leading, measure, trim size, etc.

I don't think that the interior design should be neutral. It should be attractive, a pleasure to look at. But it should not get in the way of the enjoyment or efficiency of reading. The design should not call so much attention to itself that one thinks of it with every turn of the page. It should make the reader feel comfortable, interested, delighted—unless the point of the book is to make the reader unsettled or uncomfortable. Then the design should step outside its normal role. This is in contrast to the jacket or cover design, which must make a point of being noticed. The cover's job is to sell the book, the interior's to relay the information.

I normally begin the design with the text spread and the choice of typeface(s). Everything else evolves from these selections. The initial decisions are based on my intuitive reactions to the content of the book and to suggestions offered by publisher and author. I spend time staring at samples of type, keeping in mind my emotional reaction to the book, until two or three typefaces begin to feel right—rather the way a camera comes into focus. At that point I begin copyfitting and playing with text block specs using this final list of faces. A typeface may eliminate itself by not fitting the overall format; it may, for example, need to be too large and openly leaded to maintain the required page length. I then do some sample spreads with varying faces, sizes, and leading, gradually zeroing in on the one that works. Often I will know immediately which face is right, but I have also spent as much as a day working back and forth and then had a night of contemplation before making the final decision. And if in creating the sample spreads things aren't working out, I will go back a few steps and rethink the initial decision. For me, this step is most important: if the body type doesn't work, there is no hope for the book. It would be like building a house with a weak foundation.

Choice of display type is also an intuitive decision. The book—more precisely, the way the design of the book is evolving—will tell me if special display is required. If the text face does not handle display well, I will look for something to complement it. The content of the text determines the relation between the text face and the display face. If there is a strong personality to the book, such as a cookbook, a book about the Wild West, a book about South American tribal masks, it can be mirrored in the display type, but if the content is more scholarly or contemplative, I think a quieter, more subtle allusion is appropriate. I also let the content of the book determine whether to use a centered or an asymmetrical layout. To me, a centered arrangement is formal and traditional, an asymmetrical layout more modern and informal. The word count of the display elements can also make the decision: some titles just won't work centered.

I base the chapter-opening design on a chapter title that is of typical length for the book. Once I have laid out a rough sketch, I try out the scheme on the shortest and longest chapter titles to see how they will work, and adjust accordingly. I have never asked an editor or author to alter the copy, although some have suggested a change themselves after looking at the design. I believe that it is the designer's job to make the author's words work; it would be presumptuous to ask the author to accommodate a flaw in my design or to alleviate my dilemma by rewriting.

Subheads must convey their relative importance on sight. They must also differ enough in style from the running heads for the two not to be confused when they appear together at the head of a page. Otherwise, all options are open, as long as they are true to the intent of the manuscript.

The design of the extracts is based on how closely they relate to the main body of the text. If they are meant to be distinct breaks from the text, I will set them off by a change of point size and leading, with indentation following the symmetrical or asymmetrical style established. If extracts should flow more smoothly with the main body of the text, I usually keep them the same point size but use a different font and set them off with extra leading above and below. If the book is a tight fit and there are many extracts, zero indentation and reduction in size and leading along with the use of italic (which commonly has a greater character per pica count) can save space.

Once I have a plan for all the typographic elements of the book, I write complete specs and mark the coded elements on two-page spreads, which are copies of my laser printouts. I hand-spec all the front matter elements on separate single-page laser printouts. I always specify letterspacing and word-spacing parameters. Prior to beginning the design I request an edited, keymarked [coded for the typesetter] manuscript, but rarely is that available. Often the design is completed before all the elements are finalized, which inevitably means some reworking later on. I use a separate set of uncoded laser prints as sketches, or sample pages, for the publisher. I cut and tape them together to create facing spreads and then photocopy them. Depending on whether I have control over the composition and the choice of compositor, I may ask to see sample typeset pages, and I make adjustments if the publisher allows.

Whenever possible, I try to influence the choice of compositor because the choice will influence my design to some extent. It may limit the typefaces available to me, or it may prepare me for a certain level of quality and attentiveness to detail. With a mediocre compositor I have learned the hard way not to attempt unusual letterspacing or odd line breaks in headings, because I cannot trust the compositor to be consistent.

THE BOOK OF ELDERS

To design *The Book of Elders* I was supplied with a complete manuscript on both hard copy and disk. The art director also provided me with two books previously published by another house to use as a general guide for this genre of book: Native American tradition and history. I was told to capture the feel of the earlier books, but more tastefully, not quite so preciously. I read in the manuscript far enough to get a sense of the style and content. The reading was interesting enough that I decided to save the remainder of it for the printed book.

The publisher wanted a special treatment for this book and was generous with the trim size and length: 9 × 10.75 inches, 256 pages. The book was to be printed in two colors. I was given the freedom to make it as open and spacious as I liked. The choice of type was limited only by the compositor's library. The book was to be produced in QuarkXPress. Although normally I prefer the cover design to be an outgrowth of the interior, in this case a finished cover design was presented to me with the manuscript. This frustrating practice is antithetical to the natural process of designing a book, but, because marketing drives most decisions and schedules, it is difficult to avoid. In situations like this, I try to find a cover element that can be used in the interior to create a logical and comfortable transition for the reader. The typefaces used on the cover were well suited to the feeling that I wanted to create in the interior. To avoid the precious look, I had decided to stay away from something "western" or "Native." I wanted traditional letterforms to convey the dignity and wisdom of the narratives told by the Elders. Adobe Garamond with Trajan display, as used on the cover, fit right in with this concept, as well as being compatible with each other. I also planned to set the editor's comments off from the main text with the use of italic, and the Adobe Garamond italic is a nice, readable face. Adobe Garamond also contains fonts of small caps and old-style figures, which I feel are essential to almost any design.

The main elements in this book are the narratives and the duotone photos of the storytellers. The photos are very striking portraits, and I wanted to make them large. Most are of vertical proportions, so I created a text block that was also vertically proportioned and that would play against the squarish trim size. To exaggerate the vertical impact of the text block, I decided not to use running heads or feet, thus allowing the text block to extend closer to the head and foot of the page. I turned the running head material 90 degrees and positioned it alongside the text block, again to emphasize the vertical. To make the running head recede a bit, I used the second color of ink.

The page was looking nice but a little flat, I thought. The asymmetrical layout was creating the informal atmosphere that I was looking for, with generous margins for rest and contemplation, but the page lacked spark. To portray the power of the narratives and the conflict in Indian culture between traditional and modern, I wanted something that would create an active tension on the page. So I introduced the large initial cap for the subheads and hung it in the generous margin. This gave some life to the page, but something was still lacking. The introduction of horizontal line art—a curvy geometric design—spiced things up a bit and also created some tension with the overall vertical treatment of text and photos. The graphic also added a touch of the Native American culture to help put the design in con-

When everything is cleared away and put back into the kitchen, we have social danc-ing until dawn. When it first starts to get light we have another ceremony and singing, then everybody goes home. People come from all over, from Cattaraugaus, Allegheny, Tuscarora, Niagara Falls—the whole confederacy is there to visit. And we support one another. Differ-ent nations all have this ceremony to the ancestors—*Okawa* we call it. They might have a different way of saying it, but it's the same songs. The Seneca song is the same as the Onondaga song that we sing. Different tempo, but same words. Some wear traditional clothing, some don't.

We have four major ceremonies during a year for the four seasons. During the winter is the equinox, which used to be in December, but now we have it in January because of Christmas. So many of our people have intermarried with Christians, we moved it to Janu-ary because Christmas time is a busy time for the Christians, and it's pretty hard on our youth not to celebrate Christmas. It depends on the family, how strong they are. With all the lights and the glitter, radio and television advertisements everywhere, it's hard on our chil-dren. Some give presents, and some may drag a tree home, but it has no meaning of Christ-mas. It's just an exciting time of the year. But it can be a great burden, too.

Our winter solstice ceremony takes three weeks. We don't follow the calendars, so the date that it could fall on could be anytime—the beginning of January, the middle, or toward the end—it depends on the moon. In the spring is the Planting Dance, and that takes six days. The next one would be the Green Corn Dance, which also lasts six days.

And then, besides the four seasonal ceremonies between the equinox and the planting dances, we have the Running of the Sap Ceremony. It starts in February. At the end of that, you make maple syrup candy, which is hardened in pans and made into squares. In June, for the first fruit of the year, we have the Strawberry Ceremony, which only runs one day. And then in June or July, we have the Bean Dance, for the corn, beans, and squash. We don't use the yellow corn that has been crossbred since the Europeans came over.

We also have many medicine ceremonies in between. We are known to have secret medicine societies. Only those who have been inflicted with a particular sickness or disease are allowed to go to the respective healing ceremony. I belong to four medicine soci-eties. They are held in homes. The medicine people are very strong here, but you would never know it. And we would never, never get invited if we didn't belong to that particular society. We have many in the wintertime, especially.

I belong to one society that holds ceremony only at night. I belong to another, the Bear Society, that holds ceremony in the late afternoon. I also belong to the Fish Ceremony and the Grandfather's Ceremony. The Grandfathers are healers. They are the ones that wear

83

All illustrations in this chapter from Sandy Johnson and Dan Budnik, *The Book of Elders*, HarperCollins

(reduced 25 percent)

nine or ten, they knew everything they needed to know about survival. They knew how to plant, how to harvest. They knew how to gather food and how to preserve it. And they knew how to take care of themselves and one another. All under the nurturing and protection of the women of the village.

By the time boys and girls were old enough to go out into mixed society, their talents were usually visible. Some were going to be singers, some speakers, some dancers. So all the stories about the little boy going out with his arrow and bringing home a deer were not true, because they were only taught about the bow and the arrow and the spear when they had the physical ability. The saying, "Don't send a boy out to do a man's job," came from our people. As times changed, there weren't any restrictions on a woman's physical activity. Whatever she was physically able to do, she would do. Except for sports that overdevelop the muscles and organs in a young woman's body that she needs to carry and deliver a baby. A lot of colleges began having girls' lacrosse teams a few years back. But our way does not allow us to let our girls play lacrosse; it says so right in our ceremony that this game is given to our men and the boys.

We are a very tight community because we still utilize our clan system, and that keeps everyone aware that we are all family. People still know who their family is beyond their third or fourth cousin, but it's getting more like the white society now—not as close. In our culture, your aunts are your mothers. Your mother's brothers are also your fathers, and everybody is your grandmother. All elders are our relatives.

ALICE PAPINEAU: SECRET MEDICINE SOCIETIES

My name is Alice Papineau; my spiritual name is Dewasenta. I am an Onondaga clan mother of the Eel Clan, and I have lived at Onondaga all of my life. I was born right here on August 1, 1912. My mother had six of us, and she never had a doctor or a nurse. In those days everybody used midwives. It was the way of life here.

We still have our own health laws for pregnancy, what to do and what not to do, and how to take care afterward. At birth, there was a cleansing that a woman had to do, since she hasn't had a period for nine months. She would drink about three or four gallons of these herbs. It was made from the bark of a wild cherry tree; it would cleanse the woman and make milk. That's the way that I was born. When you drink this, you don't drink coffee, tea, or water; you just take the medicine.

We didn't have big families. Six children was considered a huge family. We usually only had four in a family, because of this purification medicine we took. It wasn't made to keep text. I used the second color to cause the line art to recede and to avoid conflict with the text.

The chapter openings were a direct result of the decisions made for the text spreads. Almost all the elements were designed: Trajan for the titles, the Trajan initial caps, the line art bleeding off the page, the subheads. Each chapter begins with a note by the editor, which I set in italic to separate it from the narratives. It played nicely against the Trajan initial cap and Adobe Garamond small caps of the subhead. The only other element that I introduced was a drop cap at the beginning of the narrative following the opening note, to further distinguish the main text.

I commonly use an element of the chapter-opening display for the front matter opening pages, such as repeating the specs for the chapter title or chapter number, depending on the importance of the front matter in relation to the main text. In this case, nothing seemed appropriate—the chapter title was too dominant, and the subhead too slight—so I incorporated only the graphic and created a new head with a visual weight in between that of the chapter title and a subhead. I aligned it flush left with the text block to make it less important in placement compared to the subhead of the main text. The alignment also created the possibility for a deep indent and smaller measure for the epigraphs that precede the introduction.

The title page is a further outgrowth of the display pages. The elements and relations created in the interior are to be presented here in their best light. This is to be an exhibition of the dynamics created throughout the text so that the reader is prepared for what is to come. I decided not to use a photograph, because each one was so specific to a particular narrative, and I didn't want to highlight one person over the others. I felt that the graphic and type treatment would be strong enough. I ran two graphics, each bleeding from opposite sides, across the text measure to align with the opposite margins to subtly suggest the text block. I aligned all the copy flush right on the text measure to emphasize the asymmetry of the layout and the style of the chapter titles. As a rule, I think that the display type of the title page should be larger than, or at least as large as, any display-page type within the book. In this case, there was plenty of room, and I could treat the type as I pleased. I adjusted the size of and letterspaced the Trajan caps until they looked right, but the subtitle, at the size I wanted it set, looked bunched up with its normal letterspacing, so I broke one of my cardinal rules and letterspaced the lowercase italic text also. If I have a regret about the design of this book, it is that I did not try a two-page layout for the title page. As it stands, the title page looks a bit timid in relation to the rest of the book.

Now the last difficult problem: contents, dedication, copyright. I prefer it when an author includes a dedication page. I have a difficult time reconciling the style of the contents with that of the copyright page: they are both a departure from the basic format of the interior layout, and the main theme suggested by the title page can easily be lost in the struggle between these two pages. A dedication page, with its generous white space and subtle message, can soften the blow, allowing the contents on the following spread to begin its story without conflict from the business matter of the copyright page. I follow the basic rule of reducing the copyright text size by two points, sometimes three, but, if space allows, I like to open the leading a bit so that the copy doesn't appear so dense. In this case, for the copyright page I decided to continue the flush-right style of the title page. I usually reduce the text measure for readability, which also creates a better relation with the facing page.

I remember hearing one designer say that he *begins* his design with the contents page, and that does make a certain kind of sense. I know that in some cases, after arriving at the design of the contents, I have felt that I should rework a number of other designed elements. I first apply the front matter opening that has evolved, maintaining the same sink as for the beginning of the text. I like to lead the text out as much as possible so that it will work well for readability and open up the feel of the page as well. The layout is determined by the length of the titles and the number of levels of heads. Here, I placed everything flush right to continue the style already established, which is a neat solution because it places the folios equidistant from each title yet has them flush aligned for easy reference. I like to differentiate between the levels of the elements by using differing fonts, sizes, and leading, not indentation, to maintain a clean page. I usually avoid placing running heads and folios on contents pages, unless the contents is more than three pages long, but in this case, because these elements were in the second color, I included them to add texture to the page.

THE BOOK OF
ELDERS

The Life Stories of Great American Indians

as told to Sandy Johnson

Photographed by Dan Budnik

HarperSanFrancisco
A Division of HarperCollins*Publishers*

CONTENTS

INTRODUCTION

> The red man is alone in his misery. We behold him now on the verge
> of extinction, standing on his last foothold . . . and soon he will be
> talked of as a noble race who once existed but have passed away.
>
> GEORGE ARMSTRONG CUSTER,
> in his term paper for his ethics class at West Point

> Today, seven generations later, you turn to us as your own culture is
> failing. The land you took from us, tricked us out of, is becoming too
> poisoned to feed you. Your rivers and streams are dying. I wonder,
> why do you turn to us now? Is it because through it all we never
> stopped praying? Never stopped beating our drums, dancing and
> singing songs to the Creator? And that somehow, somehow, you
> couldn't silence us?
>
> SIOUX ELDER, Rosebud reservation

My three-year journey through Indian country had its unlikely beginnings in the bedroom
of my Manhattan apartment on what I thought must be the darkest night of my life. The
two preceding years had been filled with loss. My father and brother had died within a year
of each other, the novel I had been working on for more than two years had been shelved,
putting me in financial difficulties, and I was holding myself to blame for the failure of yet
another relationship.

SIX NATIONS

SARA SMITH: UNDER THE TREE OF PEACE

In October 1992 I flew to Buffalo, New York, and rented a car. First I visited some of the reservations in upstate New York, then my plan was to drive across the border to the Six Nations reserve (as they are called in Canada) in Ontario, where I had an appointment to meet Sara Dale Smith. The day was overcast when I arrived in Buffalo; by five o'clock the sky had grown dark with angry clouds that had swirled in from the west. Within an hour rain and sleet were pounding my windshield, all but obliterating my vision. I had told Sara to expect me before dark, so I pushed on, straining to find the Peace Bridge, the signs seeming to disappear at every turn. Rush hour traffic bore down on me, horns blaring, refusing to let me change lanes; monster trucks sped by me hurling more water onto my windshield—and all the while I was thinking, Indians were driven onto reservations to make way for this?

By the time I crossed the border into Canada it was night, and I had perhaps another hour and a half to go before I was supposed to exit. Then, carefully following Sara's directions, I found myself on long stretches of unmarked, unlit country roads, and it was getting on toward nine. I drove on, wondering if I had missed a turn, until to my enormous relief I saw the lights of a small store ahead. I called Sara and was given new directions similar to the "right-at-the-tree, left-at-the-rock" ones earlier, except that it was night, the distance great, with no one to stop and ask.

She described her house, which she assured me was only ten miles from where I was, and promised to leave a light on. It was eleven by the time I found it. Sara opened the door and

CAROLE ANNE HEART LOOKING HORSE: TOMORROW'S ELDER

My name is Carole Anne Heart Looking Horse. I am a Rosebud/Yankton Sioux from South Dakota. My Indian name is *Waste Wayankapi Win,* or They See Good, which literally means that people see something good in me.

My dad, Narcise Francis Heart, was a Yankton Sioux and my mother is a full-blooded Rosebud Sioux. The Rosebud Sioux are "Sicangu," which means "Burnt Thighs." The name traces back to the Indian wars when the people would burn the prairies for protection. Some people were burned when the fires backed up, so they called them the "Burnt Thighs." My great-great-grandfather was Horn Chips, who was one of the Rosebud Lakota spiritual advisers to Crazy Horse. My great-grandmother's name was Stands Alone by Him. My grandmother on my father's side was Aberdeen Zephir Heart.

I grew up on both the Rosebud and Yankton reservations and was a straight-A student both at St. Francis High School and at Marty, so I skipped the fifth grade and upon

Ron Costley

Ron Costley studied painting, drawing, and lithography at art school before joining the Shenval Press in London as a junior designer. At the press, a high-quality book and general printer, he learned typography on the job, designing a wide range of printed matter, including many exhibition catalogs for public and commercial art galleries. In 1977, he moved from printing to publishing, working as a designer successively at the Scolar Press, Chatto & Windus, and Faber & Faber, where he has worked since 1989. He has received many awards for book design and exhibited and lectured on his work.

Ron Costley has said about his work as book designer:

I believe in the culture of publishing, which enables us to share many aspects of our wider culture through the process of writing, printing, and reading. If I have a philosophy concerning the design of books, it is that they should be designed for readers. My main concern always is to present the text in the clearest possible way so that the reader can have direct access to the author's text without being inhibited or interrupted by my intervention. When I design a book, I aim to support the structure of the text using the typographical repertoire at my disposal, but not one element more than is necessary. At the same time, I try to give proper consideration to the aesthetic and practical aspects of scale, proportion, and materials. I am an unashamed minimalist, and if I have a motto, it is "less is more."

I interviewed Ron Costley about his working methods in 1994. Since that time he has begun using a computer.

RICHARD HENDEL: What do you know about a book when you begin work?

RON COSTLEY: For a good number of titles, the first thing I know is when the manuscript comes into me with a request from the production department asking for the layout. Accompanying the manuscript is what we call the NBI, the New Book Information, which outlines the price, format, and expected number of pages; estimates have already been made for the project.

At Faber, before a book is taken on, it's presented at a publishing meeting by the editor. The editor has to present the book, together with an estimate. So the editor would have made an estimate request through the production department, stating which format, how many pages, the expected price, the expected sales.

RH: Does the editor do a castoff [calculation of total book pages], or is that done in the production department?

RC: At this stage, the extent [length] is taken off the contract with the

Title	**The Faber Book of War Poetry**
Sub Title/Series	
Classification	Poetry Anthology
House Editor	Christopher Reid

Author/Editor	Kenneth Baker
Nat/Dom	British/UK
Illus/Trans/Foreword	
Nat/Dom	

Date to Man Editor	11 July 1995
Date to Production	i4 9 95
Date to Design	
ISBN Cased/Lam	0 571 17453 1
ISBN Paperback	

Publication Date	24 June 1996
Price Cased/Lam	£17.50
Price Paperback	(£9.99) (216×135 mm = pbk).
Size	234 x 153mm
Word Count	
Min/Max Page Extent	560pp? (544pp better).
Illus Colour	
Illus B/W	
Line/Other	

Territorial Rights	World
US Rights	ff
Translation Rights	ff
Serial Rights	ff

Promotional Points
- most wide-reaching and thoroughly detailed anthology on the subject
-KB edited best-selling FABER BOOK OF ENGLISH HISTORY IN VERSE (sales hbk: pbk:)and UNAUTHORIZED VERSIONS (hbk)
-War a subject of endless interest treated by most great poets and evoking the best from those less elevated

NBI form

author or the proposed contract. It's often a guess. When the manuscript arrives on my desk, the extent may still be based on the original estimated word count. If I see that the text is never going to get into the expected number of pages, then a revised estimate may be required.

RH: How often does something like that happen?

RC: Often enough. Sometimes the difference in length is serious enough for the manuscript to go back to the author with requests for cuts.

RH: Has the manuscript been edited by the time you've seen it?

RC: It's been edited.

RH: It really would be a lot more work to send it back and have it cut.

RC: Yes, although sometimes when the manuscript comes in, an editor will check it against the contract. They can see if it's overlong.

RH: What happens when you have an important book advertised in your catalog at such-and-such number of pages and you can't get the author to cut it? Are you required to make it work by setting it 8/9 [8-point type with 1 point of leading—small type with little space between lines]?

RC: No. The number of pages in the catalog, as far as we're concerned, is just a guideline.

RH: I would have thought that trade publishers would worry more than university presses do about their catalog.

RC: No. The big problem, actually, is short books.

RH: Making *more* pages? Why should that be a problem? You can always lead the text out or set it in 18-point type.

RC: You can, but there's a point at which an adult novel, say, begins to look like a children's book. Or you give it really extraordinary margins that are just not appropriate.

RH: Are you required to design to standard formats? Could you pick an unusual trim size?

RC: No, we're severely limited on sizes for most trade publications because of the printing process and the size of the paper. We tend to print short [low quantity] and reprint later. So paper has to be in stock in the correct sizes, because if we want, as happens very often, to reprint within a week, we've just got to have the paper there. Then, too, there are other constraints on trim size, such as racking, dump bins [store displays], etc. More than half our books are done in various established formats. [Format is a combination of trim size, typeface, and typographical style established for particular series, such as fiction, plays, and screenplays.]

RH: You are given a manuscript that you know very little about. They tell you the trim size, format, and length. Assuming that nothing seems to be a problem, what happens next?

RC: If it's one of the format books and if it looks as though it's short or long, I do a very rough castoff. Really rough. Just to make sure which side of the expected extent it is. And then I leaf through the manuscript page by page, making notes as I go along.

RH: On your transmittal sheet from editorial, do they tell you what's in there?

RC: Yes. The editor will draw attention to special problems or quoted matter, anything odd in the text, anything that needs display, markup, tabular work, and so on. Anything even very slightly out of the ordinary they draw attention to. So I can always hone in on that. But I will always go through the manuscript—every page.

RH: You say you take notes on what you see. Do you flag the pages?

RC: I flag the pages or just make a note of the page. If an editing problem jumps out, like an inconsistency in punctuation or abbreviations, then I'll make a note to raise a query with the editor. If I can see that the book is going to have running headlines and that some of the chapter titles are too long, I'll point that out and get edited headlines.

RH: They're willing to go back and change things?

RC: Oh, yes.

RH: You get your running heads at the same time you get your manuscript. I find that people don't often give them to me.

RC: Well, we invariably go straight into pages, so we need to have them. Sometimes I will argue a point with an [acquisitions] editor or manuscript editor about the structure of the book: whether the introduction is a part of the prelims or part of the text—therefore, does it number with the text, or should it be numbered with the prelims?—or how part titles and chapter titles relate to each other, or whether chapters should begin on a recto or run on.

If necessary, I may go back all the way to the author to discuss a point. Sometimes an editor will bring a manuscript to me before it goes to manuscript editing. They will have had a look through it because they need to brief the manuscript editor on what to do. And then we'll look through it together and say, "What do you think, about this, this, and this, how we should structure this," because I can then ask the editor to do some of the markup that I would, perhaps, have to do. This is particularly important with things like anthologies interspersed with editorial matter. I would just do a little pen sketch of the analysis of the text, indicating the relation of the various parts.

I turn every page of the manuscript, mark it up, and fill in the type spec sheet, and away it goes. I know who is going to typeset it. I know their particular systems, what the problems are, and whether they're best suited for this sort of text.

RH: You can make this decision, not the production department?

RC: Well, I can ask the production department to do it first. Then I can go back to them and say, "Look, given the nature of the text, I think it would be better if so-and-so set this rather than somebody else." But they have to juggle with how many jobs they have with any particular typesetter. If that typesetter can cope with another job, then it's fine.

RH: After you've done this analysis of the manuscript, do you do layouts for every book?

RC: No. At Faber, for some series a format will be used. It's not a very rigid format. But, for example, we set all our fiction in Palatino.

RH: Was this your decision?

RC: Actually, no. This is something that Jerry Cinamon established. It was very serviceable—a robust typeface, and it stands the terrible punishment of cheap printing.

RH: How did you feel about Palatino before you came to Faber. Was it a face that you used very much?

RC: I'd used it once seriously. I'd always liked the look of it. My own feeling at the time was that it's got such a classical resonance that it might not be appropriate for the late twentieth-century novel. But I think it's so commonplace now that some of that allusion has perhaps rubbed off.

RH: Does an average reader looking at a page of Palatino and a page of Baskerville know the difference? I doubt that most would. It's something that only the designer would worry about, no one else.

RC: Readers might not get the difference pinned down. But the face would certainly give the page a different color, a different general appearance.

RH: I always ask when using Palatino whether you can get a lot of text on the page. I have just the opposite situation from yours. A thousand-page manuscript is not unusual for me to deal with. I have to try to fit all of this into a reasonably sized book, which is quite an undertaking.

Palatino always seemed to me to be a very inefficient typeface until I had to redesign an encyclopedia. Then I found that 8 1/2-point Palatino worked well. I was really surprised, because I would have thought that Times Roman would have been better.

What about the option of using something like Aldus, which is a lighter version of Palatino?

RC: I know. Well, maddeningly, that option isn't open to me because our regular typesetters don't stock it.

RH: And they won't put it in?

RC: Well, they would, but I think I would have to make a very special case.

RH: When you are working on a formatted book, what do you need to do?

RC: I'm looking for the variables. In a particular book there may be part titles. And I think, "Are there just chapter numbers?" Well, we may have just chapter numbers. We may have chapter titles. We may have numbers and titles. We may even have epigraphs. So, they're the details that need to be marked specifically.

RH: Are there standard specifications for all of this?

RC: No, it would seem to me to be impossible to actually sit down and formulate specs for every eventuality.

RH: Do you find yourself changing the specifications from book to book?

RC: Oh, yes. I might often use the same solution. But then I think, "Hold on a minute. These are short epigraphs." Perhaps the epigraph is a crucial element in the story itself. This is where you've got to be alert to that aspect: It's not just an epigraph. Perhaps it is closer to being a subtitle.

RH: You are already told the trim size. Faber uses A, B, C, and D to designate the format.

RC: That's right. The D format is what used to be royal octavo (234 millimeters tall × 153 millimeters wide); C format is the old demi size (216 × 135 millimeters), which is your 8 1/2 × 5 1/2 inches. Then there's the B format, which is the normal paperback size (198 × 126 millimeters); I think it used to be called crown octavo. A format is the mass market paperback size (178 × 111 millimeters).

RH: The largest book you work with is the D format.

RC: Yes. There has been a tendency in the past few years to publish [hardcover] fiction in a large format, which creates problems when it's to be reduced to B or even mass market paperback size. Our formula used to be that we would set the book in 9.5/12.5 Palatino to 24 ems, as for a C format book. I knew that would reduce even to A format and still be reasonably legible. All of this has been superseded in the PostScript era of disk-to-plate printing. We no longer photographically reduce already set text; instead, books without indexes are completely rerun to a new specification for a smaller trim size.

RH: What size does the type become when it's reduced to mass market format?

RC: It's just over 8 point.

RH: What do you do about the front matter in books that are formatted? Do you create a unique design for each book?

RC: It depends—is it author led, or is the title important, or, again, how much text is there on the title page? Is the title long? Short? Has the author got a long name? A short name? Are there combinations of letters, say, a double "L" followed by an "A"? That would be best set in lowercase rather than caps. So I change the format, as long as it is appropriate to the book's design.

RH: How much do you feel the front matter has to follow the rest of the design of the book? Does it have to follow it *exactly* or not?

RC: The design of a book must have its integrity. Of course, the prelims [front matter] should relate visually to the rest of the book. They are the way in to the rest of the book. They lead the reader to the text, page by page. The design and the editorial sequence of these pages is very important, and they should not be used as a dumping ground nor as a playground. The entrance to the house should anticipate the rooms beyond.

RH: Do you draw out layouts for yourself, or do you know by now what Palatino will do so well that you can guess?

RC: I think that I know what it will do. Very often I'll just mark up the manuscript. I might do a couple of layouts.

Pages 111–113:
Design sketches by
Ron Costley

Chapter

CHAPTER HEAD   (ch)   16
                              ~~text~~ u+l.c

* * * * * * * * * *

high light   } 9/13 pt
intro

POET ——————— A 12/13 scs **from Title of Bk**
26 pts —}   Poem Title ——— B 12/13 u+l.c
19½ }   Epi/Dedi ——— C 8½ pT
19½ }   I ◀
½# >   ⟩—— D section head
1# →
½# →   II ◀

indent   □ Trans ———]—— E translator, etc. 8½ p

39 pts—}   POET ⟨3.05#⟩ } 12/13 pt
26 pts —}   Poem Title
26 pts }

            } 10/13 pt

½# between
stanzas

verse   □ Char: ═════
drama
            □ Char: ═════

finerule
×25 picas.

6pts #
baseline to rule

3 picas

3 picas.
back margin

22 picas

headline: 10/13 pt
S.cs letter#

122   WAR POETRY

26 pts

½ line # between
stanzas

19½ pts
39 pts

Source translator

POET NAME

26 pts   Title of Poem

E 8½/13 pt

26 pts

39 pts

NAME OF POET

26 pts   Poem Title
19½ pts   Epigraph / Dedication
19½ pts

C head   8½/13 pt

Do not begin a
new poem at the
foot of a page
with less than
2 lines of first
stanza

F bk of War Poetry · 216 × 135 mm

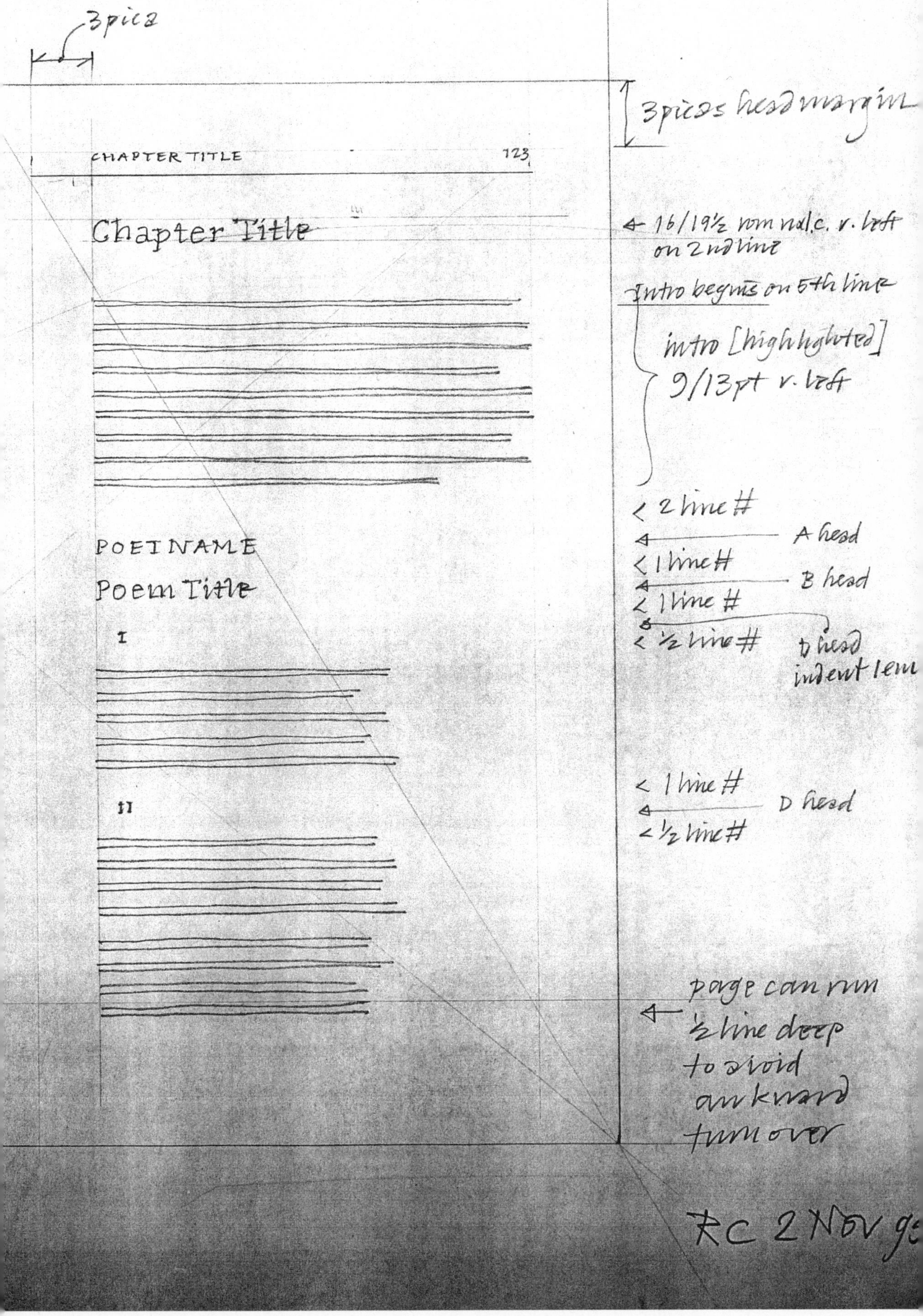

3 pica

3 picas head margin

CHAPTER TITLE   123

Chapter Title

← 16/19½ mm ndl.c. v. left on 2nd line

Intro begins on 5th line

intro [highlighted] 9/13 pt v. left

< 2 line #
← A head
< 1 line #
← B head
< 1 line #
< ½ line #   D head indent 1 em

POET NAME
Poem Title

I

II

< 1 line #
← D head
< ½ line #

← page can run ½ line deep to avoid awkward turnover

RC 2 Nov 95

RH: You don't work on computers?

RC: No. I prefer to work on hard copy even if the text exists on disk. The thing is to go through the text and make it fit to the format. We used to have fixed formats for poetry, but that's changed. At the moment, we tend to set our poetry in Sabon. The choice of size and actual format, I find now, has to depend on each book of poems. I have the most horrendous problems with a poet's work when there are 80 characters or more to a line.

RH: And you don't want turnovers.

RC: You've got to deal with turnovers. I've actually had one poet in the past year rewrite a line to avoid a turnover. But I also cheat by breaking the measure sometimes to get an extra word in. Or you discuss with the author or editor the best way of coping with turnovers—whether they're to be indented 1 em or whether the turnover hangs at the other end of the line. Turnovers are always a problem, particularly as the tendency is to publish poetry in quite small format anyway.

RH: You'd think poets would realize that books are a certain shape and would stop writing poems that don't fit that shape, but they don't.

  Of the hundreds of books that Faber does each year, how many do you really sit down and design from scratch?

RC: I suppose that it might be about fifty, but remember that every book is looked at for special problems.

RH: Fifty a year. For yourself or for you and your assistant?

RC: That's difficult. I'd have to give that real thought. I'd have to go through a catalog and count. It's not something I usually think about.

RH: I find that other designers are interested in how much work their colleagues do. It's always a measure. People often call me to find out how much staff they need. How long should it take for someone to design a book?

  The reason I was asking you about computers is because I find that sometimes, even though the computer has speeded things up for me, it gives me so many options that I may take much longer on a design than I would have earlier. After I've done a design in Sabon, I might say, "Well, I don't like it." I'll try it in Garamond. Then I'll decide I don't like that Garamond and will try a different Garamond. I have six different Garamonds that I can try. I don't know if my work's gotten better, but it's taking a lot longer to do things.

RC: The advantage, in some ways, of using a format typeface for a book is that you don't have to think about choices. You know you're going to do it in Palatino.

RH: When you have a book that doesn't fall into a format, where do you start—with the trim size?

RC: Sometimes. Very often these sorts of books will have been discussed

ERIC GILL

Fiona MacCarthy

ff
faber and faber
LONDON · BOSTON

This and the following illustrations from Fiona MacCarthy, *Eric Gill*, Faber and Faber

CONTENTS

v

BRIGHTON
1882–97

Eric Gill was born in Brighton at 6.30 in the morning on 22 February 1882 and named after the hero of Dean Farrar's moral school story *Eric, or Little by Little*. With his characteristic extremity of statement he was, in later years, to turn against his birthplace and describe Brighton as 'a shapeless mess' and 'not a place at all'. But his upbringing, as second child of the large family of the Reverend Arthur Tidman Gill and his wife Rose, was even by his own account unusually happy. It was moralistic, strict, emotional, cosy and contained.

The sense of place was always very strong in Eric Gill. In a way, this sense of place became his motivating force in adult life as he moved with his considerable entourage from one part of the country to another – from Ditchling in Sussex to Capel-y-ffin in the Black Mountains of South Wales and then finally to Pigotts in High Wycombe – endlessly in search of an ideal environment, the perfect place to live and work, which always just evaded him. Although Brighton in some ways fell so short of this ideal, seeming to Gill in later years a prime example of just the sort of urban sprawl he deprecated, his memories of childhood there were vivid and affectionate. His *Autobiography* is full of fond and careful descriptions of the scenes remembered in the little streets of Brighton in the 1880s as the family moved from Hamilton Road to Prestonville Road to Cliftonville Road and finally to the road now known as Highcroft Villas. All these houses were within a stone's throw of each other and well within walking distance of the chapel in North Street where his father was the curate.

Architecturally the district is now nothing like as cohesive as it was. Gill's birthplace, 32 Hamilton Road, a small Victorian house – two floors with semi-basement – has had modern additions which destroy completely its original character of amiable primness. But in 1960, when

3

at an earlier stage. I will know a bit about what's coming. Again, it depends on how out of the ordinary they are.

RH: You designed a biography of [the artist and type designer] Eric Gill. Was that a formatted book?

RC: No. The only aspect of format there was its trim size.

RH: Do you start with an idea—for example, "This is a book about something, and it should have this feeling, best shown in, say, 1920s or 1990s typography"?

RC: No. I think that a book published today should be in 1990s typography.

RH: I was going to ask you about allusiveness in design and whether design should suggest something.

RC: Yes, but only in a very subtle and quiet manner.

RH: The book on Gill was designed in Sabon. Why didn't you do it in one of Gill's typefaces?

RC: I think Sabon is a good, readable face. I might have set it in Gill's Joanna typeface, but the book is 356 pages long, and I thought, "No, not for a sustained read like this, written from a very 1990s viewpoint, a thoroughly contemporary biography—even though it's about Gill." But enough of Gill.

RH: What if you were doing a book about John Heartfield or somebody else who had a very peculiar photographic style?

RC: I suppose, particularly if there are going to be illustrations, that then one would choose a typeface that had a good color. And I may, in that case, choose a display face that will echo some of the sort of aggressiveness or strength of the particular subject.

RH: Do you always start with your text face—one that you feel is, first and foremost, legible?

RC: Absolutely.

RH: At that point you're not thinking about what you want to do with the display face.

RC: The first thing I want to do is analyze the text and see how the text is organized and what the hierarchy of headings is, and so on. I want to see how the whole thing is put together. For me, the whole point of book design is that the typography reinforces the structure of the text, aiding rather than hindering the reader's access to it.

RH: After you've done this, as you consider the text page, do you think about what you're going to do with the running heads, or do you wait to see what you're going to do with a chapter opening before you do the running heads?

RC: I invariably start with the text page. There are factors about the extent to consider: a book may have to make 320 pages, it cannot be 800 pages, and it's silly to make it 160. So, it's going to have, say, 424 words to the page.

RH: You talk about words in the manuscript. That's common in Britain, rather than characters per page. How come you don't work by characters per page?

RC: I will if I'm having to do a more careful castoff. I'll do a character count, because what's a word? Is it "impossible" or is it "but"? I will then look at all the headings. Are they long? Are they short? How strong do they need to be?

RH: Are you talking about subheads or chapter titles or everything?

RC: Well, chapter titles and the relations within the whole hierarchy of headings. The smallest one needs to be recognizable. Then you step up the scale to the chapter title and on to the part title, if there is one. So relations among the headings need to be established before you decide what your face is going to be. At that point, I may realize that, well, I'm not going to be able to do this with variations on the text face. I will have to pick another face of a different weight.

RH: Is your first inclination, however, to work with the text face?

RC: Yes, it is. I'm all for the absolute minimum, the smallest change that will register with the reader. There's a very big difference between *looking* at a page of text and *reading* a page of text. When you're reading, even the slightest nuance registers.

RH: Once you've got this basic page decided, do you work in facing pages?

RC: Always in facing pages. The open book is the basic unit.

RH: Do you actually draw out little lines indicating each line of type, or do you just know that if you do a box of 20 × 24 picas . . . ?

RC: I always draw up my margins making a bit of an adjustment for a thick book. I draw lines indicating text.

When it comes to lines per page, I always enjoy it when I can work in multiples of three. You could say that's my link with typographic tradition. You've got the 33-line [Gutenberg] Bible, the 36-line Bible, the 42-line Bible—all are divisible by three. If I can work to 36 lines or 39 lines, it's great, because then if I want a maximum chapter opening, I can go to a third, and I know that third will be a third of the way down the text page as well, which is where the optical center is. And, of course, the mathematics extends to the classical subdivisions of the page—1/6, 1/9, etc.

RH: I don't have any specific number of lines. I usually end up with something between 37 and 41 lines, depending on the design. A standard spec for me is 10 1/2 on 14 × 27.

RC: I would often like to use more leading, but if I can't increase the leading, I reduce the type size. I'll go 10/13. But I do usually try to get a minimum of 20 percent of type size [that is, 2 points of leading for 10 points of type].

RH: When you've done your facing pages and you haven't yet done your

31 *Hound of St Dominic*, symbol of St Dominic's Press, Ditchling.
Woodcut for poster, 1923. (reduced)

Gill's only contribution to the Guild central fund was £500 borrowed from Lord Howard de Walden. Financial control, though in theory a shared responsibility, was in reality put in the hands of Pepler, the only Guild member who was reasonably prosperous. Gill resented this. His resentment bubbled over into some notes he wrote as the background to the quarrel, by this time becoming more public and embittered. Pepler's education and background of relative affluence had, Gill maintained, left him with 'a sort of Manicheism' with regard to money: because he considered it intrinsically evil all care and method in financial affairs seemed to him unnecessary, even despicable. Gill summed up Pepler's attitude with a rather startling venom:

Everyone loves HP but *hates* his finance
      & hates his brutal methods
      his dictatorial manner
      his minding other people's business

He accused Pepler bitterly of always rushing into new projects and leaving the consolidation undetermined.

There was of course a great deal more to it than that. It was not a simple conflict of the rich man versus the poor man, a question of the person who called the tune financially, although there was certainly a little of this in it. It was more a confrontation of methods and personality.

Pepler was fundamentally outgoing, seeking opportunities to expand the craft community, to extend the boundaries from the common to the village. Gill, in spite of his talent for publicity (all the more acute the more deliberately denied), was essentially reclusive and was becoming more so.

The emotional tensions of the last few years, intensified by his resentment of Pepler and of Betty's continuing love for Pepler's son David, made their continuing partnership impossible. Gill had become temperamentally unsuited to a partnership. As Philip Hagreen, wood engraver, a new arrival at Ditchling, put it so succinctly: 'Eric had to be the Abbot.' He had begun to panic at the thought of being answerable. He could no longer tolerate the prospect of the challenges of those on his own level. He was out of sympathy with the idea of Ditchling. From now on, his mind was set on the need to be the master, and be seen to be the master, in his own house.

Gill's own official reason for pulling out of Ditchling was the publicity surrounding him and the community: his need to get away, and get his family away, from the endless stream of visitors, reporters and inquirers which had increased in volume, and in nuisance value, since the *Money-changers* controversy. It was certainly quite true that Hopkins Crank attracted visitors out of all proportion to its modest facilities for dealing with the public: Desmond Chute, in his Ditchling days, had shared with Mary the task of entertaining and distracting visitors until Gill was ready to receive them. But, like many of the versions of the truth which Gill put forward, this too was far from the whole story. There was something in Gill's nature which demanded the publicity, and this as much as anything was what he needed to escape from. Pepler, who understood him well, saw his deep-rooted and infuriating contradictions: the urge for space for peace of mind and contemplation which so bizarrely coexisted with the 'non-contemplative streak', his 'exhibitionist twist'. In one of the most penetrating passages which anyone has written about Gill he suggests 'It was that twist, which he perhaps did not fully allow for, which made him apprehensive of the publicity he unfailingly created.' It was one of Gill's great errors that in quarrelling with Pepler he rejected the one person who could see him as he was.

On 22 July 1924 Eric Gill wrote formally resigning from the Guild of SS Joseph and Dominic. It was a sadly businesslike letter:

My reasons for this are of course obvious and I think you will agree that no other solution is possible as we have lost confidence in one another. You will no

chapter openings, do you know where you want the running heads and folios to be—whether you need to center them or put the folios to the outside?

RC: I may well have reckoned on the fact that the running headlines are going to be flush left, and decided whether they will be symmetrical or asymmetrical. But where the running headline goes and where it goes in relation to the folio will ultimately depend on the number of lines on the page, whether I'm going to put the folio on the bottom and the headline at the top, whether the headline is going to be with the folio at the top, whether I'm going to introduce a rule at the top of the page—which I find useful if the text page itself is rather broken up, with, say, lots of quoted verse, or if the book is an anthology whose material is quite varied.

RH: Are you free to drop the running head if you feel that it gets in the way and is unnecessary?

RC: If it's not necessary to the reader, then I would drop it. But if it's going to be a help to the reader, I would do everything to keep it in.

RH: I often have books in which the running head is the same, verso and recto, throughout the entire book. It seems silly to put it on both

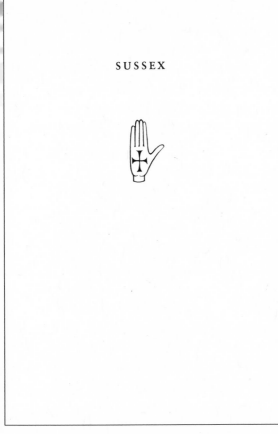

SUSSEX   SOUTH COAST

Part titles

pages, and sometimes I get away with putting it on one and not the
other and use that as a design element.

RC: In that case, what is the running head?

RH: The running head might be a book title or an author's name or
something. It's generally useless.

RC: Unless it's absolutely contributing something to the structure of the
book from the reader's point of view, I would drop it.

RH: I often do in small works of fiction, like small novels.

RC: The only argument that I've heard for retaining such a running
headline was that it was very useful to know the title of the book when
you were reading it over somebody's shoulder.

RH: The excuse in the United States is so that when the pages have been
photocopied, you know where you've stolen them from.

   Since you're a minimalist, do you tend to want to do the running
head in the same size and style that the text is set in, or do you try to
find some variant on that?

RC: The only variant I've made is to reduce it a size.

RH: In Updike's day, in the States, you would make them bigger, which I
always thought was very perverse.

RC: Very. In particular, I would make them smaller if in fact there was a lot of quoted matter in the text that was set down a size.

RH: Do you do that? Do you always set your quoted matter smaller?

RC: No, but I would use the size of the quoted matter for the running headline, so that should there be a whole page of quoted matter, then the headline wouldn't stand out too much. Quoted matter I deal with, again, as the text demands. There are two sorts of quoted matter: the sort that should be read in context and the sort that could be skipped over.

RH: The latter is the kind I'd set down, so readers can skip it.

RC: That's right. The thing that gets my goat is treating quoted matter in two different ways in one book. It seems to me that you only need to say "This is quoted matter" in one way. You either set it down, or if you're setting it text size, you indent it or even . . .

RH: Still setting it justified?

RC: Still setting it justified. If it's a book that has a lot of quoted correspondence, then I think it might be fine to set the correspondence unjustified. Otherwise it can be difficult for readers to know precisely where they are.

RH: Would you set extracts ragged right if they were lengthy and ran over more than one page?

RC: Yes.

RH: And would you set extracts text size if you felt that it was necessary to read them along with the text?

RC: Yes, I would, even in a very long book. I've done this on a couple of occasions when the quoted matter is set text size with opening and closing quotes and is really part of the main text.

RH: And is it set off from the text in any way?

RC: No. The only way you know that it's quoted matter is when you are reading it, because the context tells you that the passage is a quote.

RH: The only way I can get away with that is if the extract is shorter than about four text lines.

RC: That's commonplace, I think, if the extract is short, but sometimes I've done this even with long extracts because the author has felt that it would be critical if the reader skipped them in any way.

RH: Is this is a decision that comes to you before you start, or do you go back to the author and say, "Could you live with this?"

RC: It is something I may well go back to the author about and say, "What do you think? What is the relative weight of this?"

RH: I feel exactly the same way you do. It is editors, strangely enough, who seem to be most difficult in this connection. If you go to an author and say, "I feel this," you can generally convince the author to go along. Having quoted matter set down a size is one of those irritating practices that hangs on in the States. I think that it encourages the reader to skip extracts. Why have them if you don't need to read them?

RC: But, you see, there's a problem if there's a lot of quoted matter in a long text and it's economically important to reduce the extent of the book. The only way you can cope with the problem may be to set the quoted matter down.

RH: Let's talk about chapter openings. After you've done your text page, assuming that there are no subheadings within the text, would you then go to your chapter openings?

RC: Yes, that's right.

RH: Which one do you choose to work with, the hardest one or the most average one or . . . ?

RC: When I was making my analysis, I would have made a note of short and long titles. If there is one chapter title that is way off, then I may consider going back to the editor and saying, "Look, this is very different. Can we do something? Can we make half of it a subtitle?" Then I would just work with an optimum one-liner. But if I know that there are going to be two-line titles, I bear that in mind.

RH: Would you do a number of chapter openings when doing your layouts, or would you hope for the best with the one and see what happens?

RC: I would work out layouts.

RH: Do you trace type or do a rough sketch of it?

RC: No, I don't draw the type. I do a minimum tracing of a title, allowing for two lines if necessary. Then I go through the manuscript marking the breaks for the typesetter.

RH: Do you draw those out for yourself to see where the breaks fall, or do you feel confident that you know already?

RC: I just think, "This is going to be two lines. Where is the sensible place to break it?" If I find that I'm getting a lot of two-line headings where, perhaps, the first line is short and the second line is long, then I consider introducing a short rule as part of the chapter opening underneath in order to avoid a pyramid.

RH: What do you do about things like printer's flowers and other ornaments? Do you ever think about using them, or are they something that you feel, because you're a minimalist, you'd rather not use?

RC: I'd rather not. I tend to use rules. I do associate ornamented flowers with metal typesetting. I know that is not strictly the case, but I used them a lot when I was designing for metal type. And then for a time, of course, they weren't available. That's when I stopped using them and started to think, "Well, there are these rules that I can play with." So I started to use rules.

I did use a vine leaf for a book about Venice. But usually I think, "Do I really *need* to use an ornament?" It always comes back to whether the text demands it. If you've got a text that is divided in such a way that to use something like the old paragraph mark would highlight this aspect, I would be all for it.

RH: Would you ever use a large initial to open a chapter?

RC: I've used large initials recently for a book about the vampire story, from Bram Stoker on. There was a critical text with very long extracts from original works [legends of vampires], with short editorial introductions and linking passages. Textually there wasn't any difference between the editorial matter and the stories themselves. You were supposed to read the whole lot. A dropped initial was a useful way of highlighting the start of an extract.

RH: How big an initial did you use.

RC: Two lines. It was a small page.

RH: I might use up to six lines.

RC: On a small page with a large initial you're starting to run into a short-measure problem. You also have to watch the relation to the chapter title. A large initial is always subordinate to the chapter title.

For me, a dropped initial says, as it used to say in the manuscripts, "Here beginneth." In a way, it's a piece of punctuation. So, if a chapter opening is saying, "Here beginneth," why say it again right below? Too much design falls into tautology. It's perfectly clear that this is where we begin.

RH: Do you ever feel that you can do something bolder on the title page?

RC: No, I think the title page has got to have a certain decorum and should relate to what's going on in the text. It should anticipate the text. After a reader looks at a title page, it seems to me that things like part titles and chapter titles shouldn't come as a shock.

RH: Do you feel that most readers really look at the title page? I think only designers and librarians always look at the title page.

RC: I think that librarians look at the [title] verso [the copyright page]. And that's a page that needs to be properly designed as well. The contents page, too.

When I am asked, "What do you think of this book design?" the first page I turn to is the title verso. It gives me a clue about the control that the designer has had over a book and the care that has been exercised.

RH: That's unfair sometimes, because the designer often doesn't get to see that page. For many books that I spend many hours working on, I never get to see proof of that page. Do you usually have control over the copyright page? And how do you deal with British cataloging-in-publication data?

RC: The copyright page always comes through with the manuscript. We don't always put the CIP data in the book. I always used to center the lines. I never kept it in the sort of shape that it came in.

RH: There's no reason to, although I've had editors who insist that I break it exactly line for line, and I can't make it clear to them that it only breaks that way because the card in the library card catalog is that long. They refuse to believe me.

You don't have anything to do with the jacket, do you?

RC: Usually not. At Scolar Press I did, but those books were selling in a different marketplace. I think that in trade publishing it's pretty aggressive out there. The jacket is very much a part of the sales pitch, and it's performing a very different job than the inside is. I always think of the jacket as being the extrovert and the text as being the introvert.

For me the text is the most important point of the book, and I am perfectly happy to concentrate on that.

Richard Eckersley

After graduating from Trinity College, University of Dublin, where he studied English and Italian literature, Richard Eckersley earned a B.A. degree in art and design from the London College of Printing. He has taught or been a visiting critic at many art schools in Britain, Ireland, and the United States. From 1974 to 1980 he was senior graphic designer at the Kilkenny Design Workshops (Ireland). In 1981 he became senior designer at the University of Nebraska Press, but he continues to design for many other publishers. His work has appeared in every major design competition and has been shown in many international design magazines. He has won a silver medal at Leipzig and the Carl Herzog Prize, and his books are in several museum collections, including the Cooper-Hewitt National Design Museum.

Book design is a process so transparent and anonymous that one sometimes wonders whether it exists at all. It's a negative quantity: a book is well designed to the extent that it is not badly designed, rather like the preferred porridge in *Goldilocks and the Three Bears* that was not too hot and not too cold but just right. Confronted by such lack of definition, the designer must sometimes have doubts, and then it helps to consider the books of the past. The books made by Aldus Manutius, the Venetian publisher of Virgil and Erasmus, have a quiddity that is absolute. They are just right. And because of their modest format, they were cheaper to produce than other books of the time and thus available to the less wealthy. The importance of the Aldine editions to the establishment of the New Classicism, along with their enduring impact on patterns of readership, is incalculable. Similarly, for my generation in Great Britain, Penguin books became a sort of extra-mural university—readable and affordable editions of well-chosen texts, immaculate in their editing, design, and production. In the United States, Knopf and Houghton Mifflin managed to establish in the minds of readers a natural association between the well-made and the well-written book—a remarkably enlightened marketing strategy that saw a good return on the investment in design and production. More recent examples of presses whose authority resides at least partially in their physical presentation would include Faber & Faber; Farrar, Straus & Giroux; MIT Press; David Godine; and the small but fleet Black Sparrow Press.

Aldine Press, Penguin, Black Sparrow—these publishers have demonstrated that well-made books succeed in the marketplace. Their success suggests that readers value appropriate design and will weigh presentation and price together when making a purchase. That is certainly my own attitude as a customer. Increasingly, I find myself in the dilemma of wanting a title but not the edition that the bookseller has stocked. For example, although Oxford has an excellent list, I am reluctant to purchase Oxford paperbacks because the typesetting is a constant annoyance. Wads of space are shoved between sentences as a cure for bad word spacing—a hiatus every other line that insults writer and reader alike.

No doubt, as a designer, I am more compulsive than my neighbor about typographical integrity. I look at the front matter of any book before I buy it, and lament the copyright page that is invariably perfunctory in its design. But, as with most people, my priority is the readability of the text page.

I'm also concerned about the size of books. Most books are too big, too heavy to hold comfortably in one hand, and with type of too wide a measure. Many of these could be set in smaller type on a smaller page. Others should be broken into several volumes.

I try to apply the same standards to my own work that I demand of others, though with mixed success. Usually my approach is directed by some physical feature of the text—chapter titles of disparate length, miasmas of quotation marks, endless hierarchies of subheads. Such obvious problems make the task of design easier because they give it a focus. A plain text is the biggest challenge for me. I fret endlessly over the margins, measure, and typeface.

The choice of typeface is partly directed by the tone and argument of the text but has more to do with its physical structure. I tend to binge on a particular typeface until I sicken of it. Perhaps that is inevitable. It takes repeated use to understand a typeface, and by then, one no longer sees it freshly. Although I may abuse typefaces in this way, there are some to which I invariably return after a brief fast—Aldus, Garamond, Janson, Galliard. When choosing type, I'm not much concerned with a literal sort of chronological fidelity. The matter of the historical appropriateness of a typeface to a given text is much exaggerated. Why not a *Julius Caesar* in sans serif now and then? The equivalent is done in the theatre. But one must be deliberate about it. A great text should be treated as timeless and also contemporary.

The size of type should be decided with reference to the measure. It is also dependent on the literary style of the book. A large type size may work in a narrow measure if the vocabulary is simple, as in most fiction. It won't work for a book on Heidegger, replete with German extracts. Deciding the matter is easy enough—the computer allows one to run the actual text in the layout and to see how it behaves in a given size.

I've worked almost exclusively on the computer since about 1988 and have found it liberating. But dependence on the computer has its negative aspects. I tend to stick with the fonts that I have in the machine, whereas I used to ransack the type-specimen books for display faces and ornaments. The options seemed infinite. But generally, the computer has changed the *way* I work, not so much the look of my work.

For a simple monograph I might produce eighteen layouts, whereas before the Macintosh I would have made six but supplied a more extensive set of written instructions. The potential to control every facet draws me into an endless battle, and I attempt matters of detail that would be better left to a good compositor. I think the absence of the former relationship between designer and compositor is a terrible loss to book design. It is becoming less and less possible to revive because there are so few good compositors around and because publishers are not willing to pay the rates that good work deserves.

In theory, the production of so many layouts should allow me to dispense with lengthy written instructions. That hasn't happened, because of a lack of discipline on my part perhaps and because typesetters are becoming less visual. Many of them prefer written instructions. I write annotations in the margins of my layouts. I also provide separate written specifications. The problem is that the layouts and the written specifications are often contradictory. I'm a rotten typist, and I find the writing of specifications so tedious that my attention wanders. Often I catch the discrepancies when I come to mark the manuscript, but not always. As I mark up the manuscript, I staple the layouts to the relevant pages.

After the layouts are done, the next I see of a book is a set of sample pages. I seldom need to make changes to them. For the most part, the sample pages replicate elements that I have already fully visualized as layouts.

Some of my designs are set in-house, but most go to outside suppliers. The ability of outside suppliers varies greatly from place to place, and one may no longer anticipate a common standard even for such rudimentary elements of style as kerning and the use of ligatures. Our own typesetting equipment is limited, so I choose the least complicated manuscripts for in-house projects and keep the design as simple as possible. I've tried to devise a method of design that minimizes the effects of bad production. One defense is to lead out the lines. This mitigates the unsightliness of gappy word spacing. I make the head and gutter margins wider than is decent to compensate for bad trimming and binding. But that is like taking chamomile tea for a serious heart condition.

The examples of my work that are reproduced in these pages were well set and quite well printed. They date from some years ago, when standards of production were higher. Some are traditional designs, like the Willa Cather. Others might be called postmodern—the Motte and Ronell, for example.

My design for the Cather novels was based on the Houghton Mifflin autograph edition, designed by Bruce Rogers—the edition that Cather herself preferred. The task was complicated by the great variety of scholarly apparatus in the Nebraska edition, which had to harmonize with the text of the novel. The exercise was a revealing one. What struck me most about Rogers's design was its intuitive freedom and confidence in relating the

II

Emil reached home a little past noon, and when he went into the kitchen Alexandra was already seated at the head of the long table, having dinner with her men, as she always did unless there were visitors. He slipped into his empty place at his sister's right. The three pretty young Swedish girls who did Alexandra's housework were cutting pies, refilling coffee-cups, placing platters of bread and meat and potatoes upon the red tablecloth, and continually getting in each other's way between the table and the stove. To be sure they always wasted a good deal of time getting in each other's way and giggling at each other's mistakes. But, as Alexandra had pointedly told her sisters-in-law, it was to hear them giggle that she kept three young things in her kitchen; the work she could do herself, if it were necessary. These girls, with their long letters from home, their finery, and their love-affairs, afforded her a great deal of entertainment, and they were company for her when Emil was away at school.

Of the youngest girl, Signa, who has a pretty figure, mottled pink cheeks, and yellow hair, Alexandra is very

82

Neighboring Fields

fond, though she keeps a sharp eye upon her. Signa is apt to be skittish at mealtime, when the men are about, and to spill the coffee or upset the cream. It is supposed that Nelse Jensen, one of the six men at the dinner-table, is courting Signa, though he has been so careful not to commit himself that no one in the house, least of all Signa, can tell just how far the matter has progressed. Nelse watches her glumly as she waits upon the table, and in the evening he sits on a bench behind the stove with his *dragharmonika*, playing mournful airs and watching her as she goes about her work. When Alexandra asked Signa whether she thought Nelse was in earnest, the poor child hid her hands under her apron and murmured, "I don't know, ma'm. But he scolds me about everything, like as if he wanted to have me!"

At Alexandra's left sat a very old man, barefoot and wearing a long blue blouse, open at the neck. His shaggy head is scarcely whiter than it was sixteen years ago, but his little blue eyes have become pale and watery, and his ruddy face is withered, like an apple that has clung all winter to the tree. When Ivar lost his land through mismanagement a dozen years ago, Alexandra took him in, and he has been a member of her household ever since. He is too old to work in the fields, but he hitches and unhitches the work-teams and looks

83

From Willa Cather, *O Pioneers!* University of Nebraska Press

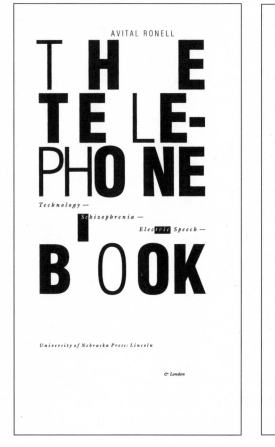

From Avital Ronell, *The Telephone Book,* University of Nebraska Press

various elements of the book. It feels all of a piece, yet it has little measurable consistency. There is a variation of type style and a play of space that goes beyond the mathematics of the grid.

Avital Ronell's *Telephone Book* might appear to be entirely in contrast with the Cather, but its design is based on the same classical conventions. Ronell challenges how we read and attempts to make us conscious and critical of the process. I tried to convey this by emphasizing the physical structure of the book. The conventions of book typography that we prefer to take for granted are either flaunted by distortion and exaggeration or conspicuous by their absence. They are always there by implication.

Warren Motte, the author of *Questioning Edmond Jabès,* was a young professor in the French department when the manuscript came into production. I knew him quite well and was wary of working with a friend, which can complicate things. In this case, my apprehension was unfounded. Motte gave me a free hand. I read his introduction and skimmed most of the main text, sometimes reading closely. I felt that I had a pretty good idea of the author and his subject.

The Motte is in a small format partly to bulk it but principally because a small page size suggested the intimacy of the dialogue. I usually begin the design of a book with the basic text page, which I use as a linear grid for the placement of display elements. With the Motte I was directed to the use of flush and hang paragraphs by the form of the extracts. Jabès visually patterns his writing very deliberately. I saw that the extract style would jar with a conventional form of paragraphing in the main text, so I built the text design around the extract style. I suppose Jabès's writing would be grouped in the postmodern school, but he doesn't quite fit there. Much of his work is grounded in the Talmud and the Hebrew tradition of exegesis. Although the design of the book might be called postmodern, the basic structure is quite classical. The word "postmodern" is by definition a ragbag of what has gone before, usually combined into inept or outrageous confections. This approach may be entirely valid for certain authors—not, I think, Jabès.

Both the Ronell and the Motte are narrow books. I don't much like the standard trim sizes, perhaps because they have become associated for me with standard designs of too wide a type measure. A trim size of 6 × 9 inches is fine if one is permitted to apply the Golden Section to the type page, but that would reduce the number of words per page to unacceptably few— unacceptable to the publisher, that is. I favor a narrow format, cut down from the standard 6 × 9 or 5 1/2 × 8 1/2. But some books need to be short and wide, or square.

For paragraph indents I usually specify the conventional em space. The em of the text might or might not be carried through to notes and bibliography set in a smaller size, depending on the design—for example, there might be a relation between the placement of the folio or running head and the text indent, and this would have to be maintained in the back matter.

I prefer old-style to lining figures almost always, except for superior note references—and perhaps that's an unnecessary qualification. The convention is to go with lining superiors, but Tschichold didn't hold with that when designing the house style for Penguin Books. On the odd occasion that a design of mine has mistakenly been set with o.s. superiors, I've found them quite acceptable. I used to set tables in lining figures, because that's what I was taught at college. Now I think that's mistaken; o.s. figs have a definite horizontal alignment, and they require less leading.

I treat extracts differently according to whether the book is on a centered axis or asymmetrical. I was hardly aware of extracts when I lived in England. There, the practice is to treat most extracts as quotations. I wish the same convention prevailed here. It seems to me that U.S. book design begins two strikes behind the count. Double quotes, unspaced em dashes, redundant punctuation in acronyms and after contractions—all this makes the Platonic book totally out of reach. I add space around extracts, otherwise they clot the page. In some books I've experimented quite a bit with extracts, setting them in bold sans serif type, of varying measure, depending on the pattern of the words. If extracts are set off by half-line spaces but set full measure, a half-point difference in size is often enough to identify them, rather than the traditional full point.

The design of running heads and folios is intimately bound to the text page solution. In the case of the Motte, with hung text, it was obvious that the folios and running heads should follow the indented text, to make a visual anchor. I would say that these elements are usually anchor points whatever the page design. In an asymmetrical page with a caption column I usually align the folio or running head with the latter, to anchor the captions that might otherwise appear to float.

Often I omit page folios from front matter and chapter openings. I'm also stingy with running heads. Frequently they are longer than necessary or entirely redundant.

The display face should have either a direct relation with the text or be strongly contrasting. Some good text faces look weak in display. Galliard is especially useful in supplying a strong text font that can bear enlargement.

The relation of running heads to subheads can be very difficult to resolve. When studying Rogers's Cather design I was immediately struck by the size of the running heads—maybe 3 points *larger* than the text. I think that design idea worth exploring. I usually set the running heads smaller than the text. In asymmetrical typography it's relatively simple to distinguish the running head from subheads. In centered books it can be tricky. I don't like using a rule, and I've come to dislike boldface in any circumstance. Sometimes I'm forced to rule off the running head or use bold to distinguish the first-level subhead. I haven't solved this problem.

dents. However, she did remember that she played a 'throwing away'
game with the patient. Julie's elder sister had played the usual version of
this game and had exasperated Mrs X by it" (*DS*, 185). (Laing had explained that "in Freud's case, the little boy kept his reel of string attached
to him when he threw it away, in contrast to the fact that he could not keep
his mother thus under contol by an attachment to her 'apron strings'"
[*DS*, 185]). Mrs. Chiasmus is quoted as saying: "'I made sure that *she* (Julie) was not going to play that game with me. *I* threw things away and she
brought them back to *me*,' as soon as she could crawl" (*DS*, 185). I could
call this a syndromic habit of reversing charges. As the self in the text keeps
dividing on automatic, Laing leads us to suppose, if by indirection, that
schizophrenia may be an effect of something intensely peculiar to our con-
temporaneity, what we are calling technology: "I am, however, describing
something that occurs in our twentieth-century Western world, and perhaps not, in quite the same terms, anywhere else. I do not know what are
the essential features of this world that allow of such possibilities to arise"
(*DS*, 180).

When you or I

get on the line

to a schizophrenic

you do not know who is there, who is speaking; in fact, one has the feeling
that no one is there, and like Ophelia, the no one that is there or not gives
you the sensation that she is not a person. Her "word salad" seems to be
the result of a recording, registering a number of quasi-autonomous partial systems striving to give simulcast expression to themselves out of the
same mouth. The overall unity of their being is disconnected into several
"partial assemblies" or "partial systems" (quasi-autonomous "com-
plexes," "inner objects"), each of which has its own little stereotyped "personality" (molar splitting). Their being is dystonic, there is a lack of an
overall ontological boundary. Listen:

---

nothing else, "obligated." Hence the acquittal footnote. And to have reproduced the necessity of différance within the triangulation of operator, other,
and addressee, means that Derrida, having been taken by the call only up to a
point, "calculated" the technology of the call in earnest. In fact, Derrida,
whose signature in this text is *j'accepte*, can be shown to have refused the call
with the same mistrust he expresses for Heidegger's assertion that "science
does not think" (*die Wissenschaft denkt nicht*).[38] If Derrida's legendary caution
indicates the value he holds for science's thinking—including the potentiality
for thinking in technology, but what is called thinking?—this is why he can
refuse a call, precisely because a decision has to be made with each technologi-
cal move on you—in this case, "you" may be an effect or defect of technology.
In this respect, all politics of moment withdraw from first place when it comes
to the call of technology, losing indeed such claims as are made for their strict
anteriority. Technology has come to rule Power: there is a politics of technology which then begins to say, among other things, that politics as such, or
ethics, can no longer be considered altogether prior to technology. Politics has
become a secondary, derivative form of telecommunications. Power-
generated by technology. This is where to start, but it's too soon to blow a
fuse. The break in the circuit calling Derrida to Heidegger is not absolute. For while Derrida refuses a call to which he nonetheless pays tributary
taxes, the call that he takes and does not take still issues from a certain Heidegger. The call comes from Jacques Derrida and from beyond him. It comes
from him because, as he confirms, he was just putting Heidegger's credibility
on the line for which the addressee pays in turn by calling in his incredibility.
The point is that Heidegger takes to the ☎, even in the fantastical scenario
which the footnote feels obliged to report, when his answerability is called to
account. Derrida's context is no doubt different from that of our investiga-
tion; yet "Heidegger" is resolutely assembled and managed according to a
telephonic logic. At any rate, the collect call, too, comes from me and from beyond me, printing out a footnote to itself and inscribing itself in the recognition scene from which the so-called unconscious can say,

All in all, the question does not amount to a locational one. We are no
longer asking where you are calling from but what is calling me from me, de-
manding my deconstruction while "I" stand by. "Where?" is a primally meta-

---

reed. *Imagine a multitude of tuning-forks of different pitch to be massed together in
front of the mouth and all simultaneously to be set in vibration. It should then be possible, by shifting the position of the tongue, to reinforce the tone—now of one fork,
now of another—at will. Indeed under such circumstances, it would hardly be possible to assume a position of the mouth, that would not reinforce some fork—at least in
a greater or less degree. Imagine the mass of tuning-forks to be placed in the Scotch-
man's throat, and similar effects would result.*

*Now the vocal cords like the hypo-
thetical forks, produce a number
of feeble tones of different pitch; when we pronounce a vowel sound, the mouth cavity
reinforces, by resonance, that 'partial tone' of the voice. (MS, 29)*

*In the final
lecture of*
the volume, "Articulation Teaching," Bell evokes a notion of maternal speech
which should form the model and program for language acquisition. A good
deal of what he has to say in closing will recall the way of training the telephone into articulate sentences, or the drawing out of the deaf toward speech.
Some may recall Heidegger's transformative grammar of Mother turned
Nietzsche.

*I should like in conclusion to say a few words upon the general subject
of articulation teaching. We don't yet know how best to teach speech
to the deaf. If we did we wouldn't be here. . . . It is certainly the case that the methods
usually employed in schools for the deaf do not even approximate to the nursery
method of the hearing child. Not one of the little hearing children whom you may
have left at home commenced by learning elementary sounds. Mothers do not begin
with elementary sounds and then combine them into syllables and words. The
mother speaks whole sentences even to the infant in arms.* **The child listens
and listens,** *until a model is established in the mind. Then the child commences
to imitate, not elementary sounds, but whole words. . . . The question is often in my
mind whether we are not making a radical mistake, and whether it would not be
better to commence with sentences and whole words, rather than with elements, and
accept imperfect speech from little deaf children as we do from hearing children.
(MS, 113; boldface type added)*

Reading like a title to a baroque *Trauerspiel* on power tools, The Mechanism
of Speech: Lectures Delivered Before the American Association to Promote
the Teaching of Speech to the Deaf, To Which Is Appended a Paper Vowel
Theories Read Before the National Academy of Arts and Sciences Illustrated

---

THE BLACK
BOX

After the **Crash: The Click:** The Survival Guide

**The Bell telephone shapes a locus
which suspends absolute departure.
The promise of death resisted,
however, destines itself toward the
click at your end. The click, neither
fully belonging to the telephonic
connection nor yet beyond or
outside it, terminates speech in
noise's finality. A shot that rings out
to announce, like an upwardly
aimed pistol, the arrival of silence
("Learning to speak is like learning
to shoot," AGB), the click stuns you.
It closes in on you, momentarily
absolving Mitsein. The phone's
nonfinitizing promise is broken.
Designed to uphold the technical
difficulty when it comes to
cathecting absence, the telephone,
whether consciously or not,
continually reinscribes its terror at
loss in such texts as are properly
designated Telephone Books, of
which ours would be merely a
teletype flash in an infinitely
crossed network.**

To avoid the crash whose site is your ear,
you hang up together, you deny the **click**.
This way, the Other is not gone but
survives the telephone, just as she was
prior to it. The telephone only places the
call. Thus Pacific Bell, offering a pacifier to
the teleconsumer, prints a Survival Guide,
whose first words are '**a major
disaster**.'[135] The last introductory word
to the directory of rescue transmissions
promises (as to the stickers on French
telephone booths), '**you can save a
life!**' (*A*, 49). The borderline zone of
temporal action cuts a path across the
decisive moments separating life from
death, as if the lines of telephony "**can
make the difference between life
and death**" (*A*, 49). This, precisely, is the
difference that Bell and Watson were
committed to making, but from the
dimension of an afterlife, which is to say
from a paranormal position or a
repression of the absolute difference. They
argued a far more uncanny projection of
the return call than we can perceive
through the iron curtain blocking our view

From Avital Ronell, *The Telephone Book*, University of Nebraska Press

On the Macintosh one may easily try all the chapter heads and find a solution that works for the longest and shortest. Routinely I do layouts for all chapter heads. Sometimes the chapter heads are so long that they must be set small, in which case one looks for another means of announcing the chapter—the chapter number, a dropped initial, an ornament, white space. Dropped initials that begin with quotation marks may present a problem, although it can be managed by manipulating the size of the quotes relative to the initial.

There need be no direct *grid* relationship between front matter headings and sinks with the rest of the book. But there must be a *visual* relationship, a rhythm. Too many books are overgridded in this regard.

The same goes for the title page relation. Harmony, but not the stifle of mathematical correctness. One has to learn to break the grid whenever it becomes a straitjacket.

The main title may well be smaller than the chapter title. There are many ways to give it emphasis. Very small type may be more emphatic than very large. It all has to do with white space and contrast.

The copyright page has been something of a hobbyhorse for me. The Library of Congress's preferred layout for the CIP data is quite irresponsible, a blemish on many otherwise well-designed books. It could certainly be reformatted to satisfy both the librarian and the typographically sensitive reader. I feel no compunction about departing from such an unreasonable standard. More and more of late, I don't have the CIP data to hand when I start on the book, in which case I interpolate the design at the galley or page-proof stage.

I see the dedication text and lay it out. Sometimes the copy changes during production. Phillipa may have left Max and Max met Juno since the manuscript entered production. Sometimes the valued spouse or parent dies. The dedication has become much overused and cloyingly predictable. In the eighteenth century the dedication was a bid for endorsement, often very witty, sometimes bitter, usually worth reading.

One has to be flexible about the relation of front matter to main text. Do whatever is necessary to make those pages work, but trust your intuition rather than the grid to find a harmony. It's like film editing. There are bedroom scenes and car chases. They vary in pace but must seem contiguous, serial, however much in contrast. I think that often we attempt too close a relation between these elements, which are physically so different.

The back matter is usually made to resemble the less emphatic parts of the front matter because it is of the same status in relation to the main text. It is an area where I spend little time, and maybe that's a mistake. On the other hand, these are reference items that vary little from book to book. To attempt innovation here might be to intervene between reader and text. I also skimp on the binding design, partly out of despair at the poor stamping that has become typical and partly because I'm usually into another

This and the following illustrations from Warren F. Motte, Jr., *Questioning Edmond Jabès*, University of Nebraska Press

Ques-tion-ing Ed-mond Jabès

Warren F. Motte, Jr.

University of Nebraska Press

Lincoln & London

Acknowledgments
for the use
of previously
published material
appear on pp xi–xii
Copyright © 1990
by the University
of Nebraska Press
All rights reserved
Manufactured in
the United States
of America
The paper in this
book meets the mini-
mum requirements
of American
National Standard
for Information
Sciences – Perma-
nence of Paper for
Printed Library
Materials,
ANSI Z39.48-1984.
Library of Congress
Cataloging in
Publication Data
Motte, Warren F.
Questioning
Edmond Jabès /
Warren F. Motte, Jr.
p.   cm.
Bibliography: p.
Includes index.
ISBN 0-8032-3125-3
(alkaline paper)
1. Jabès, Edmond –
Criticism and
interpretation.
I. Title.
PQ2619.A112Z76
1990
848'.91407 – dc20
89-14642   CIP

For Jean Alter
and
Gerald Prince

c o n t e n t s

Questioning Edmond Jabès: the participle is deliberately equivo-
cal. It is intended to figure two orders of inquiry, both Jabès's writing
and my reading of Jabès, for the Jabesian book, granted its dimensions,
its elliptical character, and its insistence on paradox and outright con-
tradiction, defies familiar strategies of reading. One is obliged to elaborate fresh strategies to approach this body of work, and that is what I
have attempted to do, largely following the canny swerves and odd

A	*Aely* (1972)
BD	*Je bâtis ma demeure* (1959; 1975)
BQ	*The Book of Questions* (1976)
BY	*The Book of Yukel, Return to the Book* (1977)
CS	*Ça suit son cours* (1975)
DD	*Dans la double dépendance du dit* (1984)
DG	*The Book of Dialogue* (1987)
DL	*Du désert au livre* (1980)
E	*Elya* (1969)
EL	*•(El, ou le dernier livre)* (1973)
II	*L'Ineffaçable l'inaperçu* (1980)
LB	*The Book of Questions: •El, or the Last Book* (1984)
LD	*Le Livre du dialogue* (1984)
LP	*Le Livre du partage* (1987)
LQ	*Le Livre des questions* (1963)
LR	*Le Livre des ressemblances* (1976)
LY	*Le Livre de Yukel* (1964)
MM	*La Mémoire et la main* (1987)
P	*Le Parcours* (1985)
PL	*Le Petit Livre de la subversion hors de soupçon* (1982)
R	*Récit* (1981)
RL	*Le Retour au livre* (1965)
SD	*Le Soupçon le désert* (1978)
Y	*Yaël* (1967)
YE	*The Book of Questions: Yaël, Elya, Aely* (1983)

a b b r e v i a t i o n s

In the interest of simplicity and brevity, I have referred
to Edmond Jabès's major works by abbreviation
accompanied by page numbers, interpolated in the body
of my text. When I have used existing translations, I
have given first the reference to the English, then the
reference to the original. All other translations are mine.
Full publication data may be found in the Bibliography.

Q.

legibility

Q...

the word

Q....

.

the book

To each book,
its twenty-six letters;
to each letter,
its thousands of books.
(PLS 19)

dernier livre) is most deliberate: the latter book is, after all, the seventh volume in the *Livre des questions* septology and constitutes one of the points where Jabès's writing comes full circle.

The circle figures God, then, but it also (and more immediately) figures the œuvre. This is implicit in the notion of the *return*, which is so insistent in Jabès's work. Gabriel Bounoure was the first to note the circularity of the first three volumes of *Le Livre des questions*, which Jabès then conceived of as a finished trilogy:

> *Edmond Jabès's three great books are joined in the unity of a circular composition. The work draws to a close in fact in a return to the book. The first volume showed the negative power of language, annihilating things in their existence. It was as if the verb of the lone I must perish from narrowness like the I itself. Then, in the second volume, after the revelation of love, the horror of history and of Evil were seen to drown individual destinies, a negativity more violent than that which plays treacherously in the ideality of the word. Finally, the poet came back to the book, moving from the* con *to the* pro, *traveling backwards, as if writing were charged with an original energy capable of overcoming so many denials.*[4]

This circularity is inscribed on the first three volumes of *Le Livre des questions*, both thematically and structurally, but it is particularly evident in *Le Retour au livre*, whose very title evokes the circular nature of the return and announces the cyclical character of the œuvre:

> *Three questions*
> *charmed the book,*
> *three questions*
> *will finish it.*
> *Whatever ends*
> *began three times.*
> *The book is three.*
> *The world is three.*
> *And for man, God*
> *is three replies.*
> (BY 210, RL 75)

134 ❖ Figures

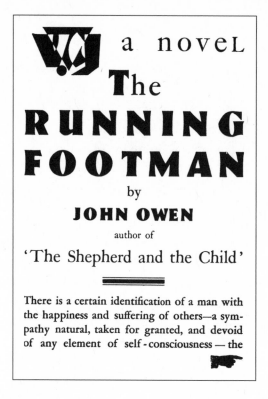

a noveL

The

**RUNNING
FOOTMAN**

by

JOHN OWEN

author of

'The Shepherd and the Child'

There is a certain identification of a man with
the happiness and suffering of others—a sympathy natural, taken for granted, and devoid
of any element of self-consciousness — the

project by the time the stamping becomes urgent. That's no excuse, of
course.

As for the relation of jacket to text, one questions whether it really exists.
Stanley Morison's jacket designs for Victor Gollanz are instructive in this
regard. They are of a vulgarity that one would never associate with Morison
the scholar. He reasoned that the jacket was an advertisement, entirely
ephemeral, and should prompt the reader by its garishness to tear the thing
off before putting the book on the shelf. Conversely, a college dean once
told me that he always removes the jacket before reading a book—to pro-
tect the *jacket!* I suppose that a jacket designer might see it the dean's way—
back to front.

Sandra Strother Hudson

Sandy Hudson graduated from Hollins College with a degree in art history. Early in her publishing career she joined Holt, Rinehart and Winston, where she eventually became senior designer in the trade division. After leaving Holt, Sandy designed for other publishers before becoming design and production manager at the University of Georgia Press. Her work has been selected for many design competitions.

Miss You is a chronicle of World War II. Spanning the years 1941–1945, the letters tell the story of two young southerners, Barbara Taylor and Charles Wooddall, who met, courted, married, and started a family during what Studs Terkel has called "the good war." The book follows Charles and Barbara from the start of their whirlwind courtship, through their chaotic months as newlyweds, through the anxious year that Charles spent on the Western Front while Barbara took care of their infant daughter at home, to their emotion-filled reunion.

There was much that I related to in this manuscript. The family snapshots reminded me of my own family photographs. Like Barbara and Charles, my parents were Georgians who met and married during World War II and served in the war effort. Because of these associations, I was very interested in the Wooddalls' letters and eager to design the book.

Although I do not often relate so personally to a text, I do find it necessary to engage with each book that I design. In various ways I try to identify with the subject of the book. I ask myself such questions as "What is this book about? What is the author trying to do or say?" I do not feel comfortable in attempting the book design until I have a real feeling for the book. The process goes something like this.

I start by reading descriptions of the book written by the acquiring editor and the author. I give the manuscript itself a complete or partial reading—complete in the case of fiction or essays and partial in the case of straight nonfiction (history, literary criticism, environmental studies). What happens next depends on the nature of the project. With scholarly books I find that I often want to do some research before starting on the design, so I make a trip to the University of Georgia library and look for books that might provide background information or inspiration. With novels, collections of short stories, and essays I stay focused on the author's text. I underline passages in the manuscript that seem to me to be particularly important—passages that reveal the author's concerns, the main theme or themes that run through the book. I mull over the book title. I jot down word associations with the book title or content of the book. I focus on the jacket as well as the text. I consider designing the jacket first—working from the outside in, rather than the opposite. I ask such questions as "What kind of image do I want for the jacket? Will I need to commission a painting or photograph? If so, who could best interpret this book? Conversely, can I find existing art that will work for the jacket? If so, where should I start looking?"

When I am designing a book that relates to an earlier period in history, I often look to the typography of that period for ideas and inspiration. I may isolate typographic ornaments in common use at that time and consider using the ornaments as decorations for the book. I look up visual material directly or indirectly related to the content of the book, and I think about how I might integrate the engravings, woodcuts, or drawings into the design. If I'm designing a book for which there are probably competing books—regional books, cookbooks, gardening books—I go to the bookstore to see what else is current in the same subject area. If I find competing books, I make mental notes on the appearance of those books and think how I can give the book that I am designing a different or more engaging personality.

After exploring the content in various ways I put the project aside. I turn things over in my mind for as long as possible—a day, a weekend, a week. During that time I think about the book. I make lists of typefaces that seem right for the book, and I look through type catalogs to see if there are newly released display faces for the Macintosh that appeal to me. In my mind, I play with various ideas for the design. I also wait to see what other ideas may surface. Of course, I am also attending to many other things during that time. I take care of production tasks related to other projects. I attend to administrative duties. I look at upcoming projects and begin thinking about those books.

Finally, I try to let the design happen. The time arrives when I must sit down at the computer. What happens at this stage does not seem to be in my control. Sometimes the design simply falls into place. My first idea works. Everything seems right and proper on the first try. I'm pleased and vastly relieved. At other times it is rough going. The design works out only after considerable struggle. Sometimes I am unable to come up with a design that pleases me entirely.

Whether or not the design works out to my complete satisfaction, my intention is always the same: In addition to presenting the text so that it will be legible and readable I want to reveal, reflect, or enhance, through visual means, the feeling tone, mood, or subject matter of the book. The various aspects of the design—trim size, typography, layout, ornaments or illustrations, text stock, binding materials, color scheme—all must work together to reflect some important aspect of the text.

I cannot be entirely objective or neutral in designing any book. My experience, temperament, and taste all come into play. My hope is that I am true to the task—that my presentation is in keeping with the content of the book.

This is what I had in mind when I started the design for *Miss You*.

I wanted the design to be upbeat and optimistic. In spite of the hardships and many uncertainties that they faced, Barbara and Charles never gave in to anger or self-pity. They maintained their youthful exuberance. They filled their letters with expressions of love, faith in one another, and hope for a future together. I wanted to honor that spirit.

By alluding to popular (commercial) typography of the mid-twentieth century I hoped to place the book in historical context. Because Barbara and Charles saved many mementos from their courtship and marriage, I wanted the book, in small ways, to resemble a photo album or scrapbook. (Originally, it was my intention to skew and overlay all the illustrations included in the photo insert in a sort of random fashion. In the end I backed off that idea and skewed only the photos that I used on the chapter-opening pages.)

The design for *Miss You* was not highly calculated. Nor was my method particularly orderly. I made some choices, such as trim size, with little thought. I reached other decisions, such as the distribution of positive and negative space and the proximity of units, intuitively by applying my own sense of proportion or taste. Still other decisions, such as exact type sizes and leading, were arrived at through trial and error.

In designing *Miss You* I elected a 6-×-9-inch trim because 6 × 9 is a standard, economical trim size for history and biography books.

In choosing margins I relied on habit. I favor a generous gutter margin (usually 3/4 inch) because I object to cracking the spine or forcing a book open in order to read the entire line. I like an ample head margin because I have found that if a book is trimmed a bit crooked or if the head margin bounces a bit, the use of a generous space at the top makes it less noticeable. I prefer to have more white space at the foot of the page than anywhere else because it weighs on me if the type page pulls toward the bottom of the page. The head margin in *Miss You* is 11/16 inch. (I can see now that it would have been better if I'd made the head margin 9/16 inch or 5/8 inch and increased the foot margin accordingly.)

For the text type I considered two twentieth-century typefaces designed by W. A. Dwiggins, Electra and Caledonia, and a third face, Walbaum. Walbaum, which was originally cut in the early nineteenth century, is also considered a modern face. I settled on Walbaum because I liked its crisp, clean letterforms and its "color." Most important, I felt that the Walbaum would mix best with the twentieth-century faces that I had in mind for the display.

After making the basic decisions regarding trim size, margins, and text type, I began the book design where I always do—with the title page. For the book title I tried out five different serif, sans serif, and script types and settled on a version of Corvinus that seemed to have the vitality and force-fulness I wanted. Gill Sans Extra Bold worked well for the subtitle, providing an interesting contrast in weight, color, and texture. For the author lines and imprint I used the text type—Walbaum. To this mix I added a photo of Barbara and a photo of Charles. (Using two photographs on the title page seemed to me to indicate the back-and-forth exchange of letters.) I centered all elements and relied on a series of horizontal rules to hold everything together. The title page then became the kingpin for the whole book design. The Wooddalls' personal photographs, the horizontal rules, the mix of Walbaum, Gill Sans Extra Bold, and Corvinus, and the centered arrangement of type and illustrations—these are the repeating elements that hold the design of the whole book together. The five numbered chapter-opening pages, for instance, with their mix of Corvinus and Gill Sans Bold, the use of horizontal rules, the inclusion of a photograph, are simply diminutive title pages. Front and back matter titles play off the chapter-opening pages in that the front matter titles are set to the same specs and occupy the same position on the page as do the chapter numbers. Subheads are set in smaller sizes of Gill Sans Extra Bold than the front matter titles and chapter numbers. The notes are set paragraph style to echo the traditional, centered nature of the design. And so it goes from large to small, down to the very last detail.

This repetition of elements/recurrence of visual themes serves two purposes in the book: (1) It makes for an integrated design, and (2) it provides a trail with guideposts and signposts for the reader to follow while making his or her way through the book. The book designer's purpose is to make the reader feel at home and comfortable. Through various means—grouping of elements, pacing, change in typeface, changes in type size, type weight, and case—the book designer tries to give the reader an idea of the relative importance of each element and to guide the reader easily through the text. In short, the purpose of the design is to aid the reader's comprehension of the text and to give pleasure.

Miss You is divided into five major chapters. By giving each chapter title full-page treatment and by mimicking the typography of the title page I made these pages diminutive title pages. Chapter titles are set in Corvinus. Chapter subtitles and chapter numbers are set in Gill Sans Extra Bold. Each chapter-opening page includes a photograph appropriate to the time period of that chapter. Again, as on the title page, all elements center, and horizontal rules hold the elements together. For a bit of relief, a pause, I followed each mini-poster with a page that contains the caption for the photo on the verso and nothing else.

The text proper in each chapter begins on the first right-hand page following the numbered chapter title page. The letters in each of the five chapters are introduced by editorial commentary that places them in the larger context of the war and American society at that time. I started each introduction with a Corvinus drop initial that relates back to the title page and the chapter-opening display. The use of a Gill Sans Bold subhead following the introductory material and preceding the letters provided sufficient notice of the change in voice and allowed me to set beginning editorial commentary in the same style as letter text. I did, however, switch to italics for editorial commentary that falls between letters.

Because *Miss You* consisted mainly of letters—with inside addresses, salutations, and closings, all of which are less than a full line in width—I realized that some pages would have to run short and that some spreads would be uneven in order to avoid widows and bad breaks. Here again the horizontal rule came in handy. I positioned a rule beneath the running heads to make a kind of clothesline on which to hang the text and to make the uneven spreads less noticeable. I also allowed the typesetter to run spreads one line long or one line short in order to give more options for solving page makeup problems.

There are two photo inserts in the book. The first insert contains ephemera of the wartime era—magazine covers, cartoons, advertisements—all provided by the volume editors to amplify the historical commentary on the war period. The second insert consists of the Wooddalls' personal snapshots from the years covered in the book. In both sets of pages the horizontal rules are developed into ruled boxes that frame the photos on each spread.

I am sure that I chose a centered design for *Miss You* because, to be perfectly honest, as a self-trained designer and a rather traditional person, I am most comfortable, and do my best work, when working in a classical idiom. Luckily, the central axis proved to be good choice for *Miss You*. It seems appropriate to the traditional nature of the book. It also provides a good underlying structure or skeleton for the text. Indenting all inside addresses to the center and positioning all closings and many signatures at the center avoids a zigzag effect for those lines of type.

In settling on the size and leading for the text type (10/14 Walbaum × 26 picas) I had the general reader in mind. Walbaum has a large x-height. The 4 points of leading is indicative of my preference for generous space between lines of type. (I like more visual space between the lines of type than between the words in the line.) The 26-pica measure allowed for a comfortable reading line of 65 to 70 characters.

For the color scheme of *Miss You,* red, white, and blue was the obvious choice. I splurged a bit on the three-piece binding and used red cloth on the spine and blue cloth on the sides. The spine stamping is black. The paper bulk being more than 1 inch thick allowed me to run type horizontally on the spine. For the spine die, as on the title page, horizontal rules separate title, subtitle, and authors. The endpapers are Liberty Red. I carried this color scheme (and the title page idea) through on the jacket.

In summary, as with any book, in *Miss You* I tried to integrate every aspect of the text and binding—to make the book a unified whole.

If I had it do over again, I'd decrease the head margin a bit and add to the foot margin. I'd also eliminate the rules on the copyright page and dedication because they are unnecessary. I'd try to make the jacket stronger. All and all, however, I'm satisfied with the book. I think that it works. The design seems to me to be appropriate to the content and tone of the book and suggestive of the period in which the letters were written. The book has a sound structure, a nice melody, and a pleasing rhythm. All of the parts of the book—title page, part and chapter openings, text pages, front and back matter, illustration pages—work together, reinforce one another, and form a coherent whole.

MISS YOU

The World War II Letters of Barbara Wooddall Taylor and Charles E. Taylor

Judy Barrett Litoff · David C. Smith
Barbara Wooddall Taylor · Charles E. Taylor

The University of Georgia Press · Athens and London

All illustrations in this chapter from Barbara Wooddall Taylor and Charles E. Taylor, *Miss You*, University of Georgia Press

Contents

Chapter One

COURTSHIP
BY MAIL

August 1941–August 1942

honeymoon" came to an end, they also had to think thoughts usually suppressed. What would be necessary to put his affairs in order in case of death or severe wounding in combat? The Army provided forms for wills, but it was also necessary to discuss insurance, debts, available funds, possible education, and a thousand other details which crowded in on their precious last hours together.[29]

As Barbara went back to Fairburn and Charles boarded his troopship, the *USS Argentina*, for Europe, they could look back on nearly three years of romance and love. In a time of great stress and anxiety their marriage was strong, sure, safe. And, as a wise observer of the day pointed out:

> Marriage at best is a tussle of wills. Given time, long, solid leisurely time, understanding and good faith emerge from the bout. War deprives marriage of time. It strips it of all opportunity to forgive and forget. It reduces it to quick, uncomplex unity. Marriage today has to do with simple sincerities. With love, understanding, patience.[30]

Those were, in fact, the hallmarks of their "marriage on the move."

Letters, August 1942–June 1944

Evansville, Indiana, August 16, 1942

My dearest sweetheart,

I am now in Evansville and it is 3:10 p.m. Guess you are well on your way to Fort Wood and I would give all I have to be with you. Darling, how will I ever do without you—even for a day!!

I went over to a cafe right across the street and got a breakfast. Sure did feel strange to be ordering for myself and not to have a pair of beautiful blue eyes looking right through me, and, oh, darling, I'm already so lonesome.

You are the most wonderful husband that I could ever have hoped or prayed for. You are so smart—you do everything just the way it should be done. Why, I could sit here and flatter you for a couple of hours or longer.

I was so proud of you when the train started moving in St. Louis. There you were smiling at me and waving, and, darling, it just made

Mary Mendell

Mary Mendell is a graduate of the Rhode Island School of Design, where she majored in sculpture. She worked at Beacon Press and Houghton Mifflin before becoming design and production manager at the University of Massachusetts Press. Subsequently she joined Duke University Press as assistant director of the press and as design and production manager. She also designs for other publishers and has won numerous design awards.

Design does make a difference. There is certainly a difference between what is readable and well organized and what is not. And for those whose aesthetic sensibilities have been developed, there is additional pleasure to be found in typographic design. A good many books are overdesigned, and that seems to me a worse fault than underdesigning. On the other hand, done with some restraint and sensitivity, arrangement, ornamentation, and invention in type can add to the pleasure of reading a book. If best-sellers are often not as well designed as the books from small presses, perhaps that reflects on the negative aspects of the capitalist system. Chairs and shoes (and just about all other products) have an equally wide range of design quality.

Only once or twice have I bought a book because of its design. I have more often not bought a book whose legibility I considered a problem. I put up with poorly designed books if I am interested in their content.

When I pick up a book, I look through the front matter and flip through the rest before beginning to read. I am interested in who published the book and want to see if a designer's name is given and if there is a colophon with other information about typesetting or printing.

We can only guess whether readers are at all influenced by a book's format and typography. I think that even the antidesign philistines are positively affected by a well-set text page with a readable number of characters per line and adequate leading. Readers must be positively affected when a book designer successfully organizes complex materials. The design for title pages and chapter openings is probably appreciated only by those with some knowledge and appreciation of the visual arts.

The typography of the book need only minimally reflect something about the contents. It should not, however, conflict with either the tone or the contents.

PRACTICES OF FREEDOM

Practices of Freedom was originally published abroad. After Duke University Press acquired the U.S. rights, the acquisitions editor and I agreed that the original design was somewhat heavy-handed and uninviting. We believed that the book had an important contribution to make in its discussion of the history of the AIDS epidemic and deserved a design that would not alienate readers. Aside from the fact that I worked from a published edition rather than a typescript, the project is typical of our books—in length, complexity, schedule, and budget.

I work on a Macintosh computer, and although in many small ways it has changed how I design, I usually start at about the same point and design elements in about the same order as I did when I designed only by hand. About the same number of elements are preset in my mind and change only for specific reasons. The computer allows for greater experimentation, and it allows me to make broad changes if my sense of the manuscript changes during the time that I am designing it.

I complete the design first and then write specifications for the book. I annotate my computer layouts with type sizes only (for my own convenience), write specifications with both sinkages and type sizes, and mark the first occurrence of elements that are not the main text and the unusual elements in the manuscript.

I most often work on unedited manuscripts, although I try to confirm with the in-house editors whether structural changes are being made in editing. I do not design books that do not have final titles or that are missing major components. I see sample pages but rarely revise them. Before I worked on a computer, I made more revisions to the sample pages.

Although I was aware from readers' reports of the importance of this manuscript, I read very little of it. In this case, I found it difficult to get past the original design.

There were no significant restrictions on format, except that the book needed to be designed promptly and had to be sent for typesetting on the same day the design was begun. Production and financial considerations dictated that the trim size be some variation of 6 × 9 inches and about the same length as the earlier edition. The typeface was left up to me. I did not have an image of what I thought the book should look like, although the goal was to give the book a more pleasant and reader-friendly look than I felt the previous edition had.

I certainly felt that this book needed a contemporary typeface, so I must feel some obligation to relate the text design to its historical context. But considering such relations is always just a way of starting to think about a project, and I don't feel totally bound to match the period described with a typeface of that exact time. It seems appropriate to me that I design some books to be not much more than legible and efficient and others whose text I try to augment or embellish in a way I believe is visually consistent with the author's intent.

I rarely read manuscripts, but I turn every page. I have done this for all but a half-dozen books in twenty-five years. Turning pages helps me develop some feel for the style, content, and tone of the manuscript. I see how the author has set up the manuscript. Sometimes it can help me develop a sense of the relative importance of the elements. Manuscripts edited on computer, where these clues have been removed, are definitely harder to work with. I take notes on the structural elements, extracts, subheads, or epigraphs. I record whether headings are all long, all short, or half and half, and whether book titles or foreign words (normally set in italic) are used within the headings. I also keep a list of manuscript pages with odd elements to mark once the basic design is done.

I don't experiment much with trim sizes. I think 6 × 9 inches (or, better, slightly narrower) makes a pleasant shape.

I work in Adobe PageMaker and have files established for various trim sizes. In most of them, the gutter is set at 3/4 inch and the line length at 26 picas. Head margin, space between running head and text, and depth of page are more likely to vary. For my own convenience, I use pages 1–10 in the computer file for the front matter. Page 11 is usually the chapter opening. Pages 12 and 13 show a text spread. This helps me locate these pages as I design.

I begin with a text spread if the manuscript has a complexity that suggests use of a multicolumn format or presents unusual typographic problems. But most of the manuscripts that I work on are divided by parts and chapters, with subheads of one to three levels, epigraphs, extracts, lists, and tables. With these manuscripts I begin either with chapter openings or the title page. Once I have something established for either of these elements, I begin the design of the other, trying to carry through a similar look. The treatment of the title page and chapter titles is the basis for how the other elements are handled. I next set up a text spread and then work on the other front matter pages.

I chose Berkeley Medium for *Practices of Freedom* because I consider it a good, clean, contemporary typeface. There are other faces that might have been as appropriate and many others that I would consider inappropriate— too dainty, too mechanical, too cold, too literary. The size, leading, and measure (in this book, 10.5/13 × 26) are standard ones for me, which I found no reason to vary here. In this case, I did not try other typefaces, but I sometimes do run out a sample text page in some alternative face. I experiment some with size and leading, although that is usually a matter of a half-point or one-point difference in the leading.

Over time I feel more and more relieved of the need to vary from standard ways of handling certain elements. I almost always use 1-em paragraph indents, old-style figures in the text, and indents to set off extracts set the same size as the text. Running heads and folios are usually at the top of the page, flush outside.

These are my defaults, so to speak, and I vary from them only for specific purposes, either functional or aesthetic, but they represent my sense of what is simplest and least disruptive to reading.

I sometimes ask the editor or the author to change the wording of running heads or titles, usually to shorten them, but not often for other reasons. In launch meetings for a new book I point out potential problems with titles: ones that are too long, that have repetitive wording, or that are partly or totally within quotation marks (which look especially unpleasant in larger display sizes).

For the display type in *Practices of Freedom* I chose a larger size of the text type. I was probably doing this in reaction to the earlier edition, which had a heavy sans serif.

I have generally come to like black sans serif display faces. Sometimes when they seem inappropriate, I feel a little lost. In this book, I wanted a softer look. Generally when I am using the text face for display throughout, I prefer to use a larger size of it, not its boldface version.

The title of the book suggested movement to me, and I tried to make that part of the total design. In fact, to the extent that there is any conscious design thinking involved here, it is about movement. In general, I prefer centered chapter openings (especially with long academic chapter titles) but asymmetrical title pages (because centered ones look a bit boring or at least static). This is a problem because I do think that it is necessary to choose between centered or asymmetrical styles for the entire book, but sometimes one can offset the centered look of the title page with artwork or selective use of boldface or caps. It may be that the series of indents in the chapter openings and title page of this book are attempts to find something a little different from the more obvious centered or flush-left formats.

I have no rule that type over a certain size is unsuitable. In the past I felt reluctant to use larger typesizes, because when they are not exactly right, they look awful. I thought that I could do less harm with smaller type. But the computer allows designers a chance to fine-tune in a way we never could before, and we can be a bit more experimental. I think that the biggest problem now is to avoid overdesigning. By some standards, the design for *Practices of Freedom* may come close to that.

I have no special style for subheads. Length, content, and number of levels have something to do with my choices. I don't think they need to follow chapter openings or running heads in style, but here I did follow through on the idea of indented lines. There are not many subheads in this book. If there were, I think the treatment would be a bit tedious. I think of caps as one way to achieve emphasis and of boldface as another. I would prefer not to see both methods used in one book.

If a chapter opening of average length exists, I start there. Otherwise, I start at either end—with the longest or the shortest—and immediately try out the other extreme. I feel that the design of the front matter display should be very closely related to that of the chapter titles. The headings in the front matter (contents, preface) should relate to the style of either the chapter number or the chapter title, whichever works best.

Practices of Freedom

SELECTED WRITINGS ON HIV / AIDS

by Simon Watney

DUKE UNIVERSITY PRESS   Durham 1994

All illustrations in this chapter from Simon Watney, *Practices of Freedom*, Duke University Press

Contents

are highly effective. That public information campaigns are unable to address this fact needs explanation together with the tendency to either stigmatise or ignore the situation of the vast majority of people with AIDS. Recent British figures describe some 533 gay men with AIDS, and seventeen (presumably heterosexual) women.[4] The enormity of the displacement of attention to the situation of non-gay people with AIDS speaks volumes in itself. As Richard Goldstein has pointed out:

> For gay men sex, that most powerful implement of attachment, and arousal, is also an agent of communion, replacing an often hostile family and even shaping politics. It represents an ecstatic break with years of glances and guises, the furtive past we left behind. Straight people have no comparable experience, though it may seem so in memory. They are never called upon to deny desire, only to defer its consummation.[5]

He concludes that 'for heterosexuals to act as if AIDS were a threat to everyone demeans the anxiety of gay men who really are at risk, and for gay men to act as if we're all going to die demeans the anguish of those who are actually ill'. A media communications industry which can only acknowledge the existence of gay men as a target for contempt and thinly veiled hatred is unlikely to be able to address itself to the issues of sexual diversity which the AIDS epidemic requires us to face as the *sine qua non* of any effective preventative strategies which alone may prevent the spread of HIV infection, or adequate support measures for the two million gay men in the UK who live from day to day through these terrible times with varying degrees of courage and fear, anger and grief.

The limits of panic

Many lesbian and gay commentators on such attitudes have favoured the influential British Sociological theory of 'moral panics' for the purposes of explanation and analysis. Drawing on the 'new' criminology developed in the late 1960s, Stanley Cohen described how societies:

> appear to be subject, every now and then, to periods of moral panic. A condition, episode or person emerges to become defined as a threat to societal values and interests; its nature is presented in a stylised and stereotypical fashion by the mass media; the moral barricades are manned by editors, bishops, politicians and other right-thinking people; . . . Sometimes the panic passes over and is forgotten, except in folk-lore and collective memory; at other times it

cultural relations between Norway and Sweden are rather like those between Scotland and England, but I cannot believe that the two countries are so very different that Norway has visible, articulate lesbian and gay teenagers, whilst Sweden apparently has none. The absence of visible gay teenagers who, after all, are the group of young people most at risk from HIV, from such materials in Sweden, closely resembles the similar amnesia affecting the British government, which demanded the withdrawal of AIDS education materials for schools for the explicit reason that they dared to acknowledge the existence of lesbian and gay teenagers. However, in relation to AIDS education such a refusal to acknowledge the reality of sexual diversity is not merely moralistic—it is potentially dangerous. Indeed, it is difficult to avoid the conclusion that a society which prefers to pretend that gay teenagers don't exist would not miss them were they all to disappear. It is important to realise the full significance of the fact that many people consciously or unconsciously consider AIDS to be an extremely convenient phenomenon, ridding the world of regrettable and unwanted minorities.

Fortunately I am sure that British and Swedish youth are not so stupid as their parents in such matters. Most young people know perfectly well that their aunt Mary is a lesbian, or that Roger and Peter who run the local garage are gay, or that Michael or Helen or Thomas in their school class are gay or lesbian. Few young people think of gay teenagers as if they were aliens from outer space, and if they do, it is a sad reflection on the power of bigotry and ignorance at home over genuine education at school and from life. AIDS education materials which fail to adequately address the real difficulties facing gay teenagers today will quite rightly be dismissed in their entirety as inadequate and untrustworthy by most young people. If AIDS educators omit gay youth from their considerations, they run the very serious risk of undermining their message amongst the rest of the population, as well as leaving young gay people feeling more isolated and vulnerable than ever. AIDS education would be much improved if adults were obliged to watch safer sex videos and to read leaflets written for them by their children, who generally have a much more sophisticated understanding of risk factors.

By telling teenagers to stick with one sexual partner, and to take an HIV test if they are worried, Swedish AIDS education fails to recognise that neither of these options provides a realistic solution to the issue of HIV. Besides, both messages are in conflict with the urgent task of establishing safer sex as a central and indispensable element of youth culture. We have to produce AIDS information which emphasises the pleasures

— 9. 'The Day After Hiroshima': Reflections on official British and Swedish AIDS education materials and government policies

Whilst it is important to understand the global impact of AIDS, as it was described at the World Health Organisation's Summit Conference in London in January 1988, I would like to emphasise that it is equally important to realise that each country affected by HIV has its own distinct epidemic, shaped according to its own national culture, access to health-care provision, health education strategies, and so on. In this respect we must recognise that the Swedish AIDS epidemic is quite distinct from that in Norway, or the Netherlands, or Britain. Furthermore, the epidemic is lived differently in Stockholm for example than in Vasteros or Malmo. We should always remember that an epidemic is a complex social and bio-ecological phenomenon. At the same time we should try to relate HIV and AIDS to the wider local framework of disease and health-care provision in any given society.

It may be instructive to begin by comparing the situation in Britain to that in Sweden. In Britain we have approximately ten times as many cases of AIDS as there are in Sweden. However, since our overall population is seven times larger, the rate of cases per 100,000 is not so very different. Yet the social context of the British epidemic could hardly be more unlike that in Scandinavia. For example, antenatal care has stagnated in many regions for more than thirty years.[1] The Royal College of Physicians recently reported that more than 2000 premature infants die unnecessarily each year in England and Wales due to cuts in hospital equipment, and staff shortages.[2] In the West Midlands, 93 per cent of hospital buildings are officially described as being in poor repair. Fire standards are not met in 33 Scottish wards for elderly and physically handicapped people.[3] Cancer treatment which was routine for women in their sixties ten years ago is no longer available. In October 1988 a government Minister of Health, Mrs Edwina Currie, was widely reported

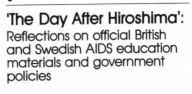

9

'The Day After Hiroshima':
Reflections on official British and Swedish AIDS education materials and government policies

Whilst it is important to understand the global impact of AIDS, as it was described at the World Health Organisation's Summit Conference in London in January 1988, I would like to emphasise that it is equally important to realise that each country affected by HIV has its own distinct epidemic, shaped according to its own national culture, access to health-care provision, health education strategies, and so on. In this respect we must recognise that the Swedish AIDS epidemic is quite distinct from that in Norway, or the Netherlands, or Britain. Furthermore, the epidemic is lived differently in Stockholm for example than in Vasteros or Malmo. We should always remember that an epidemic is a complex social and bio-ecological phenomenon. At the same time we should try to relate HIV and AIDS to the wider local framework of disease and health-care provision in any given society.

It may be instructive to begin by comparing the situation in Britain to that in Sweden. In Britain we have approximately ten times as many cases of AIDS as there are in Sweden. However, since our overall population is seven times larger, the rate of cases per 100,000 is not so very different. Yet the social context of the British epidemic could hardly be more unlike that in Scandinavia. For example, antenatal care has stagnated in many regions for more than thirty years.[1] The Royal College of Physicians recently reported that more than 2000 premature infants die unnecessarily each year in England and Wales due to cuts in hospital equipment, and staff shortages.[2] In the West Midlands, 93 per cent of hospital buildings are officially described as being in 33

82

Chapter-opening design: revised edition (left), original edition (right)

I try to have the title page relate directly to the chapter openings. Generally I feel that the type size on the title page must be as large as that used on the chapter or part titles. I am sure there are exceptions. I wouldn't want this to be a rule.

I see the text for both the copyright page and the dedication page and prepare designs for each of them.

I have no formulas for designing the contents page. I might try to pick up something that I have done with a chapter number and treat it in a similar fashion on the contents page.

I treat the display for back matter pages as I do for the front matter openings. I have a preferred style for back matter elements. I shamelessly set them in the same way unless there is a specific reason not to. I like note numbers, without periods, followed by an em space and a hanging indent. Bibliographies have a 2-em hanging indent, and indexes have a 1-em indent.

Although I recognize that the jacket has a marketing function, I think that it should be possible for the jacket to serve that function and at the same time have some modest relation to the interior design of the book. I certainly do not want just to enlarge the title-page type—which in the busiest times, is exactly what I do. I don't think that the typefaces used in the book need be repeated, although if there is a dramatic use of a display face inside the book, I would try to repeat it. I don't think that one needs to carry through the use of all caps or caps and lowercase from title page to jacket. But where choices become optional, the repetition of elements gives the book a visual coherence that is part of good design. Not to pay some attention to what has been done in the interior seems a bit of a cop-out (particularly if the interior and jacket are done by the same person). Book design is, in part, problem solving. For me, relating the jacket to the interior without denying its marketing function is part of the problem to solve.

Anita Walker Scott

Anita Walker Scott, currently design and production manager at the Johns Hopkins University Press, studied graphic design at Cooper Union in New York and calligraphy and type design with Hermann Zapf in Frankfurt. In addition to working with trade and university press publishers, she also cofounded a book publishing firm in San Francisco. She has been the recipient of numerous graphic design awards.

About two years before the great designer Paul Rand died, I heard him talk about his work. His message that evening was simple and basic, but there was obvious restlessness in the audience; his words evidently were unsettling, probably because they seemed old-fashioned. He said that if a good designer had a thorough knowledge of only five or six typefaces, that would be enough to solve any problem and create a solution that would not only be inventive but appropriate and fresh. With computer technology providing almost unlimited design choices, he said, it is easy to assume that anyone can be a designer, and tempting to experiment indiscriminately. Then, his voice rising, he added, "Experimentation is okay and necessary for growth and change, but fashion, expediency, and slickness are not to be substituted for idea, substance, typographic skill, and knowledge." I couldn't agree more.

The special responsibility of the book designer is creation of a platform that conveys, enhances, and clarifies information for the reader, with the text, not the design, as the focus. Excellent and effective design does not rely on expensive materials or fine production but rather on proper choices, intelligent judgment, the application of sound typographic principles, and adherence to standards of form and aesthetics. The design of a book should be text driven. If one design idea doesn't work with the words as the author wrote them, it is the designer's job to come up with another solution.

Good design in a book makes a difference in readability, in the organization of complex material, in the focus and order by which information is transferred from the page to the reader, and in the book's tangible and aesthetic appeal. Each part should be understood, specified, typeset, and placed with its function and use in mind. Appropriateness is a key requirement. The goal is creation of a design that represents the subject for the intended reader or user. A book of letters should suggest the form of the original; a workbook should be clear and efficient; a book for the very young or old should be easy to read; a biography should convey something of the character, time, and place of the subject. Sometimes a manuscript will clearly require a particular typeface, design approach, or style. With another project, especially one that spans a great deal of time or encompasses a variety of subjects, the appropriate choices may be more elusive.

The type finally chosen should work with the subject. It need not be of the same period or a typographic stereotype, but its size, style, and positioning should give a suggestion of the time, place, use, or attitude of the book.

Book design is, for me, a shifting and sometimes disorderly process. Elements are not necessarily considered separately or in any particular sequence. Successful design is about relationships. Each part of a book depends on every other part. Nothing can be ignored. The unifying framework that holds a good design together is sometimes quite complicated and is often invisible. Sometimes the subtleties and the small individual parts that contribute to the unity of a beautiful design are revealed only in a close study of the layout or design scheme. That is as it should be. Generally, the best designs are not obvious. Rather, the elements are intertwined and related to make one powerful image, perhaps with variations on a theme.

Tight financial considerations and small budgets often put difficult constraints on a designer. In such cases, the limits need not be regarded as a negative. Treated as only one of the elements to be considered, boundaries can be used as a challenge to the imagination. Approaching them in this way makes them part of the problem and, therefore, also part of a solution. Reliance on lavish illustration or layout must necessarily be replaced by careful typographic and graphic decisions about margins, font style and color, type size, leading, and texture—all in effective juxtaposition. Production choices, if they are to complement the design and continue the message of the book, may also need to be prudent and simple. Beautiful materials —expensive paper stocks, added colors, and lavish binding products— certainly might enhance good typography and design, but they will not rescue a book when choices have made reading difficult or the page is just ugly.

My examples are two books that, though greatly different, presented the same design challenge: how to reflect a gathering of dissimilar elements drawn together by a common thread. In *Neon Vernacular* by Yusef Komunyakaa the connection is the author. This is a book of poems written over decades from the changing perspectives of the poet as a boy, a son, a man, and a soldier, all in different parts of the world. The second book, *AAUP Book, Jacket, and Journal Show 1990,* is the catalog of an annual design selection of projects published by members of the Association of American University Presses. Each of the entries chosen for the catalog is unique; their commonality lies in their inclusion in a group of publications scheduled for exhibition throughout the United States.

I usually begin any book design by reading some part of the manuscript and whatever other background material has been provided. I often talk with the editor about the work and determine whether the author has any design preferences that need to be considered. I find out what the marketing expectations are and who might be the primary audience. Not until after I have this information in mind do I start working with the manuscript by turning over each page and looking at all of the elements of the project. This quick survey identifies problems and gives me a sense of the components while I learn the rhythm of the work. I was familiar with Komunyakaa's writing, admired it, and enjoyed reading the entire manuscript as I was doing the preliminary exploration. For the catalog, the amount of text was small in comparison to the illustrative material, but the first stage of the process was the same: becoming thoroughly familiar with all elements of the project. Designing a book is like building a house. There must be a good foundation and the recognition that a door is different from a roof and different from a wall. Each piece must be understood for its function and designed to work separately, but it must also be combined carefully with other elements to support them and contribute toward making the whole structure.

At the beginning of the design process a jumble of ideas, some well formed but most fragmentary, dart here and there in my mind on various levels of consciousness. Even when I am focusing on one part of the manuscript, I may be interrupted by an unrelated notion having to do with another element. Although these bits of thought may not make sense at the time, I try to record them (even as just a word or two) for possible use later. I have come to rely on my intuition and don't discard fringe ideas too quickly.

Specifications for a book's trim size or format and the estimated number of final book pages are usually part of the basic information received by the designer from the publisher. Sometimes the designer has flexibility to make changes, but for *Neon Vernacular* the trim had to be 5.5 × 8.5 inches. Not only was this an economical size for the printer, but the book was to be included in a series of books all of the same size. For the catalog, reproduction of the illustrations and clarity of detail were of primary importance. A trim of 7.5 × 10 inches was selected to allow effective display of the images. For both projects, the final number of book pages desired was also specified.

The poetry manuscript consisted of selections from seven previous books by the author, each with its own style, and a group of new poems. The subjects of many of the poems were the historical and social contexts that shaped the experience of the poet—a black man and Vietnam veteran. Music, particularly jazz, is a recurrent theme. A feeling, not of time or place, but of cadence, beat, variation, and rhythm pulsed through the poetry and suggested its musical inspirations. I decided to try to do something with all of that and perhaps tie it in with the title, *Neon Vernacular,* which seemed to have visual potential. The catalog was also a diversity of elements to be brought together as a new entity. Rather than reflect an amorphous feeling, as in the poetry book, this collection had to be presented as clear and direct information.

With the trim size established, the next major decision was the selection of the typeface for the text. In poetry, meaning often depends on line breaks, and it is always best for the typeset line to reflect the poet's line-by-line construction. By identifying both the longest poetic line in the manuscript and the "typical" length, I had a guide to the character count that could be accommodated by the page width. A good x-height size of the type was required for legibility. The need for a lovely ampersand (used frequently in the poetry) was also to be considered in choosing the typeface. Whenever possible, keeping entire poems on one page to preserve their integrity was preferred. Whether the poems were short or likely to run over to another page would determine the final relation of poem length to page depth, and that, in turn, would have a great influence on the amount of leading to be specified for typesetting the text.

Using actual copy from a disk, I started to plan the poetic text page. Several text faces in different sizes and with various adjustments in leading were tried for the best combination of line width and poem length. This is usually a "push and pull" process. Changing one element affects others, which then have to be discarded or refined, back and forth, until a solution emerges. Today, with the computer as a powerful design tool, this experimentation is relatively easy. Endless combinations can be tried in the time that it once took to draw out one page with pencil, T-square, and triangle on tissue paper. The typeface that I finally used was a small size of a heavy sans serif font for minor display and a more classic serifed font for the main text (Helvetica Bold and Sabon for *Neon Vernacular* and Eras Bold and Meridien for the catalog). These combinations seemed contemporary enough for the subjects and also broad enough in look to cover the diverse elements in the respective projects.

In most books, display type is used for chapter numbers and titles, on part opening pages, and in front and back matter. How the display evolves is a result of the same complex thought process used for the rest of the work—a mixture of knowledge, intuitiveness, experience, and judgment. When a design decision works, I know it; when it doesn't, that is even clearer. There are many theories and admonitions on "correct" display size and how it should relate to text, but I don't put too much faith in rules because I see them broken successfully all the time. In the hands of a good designer even the most outrageous idea can be made to work; conversely, even with all the rules in mind, a designer with unfocused ideas or poor judgment will still produce a mediocre or undistinguished design. For the catalog, display was needed only on section division pages and the title page. Rather than highlighting the copy of the individual sections, I decided that the display would carry the name of the sponsoring organization of the show in the same hand-drawn lettering that I created for the cover art. (I was fascinated by stonecutting at the time, and this cover gave me a chance to indulge my enthusiasm.) Display for *Neon Vernacular* was limited to part titles and front matter. In a book with many chapters, the type used for the display often has to be discreet so as not to become tiresome with repetition. For these two books, where display type would be used only a few times, I felt that it could be large and dramatic without losing impact and visual appeal.

Several display approaches were tried as I looked for one or more type-faces that would translate the sound and rhythm of the poetry into a typographic voice. Normally, my inclination is to use a larger size of the text type or, at least, a type of the same family. The use of the quirky display type and positioning in *Neon Vernacular* is unusual for me but was great fun to develop. It came about through two fortunate but unpredictable events as I was exploring the manuscript prior to starting the design. The first was the arrival of the cover illustration, which clearly suggested something offbeat. The second was the discovery of some interesting "junk fonts" in a compact disc that arrived at the same time. I decided to try several of these types and found some that had promise. So another decision was made—at least for the moment.

The ideas for positioning elements, just like the indications toward a typeface, usually come from the work, its subject, or its possible use. I have no preference for either a centered or an asymmetrical style of layout. In some books, either may be appropriate. For the poetry text, given the un-even line lengths and their general flush-left positioning, an asymmetric design seemed the only possible choice. It was also my choice for the cata-log, but this was more of a layout challenge than a typographic one. To accommodate the different sizes and kinds of images and copy, I designed a grid based on the width of the page divided into thirds. The grid is most clearly evident in the introductory pages of the catalog, but all elements throughout the catalog align on some multiple of this basic grid structure. The two largest sections of the catalog, which include the book selections, were designed as facing-page units to include text and four or five uncap-tioned illustrations. With the text on the left side of the verso page, the reader has immediate access to the basic information. The rest of the two-page spread could then be devoted to the illustrations, giving them the space they required. The grid ensured flexibility of size and placement but also imposed an order that, though transparent, was essential for the smooth visual flow from one page to the next.

Most books have running heads or feet included for reference, and they should be designed to meet that requirement. In Komunyakaa's book, it was important that the reader know the previous book reference, but I didn't want any copy to infringe on the poem title or text space. The deci-sion to put the reference information and folio at the bottom of the page was an easy one. The recto copy, indicating the chronology, was specified for small, but easily read, uppercase and lowercase italic. The title of the book, repeated throughout on the verso, was set in very widely spaced small caps and became, intentionally, more of a decorative element. In this fixed position, close to the bottom trim, the running feet also created a

Changes; or, Reveries at a Window Overlooking a Country Road, with Two Women Talking Blues in the Kitchen

Joe, Gus, Sham . . .
Even George Edward
Done gone. Done
Gone to Jesus, honey.
Doncha mean the devil,
Mary? Those Johnson boys
Were only sweet talkers
& long, tall bootleggers.
Child, now you can count
The men we usedta know
On one hand. They done
Dropped like mayflies—
Cancer, heart trouble,
Blood pressure, sugar,
You name it, Eva Mae.
Amen. Tell the truth,
Girl. I don't know.
Maybe the world's heavy
On their shoulders. Maybe
Too much bed hopping
& skirt chasing
Caught up with them.
God don't like ugly.
Look at my grandson
In there, just dragged in
From God only knows where,
He high tails it home
Inbetween women troubles.
He's nice as a new piece
Of silk. It's a wonder
Women don't stick to him
Like white on rice.
It's a fast world
Out there, honey.
They go all kinda ways.
Just buried John Henry
With that old guitar
Cradled in his arms.
Over on Fourth Street

Heat lightning jumpstarts the slow
afternoon & a syncopated rainfall
peppers the tinroof like Philly Joe
Jones' brushes reaching for a dusky
backbeat across the high hat. Rhythm
like cells multiplying . . . language &
notes made flesh. Accents & stresses,
almost sexual. Pleasure's knot; to wrestle
the mind down to unrelenting white space,
to fill each room with spring's contagious
 changes. Words & music. "Ruby, My Dear"
turned down on the cassette player,
pulsates underneath rustic voices
waltzing out the kitchen—my grandmama
& an old friend of hers from childhood
talking B-flat blues. Time & space,
painful notes, the whole thing wrung
out of silence. Changes. Caesuras.
 Nina Simone's downhome cry echoes
theirs—Mister Backlash, Mister Backlash—
as a southern breeze herds wild, blood-
red roses along the barbed-wire fence.
There's something in this house, maybe
those two voices & Satchmo's gold horn,
refracting time & making the Harlem
Renaissance live inside my head.
I can hear Hughes like a river
of fingers over Willie "The Lion" Smith's
piano, & some naked spiritual releases
a shadow in a reverie of robes & crosses.
Oriflamme & Judgment Day . . . undulant waves
bring in cries from Sharpeville & Soweto,
dragging up moans from shark-infested
seas as a blood moon rises. A shock
of sunlight breaks the mood & I hear
my father's voice growing young again,
as he says, "The devil's beating
his wife": One side of the road's rainy
& the other side's sunny. Imagination—

This and the following illustrations from Yusef Komunyakaa, *Neon Vernacular*, Wesleyan University Press

Blues Chant Hoodoo Revival

my story is
how deep the heart runs
to hide & laugh
with your hands
over your blank mouth
face behind the mask
talking in tongues
something tearing
feathers from a crow
that screams
from the furnace
the black candle
in a skull
sweet pain of meat

       let's pour the river's rainbow
       into our stone water jars
       bad luck isn't red flowers
       crushed under jackboots

your story is
a crippled animal
dragging a steel trap
across desert sand
a bee's sting inside your heart
& its song of honey
in my groin
a factory of blue jays
in honey locust leaves
wet pages of smoke
like a man
deserting his shadow
in dark woods
the dog that limps away
& rotten fruit on the trees
this story is
the speaking skull
on the mantelpiece
the wingspan of a hawk
at the edge of a coyote's cry

81   from *Copacetic*

strong linear anchor for poem texts of varying lengths. A different decision was made for the catalog. Because the publisher's name was the important reference, it was used as the running head copy instead of the "normal" book title and positioned prominently at the top. The page number was set in the same bold type used for the minor display, and designed to appear only on the recto page. Its position there not only allowed a clear reference point but also reinforced the strong horizontal line of the grid that connected elements throughout the pages and on which most of the type and many of the graphic elements were aligned.

When starting a design for a book, I usually begin with the full text page, go next to the chapter opening, then to the title page, and then fill in the design for the rest of the front and back matter. The jacket or cover and the binding designs are often done last. I didn't take this route for *Neon Vernacular*. When the text design of the full page of poetry and the display appeared to be resolved, I went to the first half-title page, thinking of it as an overture that would set the tone for everything that was to follow. I tried many arrangements of the display types before deciding on a final layout. The editor and the author, both of whom were to approve the design, agreed that the atmosphere created on this first page of the book reflected the work and prepared the reader before a word of the poetry was read. So the design of the first half-title page, along with that of the full text page, became the foundation for the rest of the book's structure.

Working on that foundation, I shifted back and forth through the manuscript in no logical sequence. Sometimes working on one page caused me to change much of what I'd done somewhere else, either because the design didn't apply well or because a better idea had developed during the process. The germ of a jacket idea might occur to me at any stage. Sometimes while I am working with the black and white text, thoughts on appropriate jacket colors will emerge. I may even develop a fully realized image that "only" requires translation from my mind to paper or screen. The whole process is organic and fluid, a response to each situation, and always is an effort to combine the practical and the aesthetic. And, as in creating anything, the designer must be willing to acknowledge mistakes, take advantage of design opportunities, and recognize when to stop.

The title page should reflect the book design in all respects but not necessarily imitate it. There should be a relation between the positioning of the chapter display or text and the type used elsewhere. In *Neon Vernacular,* the display used on section pages was repeated on the title page. The author's name and subtitle were designed as a large-size echo of the running foot treatment, with widely spaced capital letters. In general, I think that title-page display should be in the same size as or larger than type used for chapter titles and part titles. Chapter titles should be more important than or, at least on a visual level, similar to the contents or half-title display. Other text

YUSEF

KOMUNYAKAA

Neon
Vernacular

NEW AND

SELECTED POEMS

Published by University Press of New England / Hanover and London

Wesleyan University Press

Contents

Neon
Vernacular

from Lost in the Bonewheel Factory

New Poems

from Dedications & Other Darkhorses

from Lost in the Bonewheel Factory

vii   Contents

Yale University Press

A Performer's Guide to the Keyboard Partitas of J. S. Bach

Fernando Valenti

Dimensions 7 × 10 inches

Pages 144

Quantity 2,300

Price $23.50

Text designer Nancy Ovedovitz

Jacket/binding designer Nancy Ovedovitz

Production coordinator Cele D. Syrotiak

Copy editor/editor Harry Haskell/Edward Tripp

Compositor G & S Typesetters, Inc.

Typefaces 11½/14 Linotron Fournier; Bernhard Modern Roman display

Printer Hamilton Printing Company

Printing method offset

Paper 50 lb. Sebago Antique

Binder Hamilton Printing Company

Binding Smyth sewn; Devon 42960

Endsheets Rainbow Antique, Mauve

Jacket printer New England Book Components, Inc.

Jacket materials 100 lb. Warren Warrenflo; black, PMS metallic blue 8183, PMS 5005; lamination

Fernando Valenti

A PERFORMER'S GUIDE
TO THE
KEYBOARD PARTITAS
OF

J. S. BACH

Yale University Press
New Haven and London

Beautiful, well-designed jacket. Bernhard Modern is a perfect choice of type. It is a handsome book overall, but paper could have been more opaque. RH

Very tastefully done. DL

Clean and readable. FOW

This and the following illustrations from *AAUP Book, Jacket, and Journal Show 1990* catalog (reduced 20 percent)

Book, Jacket, and Journal Show 1990

Sponsored by the Book, Jacket, and Journal Show Committee of the Association of American University Presses

AAUP

Dana Levy

Dana Levy has more than twenty years of experience designing and producing illustrated books and graphics. After graduating from Art Center College of Design, he worked for seven years in Japan as an advertising art director and package designer, before joining John Weatherhill Publishers as design director. He has developed, acted as photographer for, and designed several illustrated books: *Bamboo, Water: A View from Japan, Kanban: Shop Signs of Japan,* and *Furo: The Japanese Bath.*

In 1976 Levy moved to New York where he designed books and exhibition catalogs for museums and trade publishers. He coauthored and designed *Anatomy Illustrated* (Simon & Schuster), which won the American Book Award in 1980. His clients include the Metropolitan Museum of Art, Japan Society, Kodansha, George Braziller, the Kimbell Art Museum, Crown Publishers, the National Gallery of Art, the Smithsonian, and Chronicle Books. He also teaches book design at UCLA.

An overwhelming number of books and jackets, along with over two dozen journals, were examined in three days by the jurors for the 1990 AAUP show.

The books were divided into two categories. The typographic books were, in general, of a higher quality than the illustrated books. This, I believe, is partly because university presses have traditionally produced more scholarly books in which the text is of paramount importance. With typographic books, there are more design and production limitations and generally lower budgets. In successful designs these restraints can become an advantage as the designer uses a narrower range of elements—paper, type sizes and styles, spacing, page composition—to create the desired effect. Most designers showed good judgment in using the more traditional typefaces—Bembo, Sabon, Garamond, Baskerville—that are still the most legible and the least distracting and self-conscious. The hallmark of good book design is simplicity and a respect for type, how it fits, looks, and feels on the page.

Judging the illustrated books presented a number of more complicated problems and challenges. An oversized volume with great numbers of four-color plates, duotones, and fine papers is very seductive. Comparing it to a moderately produced book gives it an unfair advantage. They are not on an even playing field, so time and thought are needed to evaluate the two. The big-budget book should not be rejected or accepted simply because it is expensively produced, nor should the more moderate one be accepted or eliminated simply because it was produced with limited resources. The designer who understands printing and production possibilities and uses that knowledge to create a book that is both beautiful and cost efficient should be rewarded. Conversely, one who ignores the efficiency of the printing configuration must be considered less skilled. If the budget allows only seventy pound paper that wasn't

sufficiently opaque to eliminate show-through, but the layout is designed to minimize the problem, it is a job well done.

Design of the cover or jacket and binding was sometimes treated with little regard for the design of the book's interior. Those books in which the designer coordinated the layout, typography, color, and graphics of the exterior with that of the interior were clearly the most satisfying and successful. Covers and jackets are, to a great extent, posters that must help to make the books stand out. But they can perform that very necessary task and at the same time be sympathetic to the interior. You *should* be able to tell a book by its cover!

A few presses stand out because of their unique personalities. I can usually spot a Yale Press book or one from North Carolina Press or MIT. They, and others, have developed a style over the years and, in the tradition of fine presses such as Golden Cockerell, Grabhorn, and Nonesuch, a look and consistency of design and production. Seeing their books is like meeting old friends. With consistent design direction they have established a definitive character and set high standards of bookmaking. Clearly some presses win consistently year after year. Those who do not can certainly learn a good deal by examining the books of those who do.

7

---

elements should be treated in hierarchical order according to their editorial function and use.

Chapter numbers can be necessary reference information, or somewhat incidental, or merely decorative. Determination of their editorial place affects their typographic treatment. Whether chapter numbers are single- or double-digit numerals, how often they occur, and whether each stands alone or is included with the chapter title are all questions to be asked and answered before any design decision is made.

In the catalog, one of the most difficult design issues to resolve was how the outlines of the images should be defined. Most often this is done with a hairline rule border, but in this case, that seemed intrusive, adding a device that was not part of the original design. The solution came from knowledge of production—the use of a beige-colored spot varnish. This defined the edges of the illustration and also gave it a slight gloss, which further differentiated it from the matte paper stock. The same varnish was also used on the title and section pages to help distinguish them clearly from the other text.

I feel strongly that the jacket or cover design should be, if possible, an extension of the book's interior graphic theme and should continue its typographic style and alignment. A decorative device used on text pages or a piece of supplied art may jump-start one's imagination and provide the key to an interesting jacket design. If I am really stuck for a concept or idea,

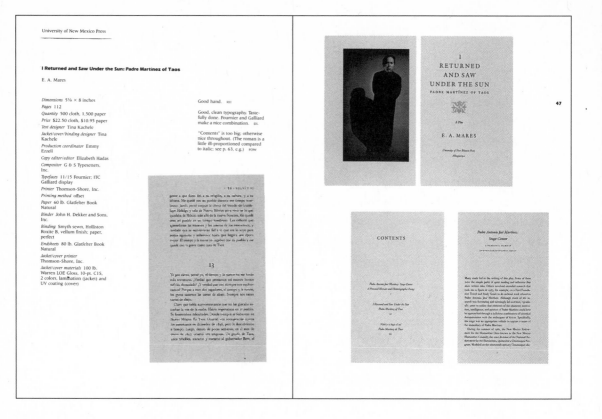

University of New Mexico Press

I Returned and Saw Under the Sun: Padre Martínez of Taos

E. A. Mares

Dimensions 5⅜ × 8 inches
Pages 112
Quantity 500 cloth, 1,500 paper
Price $22.50 cloth, $10.95 paper
Text designer Tina Kachele
Jacket/cover/binding designer Tina Kachele
Production coordinator Emmy Ezzell
Copy editor/editor Elizabeth Hadas
Compositor G & S Typesetters, Inc.
Typefaces 11/15 Fournier; ITC Galliard display
Printer Thomson-Shore, Inc.
Printing method offset
Paper 60 lb. Glatfelter Book Natural
Binder John H. Dekker and Sons, Inc.
Binding Smyth sewn, Holliston Roxite B, vellum finish; paper, perfect
Endsheets 80 lb. Glatfelter Book Natural
Jacket/cover printer Thomson-Shore, Inc.
Jacket/cover materials 100 lb. Warren LOE Gloss, 10-pt. C1S, 2 colors, lamination (jacket) and UV coating (cover)

Good hand. RJI

Good, clean typography. Tastefully done. Fournier and Galliard make a nice combination. DL

"Contents" is too big; otherwise nice throughout. (The roman is a little ill-proportioned compared to italic; see p. 63, e.g.) FOW

writing out thoughts, especially listing adjectives, sometimes helps me to think in a more creative way. Designers seem to have their individual secrets for pushing out the boundaries of graphic possibilities.

There is no question that computer technology has given the designer ways to experiment easily with fonts, sizes, space, and position of elements. The hundreds of type choices are seductive, but despite this easy availability, I still use only about a dozen text types while allowing myself an occasional flirtation—in display especially—with new faces. The things that were important to me before computers changed the creative process so dramatically—the design and proportion of letters, kerning, and letter-spacing—remain important. Combine concern for these elements with a well-conceived idea and good judgment, and the design is practically done.

Humphrey Stone

Son of the eminent wood engraver Reynolds Stone, Humphrey Stone trained at the Oxford University Press from 1960 to 1962. He then spent a year working with Giovanni Mardersteig at Stamperia Valdonega in Verona. Returning to England, he designed advertisements and jackets for Chatto & Windus and then became art editor of World University Library at Weidenfeld and Nicholson. He was next hired by P. J. Conkwright at Princeton University Press. After leaving Princeton, he joined Stanford University Press as art director, then returned to England, where he became art director at the Compton Press. He is currently a freelance book designer working for many publishers and numerous other clients, latterly Sir Robert Sainsbury.

Good design makes a difference to the prestige of a publisher even if it cannot be proved to sell more books. It suggests that the publisher cares about the products of the press, and if there is anything an author wants, needs, and frequently doesn't get, it is to be convinced of that.

On the other hand, poor design is not necessarily going to deter people from reading a best-seller. For example, in the popular fiction market, where there is a high degree of impulse buying, the front cover must be enticing, but the typography inside, provided it is comfortably legible, is less crucial. Yet with art and certain illustrated books the quality of reproduction will be an important selling factor. Guidebooks, too, will owe part of their success to clear typography and ease of reference; their appearance can often be overdesigned and fussy. The reader wants clear typographic signposts that give quick guidance.

On the whole, I aim to make a book timeless and as inviting, clear, and legible as possible. I am striving for harmony and elegance without gimmicks. Yet occasionally there are cases when one can use subtle indications that reflect the content of the book. For example, one can choose a typeface that is appropriate to the period of the book. The choice and handling of this typeface will often be enough to reflect the spirit of the book. Another technique might be to echo the title of the book with a little bit of wit. I once designed a book entitled *The Japanese Pillar Print* in which I stacked each word of the title and subtitle on top of each other. One should not slavishly copy, but draw inspiration from, the past. Having said that, I have to confess to using thick and thin rules from the 1800s perhaps once too often!

The key to good typography is always to allow the words to dictate the design. Imposing your own rigid design and making the words fit is unwise. However unpromising the copy may be, there are always ways of making the typography elegant and consistent—virtues that are probably old-fashioned, like being courteous. For example, judicious arrangement of the lines on a title page can transform an awkward shape into a pleasing one. Avoid stacking two display lines of equal length or a very long line followed by a very short one. Too many sizes of type on a page should also be avoided. Letterspacing of capitals as well as space between lines are other key factors. Finally, detail is everything.

It has become necessary for the typographer to be a good proofreader, for typesetting firms now often seem to be run by people who have had no training in traditional typography. They cannot be relied on to tell a bad word break from a good one. One has to be vigilant, with laser eyes, to pick up mistakes. Some typesetters have a habit of dropping the imprint on the title page to the base of the text area despite instructions. It is also important to follow through on every detail of production until the book is bound; otherwise, there will be gloom at the breakfast table when your book arrives with an awful howler perpetrated at the eleventh hour without the knowledge of the designer.

My working method involves drawing sample layouts in pencil of the prelims, chapter headings, part titles, and subheadings. So far I have managed without a computer, for I can visualize type sizes and have a friendly local typesetter to fax me proofs. But the advantages of playing around on a screen and being able to control the final result on a disk are obvious, so it won't be long before I have one. [Stone has since acquired a computer and has changed his working method.] Of course the new technology is only a tool, and the basic principles of typography do not change with it. I only mark the layouts to indicate the space between lines (from base of x-height), margins, etc., and mark up the manuscripts for type size. Specifications are also written out on a preprinted specification sheet. I work from an edited manuscript and often discuss problems with the editor and, ideally, the author. With the latest novel by A. S. Byatt, *Babel Tower,* it was crucial to understand the author's intentions that weren't obvious from reading the manuscript. In this case, there was a novel within a novel and a curious item that the author called "laminations," which were like jottings in the heroine's mind. We ended up printing the novel within the novel in a different typeface and setting the laminations apart by differing indentions.

I get sample pages only if the author or publisher requires them to approve my design. I need them only to ensure that the typesetter has followed my instructions. Knowing who the typesetter is in advance influences my design only in terms of availability of typefaces, proper small caps, non-lining figures, and so forth.

For the book *Mea Cuba* by G. Cabrera Infante I didn't know anything about the manuscript before I began the design, so it was necessary to familiarize myself with it by browsing through it. The book is an anthology of short pieces written by Cuba's most outstanding living novelist. Publishers would not want to pay me to read the manuscript all the way through, so reading the introduction gives me a good idea about the nature of the book. The contents page gives me a clue to the shape of the book and the beginnings of the design. The publishing house lists the basic production details and any editorial points that need attention.

Other than the trim size of the book, which was determined by the publisher, there were no restrictions put on the design. The publisher preferred the book to be a certain length but was flexible. I experiment with book trim sizes only if the publisher encourages it. So, often for economic reasons, it is a question of sticking to the basic sizes, like royal octavo (234 × 156 millimeters). Where illustration and an integrated text are concerned, there is much more need to experiment and indeed reflect the shape of the illustrations. All clues to the design of this kind of book come from the words of the manuscript. After familiarizing myself with the manuscript, I might, if there is time, put it aside and allow ideas to ferment in my mind.

In any case, I would never begin the job without a clear idea of its general design—centered or ranged [flush] left, for example. Obviously, details of copy will dictate further aspects of the design, such as the length of the subheads.

I draw out the text spread first, then the contents page, which will dictate the sink of the chapter opening. I often make use of a tried and trusted standard page layout, which is the block of text of a certain number of lines and measure [length of the line of type]. With illustrated books, no standard layout would apply. The choice of typeface depends on the length and character of the text. I may flirt with the idea of choosing a face that I haven't used very much, but I tend to use a few choice faces in the end—Sabon, Palatino, and Ehrhardt. I reject so many out of hand as being idiosyncratic. Bembo is now too thin, as is Baskerville. It is not only the face itself that gives character to a book but the way space is used. In other words, I don't need to change typefaces all the time to make a fresh design. I experiment with leading, tending to increase the leading rather than the type size. I find the half-point increments now available very useful.

I use type books or specimen sheets that show various sizes of different types, but in many cases, I can visualize the appearance in my head through years of familiarity. I draw a single box to indicate the type area on the layout page. For title pages I often draw thumbnail sketches, trying out variations in caps or lowercase and different line breaks. I always end up drawing an accurate pencil sketch of the title page.

For *Mea Cuba* I chose 10.5-point Ehrhardt, for I wanted a dark, strong type that was also economical in the number of characters that it makes on a line. The 13-point leading and 26.5-pica measure were dictated by the trim size, and with the widish measure I felt that the lines needed decent leading to be readable.

I specify every typographic detail except those specified by the editor. I consistently use 1 em for paragraph indents. I always prefer old-style figures within the text. Lining figures I use for tables only. Authors and editors often have strong preferences when it comes to styling extracts.

As long as there is not a mass of block quotes, I prefer to reduce the type size, keeping the extracts full measure with a half-line space above and below. If they are numerous and almost part of the text, however, it is better to avoid the choppy appearance of reduced size and to set extracts the same size as the text, indented 1 em from the left and also indented 1 em from the right when a centered subhead above would otherwise be unbalanced. In *Mea Cuba,* with just a few block quotes and with a relatively wide measure, the quotes are reduced by 1 point and indented 2 ems from the left.

A number of factors affect the design: the length of the running heads and chapter titles, their nature (that is, whether they contain italicized words), quotations on chapter-opening pages, and so on. In *Mea Cuba,* the chapter titles varied enormously in length, some had subtitles, and some had italicized words. So I set the chapter titles in 18-point uppercase and lowercase roman, allowing for italicized words to remain in italic. The subtitles could then be set in 14-point italic as a contrast.

I used a raised, indented initial to highlight the first words of the chapter following the quotes and dedications that appear at the heads of the chapters. For the display I stuck to my usual style of choosing different sizes of the same type as the main text type. For this book I was tempted to try a bold sans serif but rejected that because there were italicized words in the chapter titles. I rarely use bold in display, for, apart from Dante and Sabon, which have a semibold, the bold versions of old faces such as Bembo are ugly.

I decided on asymmetry because of the nature of the author's writing; the quotes on the chapter-opening pages, which lent themselves to a ranged-left style; and the contents page, which was best set out ranged left because very short titles were followed by very long ones. I don't like centered and uncentered styles in one book. I prefer a centered style. You can box yourself into a corner with asymmetry, particularly on the title page, where it can be difficult to avoid a certain loss of weight and authority because of the less formal nature of asymmetry, aside from the difficulty of achieving a happy balance.

All parts of the book should relate. If in doubt, I choose a smaller size for display, but a smallish type on the title page shouldn't be followed by much larger chapter titles. I do not like to see the length of a line of display stretching to the width of the measure of the book. I would always break the line into two unequal lengths, with the first being longer. I do like elegance in the shape that the lines make.

I usually set subheads in the same type size as the text, with either a half-line space below and one and a half line spaces above or 3 points extra space below and 10 points extra space above, if I am using 10/13. I don't like to see a subheading floating with equal space above and below it because this creates ambiguity for the reader. I believe that spacing above and below subheads should add up to whole lines, which reflects my training from hot-metal days. The style of subheads and running heads should contrast to avoid confusion when they are close to each other. The relation of subheads with chapter openings is dependent upon whether the subhead is above the first line of text, in which case it would be best to avoid setting the chapter title and subhead in the same style (for example, both in italic). Subheads, in any case, should be designed in harmonious relation with such elements as running heads and chapter openings.

Determining the chapter-opening style requires a review of the contents page to check length and composition of all the chapter titles. I end up designing chapter openings based on the most representative of them all.

I would never alter copy without consulting an editor. In fact consulting and working with a good editor who appreciates the finer points of typography is one of the most rewarding aspects of book design. So often decisions of style, albeit minor ones such as the arrangement of the prelims, should be made jointly by editor and typographer.

I like to see chapter openings and part titles share the same spatial relation and style as front and back matter display. If they are not in the same exact style (roman or italic), all should sit in the same position on the page throughout the book.

The design for front matter should parallel the chapter-opening style closely. In *Mea Cuba* I use the same display type size as on the chapter titles, in the same position on the page, with the same sink to the first line. When I have chapter numbers above the chapter titles, I align the display for the prelims with the chapter title.

I try to relate the title page closely to the other design elements in the book. In *Mea Cuba* the first line on the title page is in the same position as the prelim and chapter headings. The type size of the title must be as large as that of the chapter titles and should usually be larger, as in *Mea Cuba*.

The copyright page copy is usually available with the manuscript. I indicate on the layout only where it sits on the page, either backing up the title page or aligning with the first line of the contents page. I like to bunch the copy together with half-line spaces between blocks of information. The copyright always relates in style to the rest of the prelims, and it is set two sizes smaller than the main text. So many copyright pages are poorly designed, set in overly large type sizes and in a different style from that of the rest of the book—ranged left after a centered title page.

The dedication page copy is usually given a separate page in the prelims but can be combined with the copyright page to save space. I always indicate where it goes on the page and sometimes draw it out line for line. Rather like a colophon, it can be an opportunity to set an elegant shape of lines on a page.

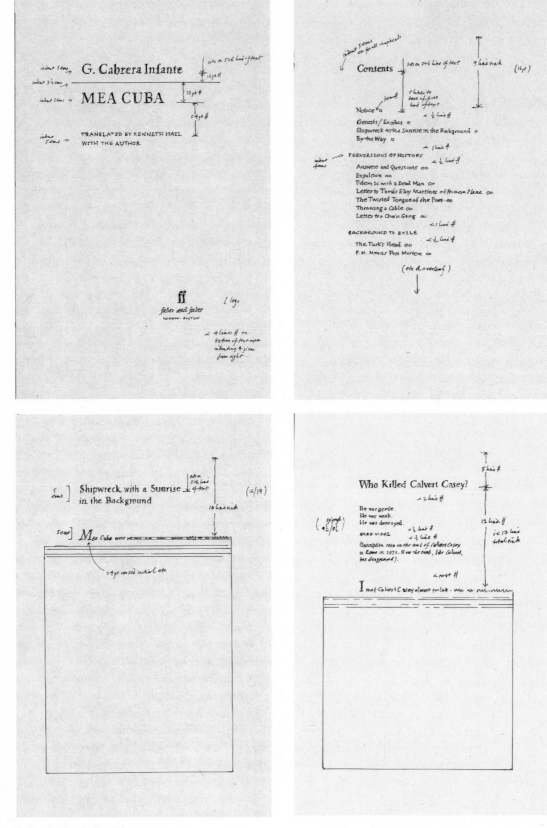

Design sketches for *Mea Cuba*

Who Killed Calvert Casey?

He was gentle.
He was weak.
He was destroyed.

GORE VIDAL

*(Inscription seen on the tomb of Calvert Casey
in Rome in 1972. Now the tomb, like Calvert,
has disappeared.)*

I met Calvert Casey almost too late. That is, almost too late
for me. Everyone who met Calvert believed they too had met him too late.
Like that privilege that one always believes one has not had in time, that
one hasn't enjoyed properly or has received late, Calvert seemed not to last
us at all. I don't know of anyone who knew Calvert who didn't consider
him to be a gift. One of those precious presents that gift-giving gods
concede to humans because they know that they will have it (or will enjoy
it: the terms are interchangeable) much, much less than an eternity. It was
the shortness of Calvert's life in my life that made this gift unappreciable
for me and at the same time let me see the brief time that the gift would
last. It is true that Calvert Casey lasted us all a short time. But we must not
lament the brevity of his life but celebrate that there existed someone
called Calvert Casey who was unique and extraordinary and that we are
able to say with Hamlet: 'I knew him well.' Without having to lament to
Horatio: 'Alas, poor Yorick.' Not poor Calvert. Poor those who did not
know him.

But I met him late, it's true. In 1960, in fact, when Virgilio Piñera was
insisting that I had to meet Calvert Casey by whatever means and I was
afraid that he would be one of those sterile hybrids, a Cuban-American. I
had already personally endured one of those mules in the abyss who had
tried to insert himself into American literature – 'to which I belong' – and
had got no further than writing trite stories in New York, where they were
never published. He ended up writing for one of those 'Latin American

This and the following illustration from G. Cabrera Infante, *Mea Cuba,* Faber and Faber stripe, brought to historical judgement and condemned as counter-revolutionary. That there has been no criminal more innocent in the history of relations between the Cuban Government and the culture of the country, only emphasizes if not its nature at least its destiny: chosen as unique by a historical process that started out being a-totalitarian. The political trial to which *P.M.*, its makers and the defenders of both were submitted has not ended. Ten years later many of those who participated in that process are still being persecuted for crimes as diverse as 'left-wing infantilism', 'homosexuality' or 'application for counter-revolutionary emigration'. It is an indication that the accusations against *P.M.* were labels to cover up a design which was not merely political but made in a police state.

THE PROTAGONISTS

Sabá Cabrera was born in Gibara, Oriente province in 1933. In his adolescence he was one of the most interesting painters to be found in Cuba in the forties. Praised by the masters of the time – Víctor Manuel, Wifredo Lam, René Portocarrero – he gave up painting when he found himself impeded by the tuberculosis that he suffered between the ages of fourteen and twenty-one. After being completely cured, he abhorred painting, perhaps from associating it with his illness. He studied journalism, which he had to abandon when the school was shut down in the last years of the Batista dictatorship. Connected in the school with students like Guillermo Jiménez, Santiago Frayle and Ricardo Alarcón, he found himself involved in more or less clandestine activities from 1956 on. In 1957 he was invited to the World Youth Festival in Moscow. In 1958 he started work as a newsreel editor at Channel 12, which was beginning the transmission of colour images on television in Cuba. With the triumph of the Revolution and with Channel 12 shut down, he moved over to work for Channel 2, also as editor of its newsreel and later as curator of its film library. He met Orlando Jiménez-Leal at this time. After the *P.M.* affair, he was sent to Madrid as commercial attaché. When his mother died in 1965 he came to Havana, where he was sacked without explanation. Sent to Madrid to 'collect his things' – a diplomatic-revolutionary euphemism for being dismissed from one's post – because of the Minister of Foreign Trade's desire to show a degree of independence from the security services, he decided not to return to Cuba and flew to Rome where he made counter-revolutionary statements. Later he travelled to New York, where he now

The contents page can pose the most difficult design problem in a book. I have evolved several layouts to overcome inherent problems, such as the yawning gaps between short lines and folios, without using the dreaded leader dots. For a start, I always use an extra half-line space between lines, and I indent on left and right sides to bring the lines and folios closer to each other.

I use three basic styles:

1. Folios are flush right; text is flush left. Indent the whole on either side and center on the overall measure.
2. Text is flush left. Folios run 1 em space between text and folio. Treat like poetry and center the whole block optically.
3. Chapter numbers, text, and folios have 1 em space between them. Each line is centered on the measure.

Back matter heads usually parallel the chapter openings and front matter headings. I usually set the back matter text one or two sizes smaller than the main text.

If given the chance to design the jacket as well as the inside, I like to echo in some way the typography of the inside. This is possible, particularly with type-only jackets. But the jacket designer and the text designer are often different people, and the brief from the publicity department regarding the impact of the jacket may be at odds with the typography inside the book.

Heavily illustrated art books present quite different demands on the typographer. A generous book size will be dictated by the need to reproduce the illustrations as large as possible, and consequently traditional placing of the text will become inappropriate in the large format.

The catalog, in three volumes, of the Sainsbury Collection was a complex undertaking that took many years to complete. It was obvious that a catalog of a collection of this size could not be contained in one volume without a crane being offered with every book. It was also obvious that the typographer needed to come up with a flexible grid to accentuate the vastly different shapes and sizes in the collection, ranging from totem-shaped African sculpture to paintings by Francis Bacon. Furthermore, although the pieces had captions of a consistent length, they were followed by descriptive text of wildly differing lengths.

Yet somehow we wanted the reader to view the text and its accompanying illustrations on the same page or, as in many cases, across facing pages. To have had a variable measure for every page would have set up a confusing rhythmic inconsistency for the reader. Having just two basic measures (20 and 27 picas) allowed for flexibility without destroying the integrity of the style. To avoid visual disharmony, the two measures were never mixed on the same double-page spread.

The editor was particularly keen to show sculpture in the round. So,

20

Hawaiian Islands

Neck ornament
Late 18th/early 19th century
Whale ivory, human hair, fibre
l. 11½ in (29.2 cm);
Pendant l. 4⅝ in (11.8 cm)
Acquired 1984   UEA 876

A number of traditional Hawaiian art forms underwent an increase
in scale and technical refinement during the period following initial
European contact in 1778 and prior to the dramatic religious and political
changes of 1819. This was in part a response to the political and ritual
centralisation which was taking place in Hawaii at the time and was also
facilitated by the increasing availability of metal tools. This trend is
noticeable in wood temple images and also in hook-shaped ornaments of
the type shown here (*lei niho palaoa*), for only smaller examples in whale
ivory, wood or shell were collected during Captain Cook's visits (see
Kaeppler, 1978: 91–3).

The Hawaiians did not hunt whales, but relied on stranded sperm
whales as their source for ivory. However, in the last years of the
eighteenth century, European traders began to supply large whale
teeth and even walrus tusks to Hawaiian craftsmen, thus allowing the
development of the larger form. Choris (1822: 19) made an interesting
observation on the type during his visit to Hawaii in 1816. He wrote:
'Les femmes portent souvent au cou des tresses de cheveux d'hommes,
auxquelles est suspendu par devant un morceau d'os taillé en forme de
langue; c'est ordinairement de la dent de cachalot que les Américains
vendent très-cher aux insulaires.'

Of these larger necklaces this example is unique, for the artist has
refined the basic form by adding two ridges at right angles to one
another on the underside of the hook pendant. It is suspended between
thick looping bunches of 8-ply braided hair, which are joined by a fibre
cord passing through a hole in the pendant. Walrus ivory pendants can
normally be distinguished from whale ivory ones by the crystalline
core which runs down the centre of the tusk.

The hook shape is an ancient Polynesian design form. An example of
a hook neck pendant, possibly dating to AD 1000, has been excavated on
Hawaii Island (Rose, 1980: 126,197), and related objects were also made
by the early Maori (Mead, 1984: 179; Duff, 1950: 110–22). The significance of the form is not clear, though Choris's reference to the tongue
is quite feasible, since the tongue was also important in New Zealand
Maori iconography.

PACIFIC: POLYNESIA   31

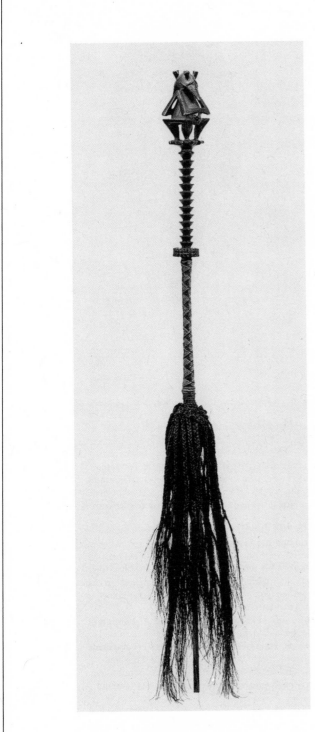

13

Austral Islands, Tupua'i or Rurutu

Chief's fly whisk
Late 18th/early 19th century
Wood, human hair, coir
l. 28½ in (72.4 cm); figure h. 3¼ in (8.3 cm)
Acquired 1984   UEA 895

Until comparatively recently much of the fine early wood sculpture brought back by Europeans from the central Pacific was generally attributed to 'Tahiti', which for a long period had been used as a catch-all term not only for the Society Islands (of which Tahiti is the largest island), but also for the whole of central Polynesia. It is now clear that many of these carvings originated from the Austral and Cook Groups, and this elegant type of fly whisk is a case in point. For long known as 'Tahitian' fly whisks, ethnohistorical analysis by Rose (1979) and others has shown that they were almost certainly made in Tupua'i or Rurutu in the Austral Islands. However, it is probable that many examples were collected in the Society Islands, since it appears that drums, whisks and other ritual items were supplied to chiefs on Tahiti and other islands by craftsmen on the Australs.

This attribution to the Austral Islands is further strengthened by evidence from an unpublished example in the Peabody Museum, Yale (no. 7154. 209919), which was collected on Tupua'i in June 1826 by Lieutenant Hiram Paulding of the United States Schooner *Dolphin* (information courtesy of David Kiphuth). Paulding wrote a lively account of his voyage, in which he describes his visit to Tupua'i, his friendship with 'King Dick', and their exchange of presents. He also makes direct reference to this type of fly whisk. He wrote: 'At Toubouai, we added considerably to our collection of curiosities. The most ingeniously wrought article, was a lash, used by the natives for brushing the flies off their backs. The handles were carved to represent a man's face, or some animal familiar to them. The lash itself, was, in several strands, finely braided from twine of the cocoa-nut husk' (Paulding, 1831: 249).

There are two basic varieties of double-figure fly whisk, large and small, both of which have a similar general form: twin figures sit atop a columnar grip, which is separated from the decoratively bound shaft and coir whisk by a raised disc, the rim of which is engraved with tiny heads. Rose (1979) describes these whisks in detail and designates three types (A–C), dividing the smaller variety according to the form

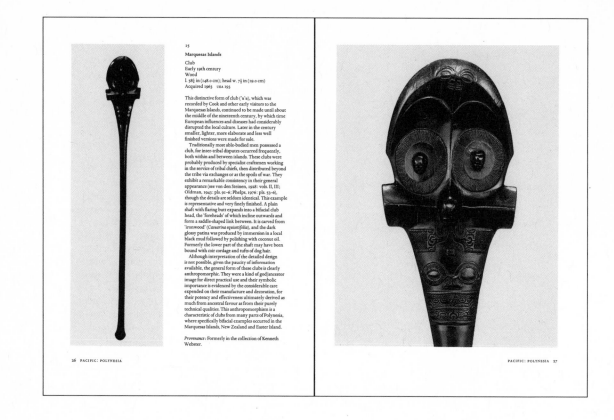

Marquesas Islands
Club
Early 19th century
Wood
l. 58¼ in (148.0 cm); head w. 7½ in (19.0 cm)
Acquired 1963   UEA 193

This distinctive form of club ('u'u'), which was recorded by Cook and other early visitors to the Marquesas Islands, continued to be made until about the middle of the nineteenth century, by which time European influences and diseases had considerably disrupted the local culture. Later in the century smaller, lighter, more elaborate and less well finished versions were made for sale.

Traditionally most able-bodied men possessed a club, for inter-tribal disputes occurred frequently, both within and between islands. These clubs were probably produced by specialist craftsmen working in the service of tribal chiefs, then distributed beyond the tribe via exchanges or as the spoils of war. They exhibit a remarkable consistency in their general appearance (see von den Steinen, 1928: vols. II, III; Oldman, 1943: pls. 91–6; Phelps, 1976: pls. 53–6), though the details are seldom identical. This example is representative and very finely finished. A plain shaft with flaring butt expands into a bifacial club head, the 'foreheads' of which incline outwards and form a saddle-shaped link between. It is carved from 'ironwood' (Casuarina equisetifolia), and the dark glossy patina was produced by immersion in a local black mud followed by polishing with coconut oil. Formerly the lower part of the shaft may have been bound with coir cordage and tufts of dog hair.

Although interpretation of the detailed design is not possible, given the paucity of information available, the general form of these clubs is clearly anthropomorphic. They were a kind of god/ancestor image for direct practical use and their symbolic importance is evidenced by the considerable care expended on their manufacture and decoration, for their potency and effectiveness ultimately derived as much from ancestral favour as from their purely technical qualities. This anthropomorphism is a characteristic of clubs from many parts of Polynesia, where specifically bifacial examples occurred in the Marquesas Islands, New Zealand and Easter Island.

Provenance : Formerly in the collection of Kenneth Webster.

of the hand grip. T
(represented here:
crisply carved and
through the body
whisks. It is possibl
post-contact devel
century, since only
during Cook's voy:
the availability of r
greater precision ir
both varieties of w

Monotype Dante

paradoxically, having several views of a piece allowed for further flexibility in the layout. For example, a side view could have text down the side, and the page opposite could be filled with two or more views rather than the next item, which might have an illustration whose shape would not allow the text to appear on the same page.

The editor was brilliant at cutting copy or rearranging the strict chronology of the entries. Further freedom was achieved by divorcing the caption from its text and placing it by the side of the illustration.

I chose Monotype Dante, which has just the right robust but refined sculptural quality to match the subject matter. Sir Robert Sainsbury was keen to ape the quality of the books of the 1920s and 1930s, so hot metal was initially chosen. Reproduction proofs were made from the metal type and printed by offset. By 1994 Dante had been digitized, and it was decided to typeset the third volume on computer. Laborious work was necessary to adjust individual characters to improve the match, but fortunately Martino Mardersteig had created his own digitized version, which corresponded closely to his father's hot-metal original.

Unjustified setting, chosen to match the asymmetrical style of the book, gave a less boxed-in look to the page and an even color to the type from the even word spaces. Unjustified setting has its problems. Luckily our typesetter was highly skilled in achieving a balanced look for the line endings.

Virginia Tan

After graduating from Pratt Institute with a BFA in book arts, Virginia Tan was employed at Hallmark Cards, where she worked on a new line of gift books. At that point, she was still undecided whether she was more interested in design or illustration, but she quickly discovered that her greater interest lay in design. Hallmark had all its production facilities on site, and she was able to set some of her own type and be closely involved in the production process. The most fascinating part of the job was working with Hermann Zapf on a deluxe binding project.

After leaving Hallmark she returned to New York to be the assistant designer at Knopf working with Betty Anderson. She is currently art director at Knopf.

Many American books seem overdesigned. Many British books look as though they've never been touched by a designer. I don't think that every book needs or should have a noticeable design. I do think that books should be readable, and I think that consistency in design goes a long way toward achieving this. It allows the reader to ignore the design because it has rhythm — it carries the reader, lessens the burden to tired eyes. What I mean is that there should be an order to heads and levels of display. I work with many British books, which we change for the American market. So many of their books don't do this. Many British books don't skimp on type size, but they do on leading, which I think is the worse of two evils. I find their page makeup and copyediting incredibly sloppy.

I get fan mail or hate mail from people who have bought Knopf books; they praise the design or complain about things like scant margins, which are the bane of modern publishing — even for Knopf.

I doubt that most people notice design except when they find the text uncomfortably small, unleaded, or disappearing into the gutter. Good design probably goes unnoticed, as it should. I think readers are affected by design, but only subliminally.

Typography should reflect something about the contents, but subtly and as neutrally as possible.

I used to trace type and draw layouts and then switched to photocopying and pasting type. For the past eight years I have been designing on a Macintosh in QuarkXPress. I was concerned when there was speculation about moving to computer design, for I was afraid that I would be forced to do "nontraditional" design or that I wouldn't be able to do the kind of designing I was accustomed to. I came from a hot-metal–letterpress background and had suffered through the cold-type revolution. I was skeptical about the design of the fonts and the availability of things like old-style figures and true small caps. In fact, font suppliers have exceeded my expectations in meeting these needs, and with applications like Illustrator and Fontographer the possibilities seem endless.

Designing on computer works well for me. I used to visualize a design and put it on paper, and found the process painstakingly slow. Now I visualize only enough to choose some typefaces that I think might work well, load them up on my computer, and launch into designing. I can make an infinite number of small changes until I feel the balance is just right, whereas before I might have stopped just short of that point because I couldn't bear going back for more stats or photocopies. Or, if I wasn't sure about the design, I would have had to order slight variations from the typesetter for galleys, pages, and repro—a costly way of getting the design right.

I have always marked specifications directly on my layouts, on the manuscripts, and on a spec sheet.

I usually work from an unedited manuscript.

I do see sample pages when the book is being set by an outside vendor. I especially like to see the density of the output and the tracking of the text [the tightness of the overall fit of the letters] and the kerning. I usually have some revisions, most often because my specifications were not followed or because of castoff considerations (to make the book longer or shorter).

Who will typeset the book does make a difference to me, but less now than in the past. When we set books hot metal, especially in letterpress printing, we were far more limited in our choices. For letterpress we had to design only with the one hundred or so faces that a typesetter had available, only in those sizes available, and only with the ornaments stocked. Otherwise, we would have had to pay a lot to have special dies made. With cold type the considerations had more to do with the typesetters' ability to do proper page makeup and to interpret specs properly. With computer design and setting it becomes a matter of who can output with the least aggravation. *The design is really under the designer's control through output to film.*

I get a planning manuscript from which to work. I usually get a summary as well. I read the summary and a bit of the manuscript until I have a feel for the book. Sometimes I never do, and that's frustrating, because I still have to come up with something but am unsure of its appropriateness.

I nearly always have a given trim size and expected length. This is flexible, but the price must often be changed to accommodate a different castoff. Sometimes editors or authors will request or demand a particular typeface.

I do visualize a design in my head. I feel confident that I can even spec a manuscript with sinks and everything without putting anything on paper. However, I have to be able to show the design to others for approval. I do less visualizing working on the computer because I can make changes so much faster. I think I work more spontaneously on the computer, which, aside from speed, is its main advantage for me. I must still do a little preview in my head in order to load the necessary fonts.

With the planning manuscript, I receive from the production editor a listing of various design elements. This tells me all the levels of heads, extracts, footnotes, sections, etc., that need to be styled. If I don't get this list, then I have to go through the manuscript myself to find this out.

Most often I start with the text spread and do a castoff to see if the book will make the expected length. I then design the chapter openings, part titles, and the title page. I may have to revise the chapter openings, part titles, and even the running heads after I have designed the title page. I reserve the design of the ad cards, contents, dedication and quotes, and other front and back matter until I mark up the manuscript.

I choose the typeface based on my perception (or the editor's) of the content of the manuscript. I try to reflect period, mood, gender, age—any number of things—in the text and display faces and in the way the type is used. An allusive design can be unobtrusive if it fits the content so well as to be a part of the experience of reading.

Size, leading, and measure are based first on readability within a certain trim size (which is a given for each individual manuscript). The next considerations are achieving an atmosphere and, unfortunately, fitting the text into a predetermined length. In fitting to length, I find that a nice round cut of type and generous leading make for greater readability than increasing the type size does.

I usually experiment less with my text faces than with my display faces. There are far fewer faces appropriate for use for text in books than there are for display. Display type is used larger and presented in far smaller blocks of copy. I also check to see if there are many italic passages and of what length, and if there are figures and small caps, etc., before I decide on a typeface. I do this before I really begin to visualize the design, and rarely need to change the text once I have chosen it. Now that I am working on the computer I may change the display a lot simply because I can do so with no pain. That means less visualizing ahead of time and more considering of the page layout and all of the choices possible in using a typeface (all caps, or caps and lowercase, italic).

I don't get too involved in specifying every typographic detail, such as the space between columns in tables, for I prefer to work with typesetters who have a reputation for doing those things well. However, now that I am actually setting a number of my books myself, I like this aspect of typesetting—except for making kerning pairs, which is an endless task once you begin doing it. I kern only display or repeated elements, like running heads. Much of this falls under Knopf house style; some is my own choice, such as the use of old-style versus lining figures. I'll almost always choose old-style, except in cookbooks, where you need cap-height fractions next to lining figures. Sometimes a period look requires lining figures, or there may be lists or other features that will be more readable with lining figures.

I almost always use the same paragraph indent with a given type-page width unless it is customary to do something different for the period look that I am trying to achieve. I like a paragraph indent of 1 pica 3 points for a type-page width of 27 picas and an indent of 1 pica for a width of 24 picas. These are my two standard type-page widths. I'm satisfied that these indents look good.

I did not use to visualize the text, and I would draw only a box for the text area. I would attach to the layouts a small sample of type showing the size, leading, and width but would draw out or paste up display elements. Now I set dummy copy on the computer to cover all aspects of the design.

I usually set extracts in the same size and leading as the text, justified, indented, and set off by a line space above and below. This eliminates problems with backup and alignment at tops of pages.

Although I include the running heads or running feet when I first design the double-page spread, I may revise them after I have styled the display. I do sometimes ask an editor for abbreviated running heads when they don't fit at all or when they are so long as to look out of balance with the page.

The choice of display type is based on content, readability, and the cut of the individual letters in the face and how it combines with the text, how titles break. There are a lot of different considerations, and for that reason, the choice is subject to change after my first visualization. I don't think that I have set preferences regarding display. I know that when I hate a typeface, inevitably I or someone else eventually comes up with a good use for it. The same is true about saying that I would never use all-cap italics or drop shadows or whatever. Options are the heart of book design. Otherwise, you would be just as well off with a standard design for all fiction or all art books or whatever. What I am saying is that I don't generally prefer anything when it comes to display type; I start with a clean slate.

This is also so for subheads, except that they should get progressively smaller for the various levels, going, for example, from bold to semibold to regular, from all caps to caps and small caps to caps and lowercase, from roman to italic, from a line alone to run-in—all depending on the level of preceding subhead. I don't think particularly of their relation to the running heads *unless they are to be the running heads*.

When designing chapter openings I like to consider the extremes, longest first, then shortest. Or I show the one that has the oddest-looking figure. Some typefaces have slanting 5s or perfectly round zeroes, or 4s with serifs. Some chapter titles have other titles within them that need to be set off. I show these problems in design layout to the editor so he or she won't make a change in galleys that could cause big alteration charges. It would be a rare case for me to ask for a copy change for design purposes and expect to get it.

I think of the title page as being the first level of display; it is followed by part titles and chapter titles, with the front and back matter heads equal to or less than chapter titles. This is especially so with long front matter titles like "Acknowledgments" or "A Word from the Translator."

I feel that all the display in the book should be closely parallel and that front and back matter heads should be handled the same, *as should the running heads throughout the book*. The display type for front and back matter should match, although it may or may not match the chapter number or chapter title.

I usually sink the text of the contents, introductions, etc., to match the chapter openings, but not always—especially not when I need the space. Sometimes I change the front and back matter design when I find that I need more room for the index entries. Ideally, I like notes, bibliography, and index text to be in the same size, but if that isn't possible, the index should be smaller than the others.

Even though I usually design the title page last, I may go back and change everything else to reflect the needs of the title-page design. As a rule, I do think the title-page type should be as large as that used on part titles and chapter titles. I recall one design by Betty Anderson that I really loved in which the display type for the title page and the chapter openings was in small caps the same size as (or perhaps a point or so larger than) the text.

I tend to do the same design with minor variations for all my copyright pages, probably because I do most of my work for the same publishing house.

I style materials such as dedications and quotes individually, and although I see the copy in the planning manuscript, I rarely draw a design. When seeing the material in galleys, I may make adjustments. I very often leave adjustments to sinkages until blues, for I find that these refinements are hard to see until the design is in a sort-of-book form.

I try to set up the contents pages with miniature versions of the part and chapter titles in the text face. For example, if I have used full caps for the part title, I try to use full caps for the same words on the contents page. If I have used italic for chapter titles, I set the chapter titles in italic on the contents page.

I try to get the editor to eliminate redundancies like "chapter" before each chapter number, and I like the fewest number of indents, so I usually align all part and chapter numbers flush right over one another. I align all the part and chapter titles flush left with an em or so space between them and the part and chapter numbers. I align the folios flush right. Of course, there are variations for centered layouts, but this is my usual style. I also like the contents list to be more openly leaded than the text, with turnovers leaded the same as the text. I use space to separate front and back matter headings from the chapter titles—more space than between chapter titles.

In an ideal world, the book and jacket would be designed by the same person with the same concept, but perhaps not. A jacket may be viewed as advertising. It may be the only thing that a prospective buyer sees, especially if the book is shrink-wrapped. I have had books which I was instructed by the editor to view one way and to make that viewpoint clear to the reader, whereas the jacket designer was told to do the exact opposite. This makes for an oddly disparate package.

One way to relate the book to the jacket when the designs are done by different people is in the binding. The binding should echo the interior design, for it is an inseparable part of the book, but the choice of colors for cloth, paper, headbands, and topstain should reflect the jacket.

For *The Devil's Own Work* I was given the usual transmittal sheet requesting a specific number of pages and trim size. This book had very few design elements, just the usual front matter, chapter openings, and space breaks. There were no illustrations. I read the editor's summary, which called the book "a subtle, eerie novel about a writer's possession by a mysterious literary spirit." I also read enough of the manuscript to give me a feeling. The book struck me as being Victorian and dark. The author had previously written a biography of Ford Maddox Ford, but I was also reminded of John Fowles. The editor was unsure about the size, so I did the same design for a 5-×-7 1/2-inch and a 5 5/8-×-8 3/8-inch trim.

I wanted to do a design that looked stylish, late nineteenth century, a bit gothic, and relating to the devil in the title. I think that I decided immediately on Nicholas Cochin for the display. It is definitely stylish and dated and has those quirks of exaggerated ascenders and serifs. We were going to set the job PostScript, so for the text face I chose Adobe Garamond, which looked good with the Cochin and kept a clean, stylish appearance. I searched though all of my fonts for the right ornaments. On the title page and binding I used a Monotype Arabesque with a small modification. I removed a small **V**-shaped piece from the top of the ornament and set the ornament at a 45-degree angle, which made it look like the face of the devil.

In Cochin, the caps are nearly the same height as the ascenders. On the chapter openings I modified the height of the cap "C" in "Chapter" to make it slightly shorter and accentuate the height of the ascenders.

I wanted a second ornament for the chapter opening, along with caps and small caps for the first phrase, just to add something to such a spare design. I wanted something creepy, but not overtly so. The Poetica ornament fit my needs, and its weight related nicely with the other type. I also wanted an open, airy text page, especially with the smaller trim size that was finally used. The intimacy suited the sort of fireside ghost story aspect of the book. I pushed the leading to its limit (12/16 × 21), beyond which it would have looked as though I was trying to fill out the book. I also recommended no running head to give it that British look, and a centered layout.

The Devil's Own Work

A NOVEL BY

Alan Judd

Alfred A. Knopf
New York   1994

All illustrations in this chapter from Alan Judd, *The Devil's Own Work*, Knopf

Chapter 1

I HAD IT, YOU SEE, from Edward himself; though not all at once and never, I am sure, all of it. I don't suppose anyone could tell it all, except perhaps Eudoxie, and she was—is—part of the problem. The origins pre-date my marriage and Edward's fame. I now regard that time as our first youth but it seemed to us then, fresh from university and in London, the time of entry into full estate. Nothing was impossible and nothing unimagined, except failure. In my case you could say that I was merely wrong but Edward's is more complicated. He had every success an ambitious man could wish; it was the cost that got him.

Of course, when he purchased that particular ticket he had no idea—which of us could have?—of what compound interest can mean, over a lifetime. I don't suppose it even felt like a transaction, more another gift from a kindly Providence to add to his health, his looks, his charm, his winning disposition, his talent—

I

his genius, it came to be called, but I at least am more cautious now. Everyone liked, even loved him, or perhaps I should say that no one disliked him and everyone felt drawn to him. I think I love him, though what it was in him that I loved I am only now beginning to grapple with. I also envied and for a while hated him but my knowledge of the price he paid makes it impossible for those feelings to last. And there is a coldness that slows my blood at the thought that he might still be paying it.

He had a flat in a Victorian house in Kennington, down one of those dirty Lambeth streets that for decades were described as 'coming up' but which never quite seemed to arrive. I shared a flat with two other teachers in a modern block not far away. Edward was not a teacher, of course; from the start, he was to be great writer. He never actually said as much but the knowledge of it somehow spread around him like a personal aura so that no one ever thought of him as anything else. Perhaps we assumed that you become a great writer simply by being intent on it and by keeping at it until your greatness became apparent. Perhaps even Edward assumed it. After all, the intellectual world is credulous enough to take many of us at our own evaluations and people can become very successful just by believing in themselves and so persuading everyone else. I think Edward did believe in himself.

2

He was lucky in that he had money from his father, so that while working on his first novel he didn't have to get a regular job but could do freelance reviewing, which was as useful for getting his name known as for what it earned. In those days there was nothing to distinguish him from the shoals of Eng. Lit. graduates who feed off the scraps of London publishing and journalism. The more fortunate and determined grow into big enough fish to join the literati and become editors, columnists, presenters and, usually in a small way, writers.

EDWARD AND EUDOXIET were itinerant from then on. They kept the house at Cape Ferrat and occasionally revisited but never for long. When I saw him there was never much said. Not that there needed to be. Our friendship was an acknowledgement that we went back a long way, that there was more behind than to come. I don't think either of us had the linear view of relationships which demands progression towards—well, what? That is always the problem.

He put on more weight and became a heavy, bloated figure although his basic good looks could still be traced beneath the distended flesh. his skin became red and shiny, his hair silvery and thin but his eyes kept their colour—blue and white islands in a red and wrin-

3

Glossary

The definitions of technical terms used in this book are based on those in *Glossary of Typesetting Terms*. Cross-references to terms defined in the list are in italic.

Ascender: The upper part of a lowercase letter that extends above the *x-height,* as in "b," "d," "f," "h," "l." Compare *descender.*

Back matter: Part or parts of the book that follow the main text, including appendixes, glossary, endnotes, bibliography, and index.

Baseline: The horizontal on which the letters of the alphabet optically range and below which the *descenders* fall.

Bastard title: A page, usually the first page of the book, containing the main title of the book or, occasionally, the series title or an epigraph. It is commonly called the *half title* or first half title.

Bleed: Description for an image or *rule* that extends off the edge of the page.

Body: Text matter, as opposed to *display.*

Bold: A heavier weight of a typeface, as in **bold**.

Bullet: A heavy centered dot: ·.

Cap height: The height of a capital letter from the *baseline* to the top of the letter.

Caps: Capital letters, uppercase. ABC as opposed to ABC (*small caps*) or abc (*lowercase*).

Castoff: The calculation of the number of typeset pages that a manuscript will make based on the *character count.*

Character: A single letter, numeral, punctuation mark, or word space. The equivalent of one keystroke on a typewriter or computer keyboard.

Character count: The total number of characters in a manuscript or the total number of characters in a given unit of measure (for example, characters per *pica*).

Color: A vague term when used by typographers but generally a reference to the design and weight of a typeface, especially when it is set in a block of text.

Descender: The portion of a lowercase letter that falls below the *baseline,* as in "g," "p," "q," "y."

Dingbat: A typographic ornament.

Display: The type used for the title page, chapter titles, epigraphs, and other elements besides the text proper. Compare *body.*

Drop cap, drop or dropped initial: A large capital letter dropped into text at the beginning of a line, usually at the beginning of a chapter.

Drop folio: A page number positioned below the normal text page.

Em: A unit of measurement that equals the point size of the type. For example, in 10-point type an em is 10 points wide. The em is used to specify size, as in *em dash*.

Em dash: A typographic rule (—) usually measuring the width of an *em*.

En: A unit of measurement that equals half the width of an *em*.

En dash: A typographic rule (–) usually measuring the width of an *en*.

Face: Short for *typeface*.

Flower: A typographic ornament of floral design (❈ ▩ ▨), also called a fleuron or printer's flower.

Flush and hang: Set with the first line flush left and the following text indented, as in many bibliographies and this list.

Flush left, flush right: Aligned to a common edge, as here:

xxxxxxx	xxxxxxx
xxxxxxxxxx	xxxxxxxxxxx
xxxxxxx	xxxxx

Folio: The page number printed on the text page.

Font: Particular cut of a typeface. Often used interchangeably with *face*.

Gutter: The inside margin of the page, closest to the binding.

Half title: Often the first page of a book (same as *bastard title*) and repeated as either the last recto page in the front matter or as page 1 of the text, in which case it can be called the second half title. The text on the bastard title and the text on the second half title sometimes differ.

Hang: To position beyond the normal outer margin of the text page. For example, opening quotation marks can hang in the margin.

Italic: A style of type—different from upright roman type—that usually slopes forward, as in *italic*.

Justified: Aligned on one or both sides of a block of text, as in "right-justified." Compare *ragged*.

Kern: To adjust the space between selected pairs of *characters*.

Lead: The space between lines of type, now usually measured from *baseline* to baseline.

Letterfit: The spatial relation of letters. The letterfit may be too loose or too tight, for example.

Letterspacing: The adjustment of space (usually the addition of space) between the letters of a word, as in l e t t e r s p a c i n g.

Ligature: Two or more letters combined to make a single character, as in "fi," "fl."

Lining figures: Numerals of the same height (generally cap height), as in 1234567890. Compare *old-style figures*.

Lowercase: The small letters (abc), distinguished from *caps* (ABC) and *small caps* (ABC).

Measure: The width of a full line of type, usually measured in *points* and *picas*.

Mise-en-page: Layout or design of the elements on the page.

Monotype: In this book Monotype refers to the company that made typesetting machines that cast individual pieces of type. Compare Linotype, which refers to the company that made typesetting machines that cast metal type into a single line of type.

Old-style figures: Nonaligning numerals, as in 1234567890. Compare *lining figures*.

Pica: A typographic measurement equal to 12 *points*. Six picas equals approximately one inch.

Point: A typographic measurement equal to approximately 1/72 inch.

Ragged: Not aligned on one or either side of a block of text (ragged right, ragged left, ragged center). Compare *justified*.

Recto: The right-hand page of a book. Compare *verso*.

Roman: The upright style of type. Compare *italic*.

Rule: A vertical or horizontal line.

Running head, running foot: Book, part, chapter, or section title or any other reference positioned outside the text area, usually on every text page of a book. A running head appears at the top of the page, a running foot at the bottom.

Sans serif: A letter or typeface without *serifs*, as in **sans serif**.

Serif: The short ending stroke of a *character* in a typeface.

Sink, sinkage: The space from the top margin of a type page to the first printed element on the page. On a chapter opening, for example, the chapter number or title will not usually begin at the very top of the page but will sink from the top.

Small caps: Capital letters approximately the same height as the *x-height*. (x SMALL CAP). Compare *caps*.

Trim size: The finished size of a book, generally given width by depth, in inches, in the United States and depth by width, in millimeters, in Britain.

Turnover: A line of an entry or a poem that does not fit in the allotted space and continues over to the next line. Also called runover.

Verso: The left-hand page of a book. Compare *recto*.

Word space: The space between words in a line of type.

x-height: The height of the lowercase letter "x" in a particular typeface.

Further Reading

The books listed here, all of more or less recent vintage, are among the most useful references available on typography and book design.

Bringhurst, Robert. *The Elements of Typographic Style*. 2d ed. Port Roberts, Wash.: Hartley & Marks, 1996.

Carson, David, and Lewis Blackwell. *The End of Print: The Graphic Design of David Carson*. London: Laurence King Publishing, 1995.

Carter, Sebastian. *Twentieth-Century Type Designers*. New York: Norton, 1995.

The Chicago Manual of Style. 14th ed. Chicago: University of Chicago Press, 1993.

Dowding, Geoffrey. *Finer Points in the Spacing and Arrangement of Type*. Rev. ed. Port Roberts, Wash.: Hartley & Marks, 1995.

Eckersley, Richard, Richard Angstadt, Charles M. Ellertson, Richard Hendel, Naomi B. Pascal, and Anita Walker Scott. *Glossary of Typesetting Terms*. Chicago: University of Chicago Press, 1994.

Gill, Eric. *An Essay on Typography*. Boston: Godine, 1993.

Hochuli, Jost, and Robin Kinross. *Designing Books: Practice and Theory*. London: Hyphen Press, 1996.

Kinross, Robin. *Fellow Readers: Notes on Multiplied Language*. London: Hyphen Press, 1994.

———. *Modern Typography: An Essay in Critical History*. London: Hyphen Press, 1992.

Lawson, Alexander. *Anatomy of a Typeface*. Boston: Godine, 1990.

———. *Printing Types*. Boston: Beacon Press, 1990.

Lee, Marshall. *Bookmaking: The Illustrated Guide to Design/Production/Editing*. 2d ed. New York: Bowker, 1979.

McLean, Ruari. *The Thames and Hudson Manual of Typography*. London: Thames and Hudson, 1980.

———, ed. *Typographers on Type*. New York: Norton, 1995.

Spencer, Herbert. *Pioneers of Modern Typography*. Rev. ed. Cambridge, Mass.: MIT Press, 1982.

Spiekermann, Erik, and E. M. Ginger. *Stop Stealing Sheep and Find Out How Type Works*. Mountain View, Calif.: Adobe Press, 1993.

Sutton, James, and Alan Bartram. *An Atlas of Typeforms*. London: Lund Humphries, 1968.

———. *Typefaces for Books*. New York: New Amsterdam, 1990.

Tracy, Walter. *Letters of Credit: A View of Type Design*. Boston: Godine, 1986.

Tschichold, Jan. *The Form of the Book*. Ed. Robert Bringhurst, trans. Hajo Hadeler. Port Roberts, Wash.: Hartley & Marks, 1991.

————. *The New Typography*. Trans. Ruari McLean. Berkeley: University of California Press, 1997.

Updike, D. B. *Printing Types: Their History, Forms, and Use*. New York: Dover, 1980.

Williamson, Hugh. *Methods of Book Design*. New Haven: Yale University Press, 1983.

Wilson, Adrian. *The Design of Books*. San Francisco: Chronicle Books, 1993.

Zapf, Hermann. *Hermann Zapf and His Design Philosophy*. Chicago: Society of Typographic Artists, 1987.

Index

Walbaum, 147–48, 149

Warde, Beatrice, 5, 27, 28; "Crystal Goblet," 27

Weidenfeld and Nicholson, 177

Williamson, Hugh, 27, 34, 48, 52, 58

Willow, 67, 68, 69, 73, 76

Words: design choices dependent on, 33, 37, 39, 49–50, 52, 56, 63, 92, 177, 179; design in service of, 3, 6, 11, 33, 93, 177

Word spacing, 28, 39, 41, 45–47, 82, 93, 128, 129

Zahn, Carl, 21

Zapf, Hermann, 27–28, 165, 189

Zapf dingbats, 67